Taking the War
Out of Our Words

Taking the War Out of Our Words

The Art of Powerful Non-Defensive Communication

SHARON STRAND ELLISON

Wyatt-MacKenzie Publishing, Inc.

Taking the War Out of Our Words
The Art of Powerful Non-Defensive Communication

Library of Congress Control Number: 2008943770

ISBN: 978-0-9820518-2-5

Published in hardcover as *Don't Be So Defensive!* (Andrews McMeel) Published in paperback as *Taking the War Out of Our Words* (Bay Tree). First paperback printing, August 2002. Second printing 2005. Third printing 2008.

Wyatt-MacKenzie Publishing, Inc.
www.WyMacPublishing.com

Designed by John Reinhardt Book Design
Composed by Kelly & Company, Lee's Summit, Missouri

The names have been changed and the circumstances altered enough to protect the identity of the people whose stories are told in this book.

For
Edythe, Monza, and Ami

Contents

PART II

THE NON-DEFENSIVE MODEL
Tools Instead of Weapons

List of Charts

Acknowledgments

Many people have given me support and guidance in the development of this theory and this book. I want to give special thanks to these:

Edythe Strand Ellison. Mom, you gave me the strength to live by my own values, no matter what others said or thought, and you had faith in my potential to make a difference in this world. I wish you were here.

James Ellison. Dad, you always taught me that no matter what we do in life, communicating well is one of the most important skills we have. When I was in high school, you sat by my side, teaching me how to craft a speech, listening to me practice, giving astute feedback until my speech was original, polished, and heartful.

Dr. Monza Naff. For a dozen years, you guided and supported my efforts to write this book. You have healed my heart, challenged my mind, and strengthened my spirit. You've taught me how to keep my soul in my words, and to make them concrete, concrete, concrete. Without you, this book would exist only in my mind. Thank you for giving my heart a home while I devote so much of my life to this work.

Ami Atkinson Combs. You told me recently that this book has been your sibling, and it's true. Since you were born, this project has been a member of our family. I want you to know you've been a great sister to it, never jealous and always interested. You've believed in me and my work in ways that inspire awe in me. Your decision to make this your life work, too, is a gift greater than I could have ever dreamed. Having you as my daughter is a blessing.

Jesse Combs. You are the best husband to my daughter and son to me that I could ever have hoped for. I appreciate your loving, skillful "high tech" work that has so enhanced my website and makes "Powerful, Non-Defensive Communication" accessible in new ways.

Judith Cope. As my editor, you've been a consummate sculptor, shaping my words and thus always enhancing my message. In your art, you combine gifts of the poet and the surgeon. I thank you, my friend, for your challenging questions, your unflagging commitment, your generous spirit.

Regula Noetzli. I cannot imagine a more gifted agent. You understand this endeavor, and believe in it, and have consistently worked in the best interests of my vision. For your guidance and your skills, I am deeply and increasingly grateful.

Chris Schillig. I'm grateful for your willingness to publish the original hardback edition of this book. It meant the world to me.

Jean Zevnik and *Janet Baker.* Thank you for your excellent editing.

David Cole. You have my deep appreciation for publishing the first paperback edition and for respecting my integrity as an author.

Nancy Cleary. As the publisher of this new paperback edition, and the forthcoming *Taking Power Struggle Out of Parenting*, you are creative, proactive, tenacious and seemingly tireless. Your graphic designs always reflect your own unique creativity while honoring the essence of my work. At the same time, how you envision and live out your own goals for creating change in the world is remarkable. You are a joy to work with.

Caroline Pincus. Thank you for your faith in this project and for your generosity in leading me to Regula. Working with you on revisions for this paperback edition deepened my already keen respect for your craft and vision. Caroline, I value our friendship a great deal, trust your astute judgment, and look forward to many more stimulating conversations.

Canyon Sam. Just as I believe in the wisdom of your work (*One Hundred Voices of Tara: Tibetan Women Speak*), you believed in mine enough to send me to Caroline. Thank you!

Jennifer Biehn. I credit you with bringing the work I do into wider spheres. Thanks, Jenn, for taking the risk to invite me to the Bay Area to share PNDC in a myriad of settings and for supporting my ideas with your enthusiastic spirit.

Dr. Kostas Bagakis. You saw the potential of my work to help us all move toward living as a cultural democracy. Thank you for encouraging me to create a curriculum based on this theory and for teaching the first college course to use it.

Vicki Dello Joio. I am in awe of your vision of the importance of this process and your commitment to it. Thank you for your brilliant mind and your tender, generous heart. You have not only made my path easier, you have strengthened me with your wisdom and your friendship.

Sherry Mouser. You have spent countless hours developing my website, making it truly represent the spirit of my work. Your generosity touches me deeply, and I am grateful for your friendship.

Randy and *Helen Ellison.* Randy, you have sustained me and my vision through many hard times. Having a brother like you is a special treasure. Helen, you have been a sister to me. Thank you both for making your home a safe harbor.

Nancy Gallagher. I will never forget how long you held the lifeline, reminding me of the importance of this work even in moments when I forgot.

Jane Mara, M.S.W. Before other professionals recognized it, you described learning this non-defensive communication process not only as revolutionary but also as "an evolutionary change." Your faith in my work and your friendship helped me hold my vision.

Mady Shumofsky: You are the first person besides me to be out in the world teaching PNDC on a regular basis. I so respect you, admire your gifts, and treasure your friendship.

Michael Bell and Mercedes Martin: Thank you for how you have expanded my understanding of issues of diversity and cultural competence and strengthened my ability to incorporate it into my work. You have sustained my spirit in so many ways. I am honored that to have you as my mentors and friends.

Jane Grossman and Teresa Edmondson: You have given me vital insights and tools for using technology more effectively in my work and creating materials that augment people's learning. You have guided me in envisioning my work in new ways. Thank you for your dedication and friendship.

Nancy Foster and Maureen Tighe: You have each brought me to whole new communities, in ways that have spread the word about my work, both nationally and internationally. I treasure my friendship with each of you.

I also want to name others who have given me and this theory special gifts:

Emma (Grandma) Strand, Candy and Mike Smith, Rose Mary Pearson, Dorothy and Elmer Willmore, Eleanor Borg, Regan Olsen, Patty Ryan, Susan England Henderson, Dr. John D. Atkinson III, Dr. John D. Atkinson Jr. and Cecile Atkinson, Steve and Emily Chandler, Dr. Owen White and Peggy White, Betsy DeMartini, Molly Jensen, Terry Ezell, Paget Engen, Kathy Smith, Sue Redbird Cochran, Nathaniel Sperry, Becky Smith, Julie Hale, Virginia Filley, Maggie Rose, Carole Jackson, Barbara Baird, Marsha Mabrey, Stephanie Wittman, Vicki Brabham, Marilyn Garber, Kris Kennedy, Nancy Louise, Sonja Vik, Valerie Haynes, Nancy Clark, Caroline Parke, Sid Magee, Lynn Fetherstonhaugh, Jill Fetherstonhaugh, Laura Parrish, Dr. Gisela Bergman, Donna Albro, Don Ross, Gayl Bowser, Kate lyn Hibbard, Lisa Tomlin, Dorothy Rollins, Dr. Linda Hansen, Dr. Annette Atkins, Barton Sutter, Dr. Mary DeShazer, Dr. Martin Jacobi, Joan Lohman, Shakti Butler, Fabienne McPhail Naples, Papusa Molina, Margaret Thompson, Mady Shumofsky, Emily Doskow, Alicia Wills, Dr. Sandra Lewis, Lauren Kucera, Jim and Phyllis Whiteside, Yeshi Sherover Neumann, Bobby Rothschild, Rebecca Kutlin, Robert Brownstone, Evelyn C. White, Amy Levine, Edith Ng, Dale Marie Golden, Barbara Rowles, Maria Mears, Carol Sachal, Dr. Ragna Boynton, Liz Raymer, Karin Kelly-Givens, Jan Herzog, Pat Barrett, Catherine Riedel, Johanna Harding, Irene Nexica, Tina Marie Santos, Carol Olwell, Donna Belk, Donn Davy, Meg Sanders, Sue Floethe, Sterling Newberry, and Mary Koloroutis.

So many of you, family, friends, and colleagues, have helped me to conceive this work. Love and gratitude fill me for the gifts each one of you has given. I believe that together we have given birth to this book.

It has been impossible to list everyone who has helped to make this new edition possible, but I am thinking of you and thankful for you.

INTRODUCTION

It's Just Human Nature— or Is It?

By the time I was six, I realized something was curiously wrong about the way people talked to each other. When called ugly names, kids would taunt back, "Sticks and stones may break my bones but words will never hurt me." I didn't believe them. I could tell that they were really upset. I also remember my friend Patty saying, "I would never let that stupid Sarah know she made me feel bad!" I squinted at her, as if to say, "How will you get over it if you don't talk to her about it?"

I watched adults act the same way. When I heard my mother's friend Clara say, "I'm not going to let him hurt me," I could tell that she was already hurt. Behind her tough words, she struggled not to cry. What puzzled me was why people so often tried to act like they didn't care when someone hurt their feelings. Why would people hide their feelings instead of showing them?

While people often hid their feelings, I was also jarred by how accepting they were of violence. It sometimes came in mixed messages. Parents would chastise boys when breaking up a neighborhood fight, only to make sidebar comments such as "Boys will be boys," "They were just feeling their oats," or "Johnny got a few good licks in, didn't he!?"

I wasn't a passive child myself, although I had my own host of insecurities. I was inclined to jump into the fray, and could argue with the best of them. In fact, my mother used to joke that I was behind the door when God passed out the sensor between the brain and the mouth. Today, I might well have been labeled hyperactive. But there was always a quiet place inside of me where I was pensive, wondering, thinking.

The idea that violence is just a part of human nature seemed to float through the airways of my childhood. I remember responding with wide-eyed horror when I heard people actually say, "It's just human nature to be violent." Violence didn't seem normal to me; it seemed like an illness. The fact that people could say those words so casually made a lasting impression on me.

I was always appalled by the amount of needless conflict and pain in people's lives. From childhood on, I carried the thought, "It doesn't have to be this way." Despite all evidence to the contrary, I felt certain of this.

When I was in college, a friend gave me a puzzle test as part of a psychology experiment. The puzzle had no exterior frame, merely pieces with soft, rounded sides like those of a child's puzzle. How the pieces might fit together wasn't obvious. I played with them, moved them around, and gradually arranged them next to each other in a still-unidentifiable form. The last piece was long, narrow, and curved, not as round as the others. I found a spot where the curves fit, placed it, and suddenly realized that I was looking at an elephant, now lying upside down in front of me. "Ah," I said, "I get it! It's an elephant!"

"You can't do that," my friend retorted.

"What do you mean?"

"You can't put it together without first figuring out what it is. It can't be done. They told us in class. No one would be able to put it together without first figuring out that it's an elephant."

"But I just did."

Likewise, without being fully conscious of what I was doing, I have put together a new way for people to talk to each other. Putting the elephant together took about five minutes. Putting together the approach to communication outlined in this book has taken me most of my life. My thirty-four-year-old daughter, Ami, calls this book her sister.

After studying psychology in college, I worked as a juvenile court counselor, play therapist, and parent trainer. I came to understand that people were often reluctant to tell the truth about how they felt because they were afraid such honesty might give someone power over them, or conversely, might be hurtful to the other person. I saw therapists nod in agreement when people said they wouldn't feel "safe" opening up to someone with whom they were in conflict.

No one ever asked, "Why are you safer if you don't speak than if you do?" Or, "How does saying what you feel and think give someone else more power over you rather than less?" I still didn't quite understand why people felt safer being closed. What I observed, in frustration, was that all this hiding and maneuvering caused much of the misunderstanding, conflict, and ongoing power struggles in people's lives.

In my late twenties, I began to train other professionals, many of whom were teachers and therapists. Participants in my workshops would often say to me, using almost identical words, "This is so revolutionary and disarming!"

I didn't have the trunk on my own elephant yet, so I didn't know what they meant. I just mused about it. Finally, one day, I sat down in my living room and asked myself, "If I were going to disarm, what would I do? . . .Well, I guess in the most literal sense, it would be like taking a rifle off my shoulder and laying it down." Dis-arm. I went through the physical motions.

Over and over, I took an imaginary rifle off my shoulder and laid it on the carpet, asking myself each time, "What am I teaching about communication that is disarming?" Finally, the light bulb clicked on: "Oh! To put down the rifle means I don't have to defend myself anymore."

I suddenly had a vivid picture of how people use defensiveness as their way of protecting themselves when they talk to each other. Of course. Being defensive would require putting up a shield of armor. What I was teaching was a method of communication in which people would not have to resort to defensiveness to protect themselves.

Then the larger light bulb went on. Wow. We have been using the rules of war as the basis for human conversation. War creates and accelerates conflict, so using those rules in conversation would get the same results. We might not notice it when we are on the "same side" with someone, have just fallen in love, are proud of our child's accomplishments, or gossiping with a co-worker. But as soon as conflict arises, that's when people can shift instantly to defensive reactions. Our use of language prescribes being defensive as our primary means of self-protection and thus leads us directly into power struggle. That's what I saw in that moment.

The trunk was finally on my elephant. The revelations I had that day explained both quandaries I had puzzled over since childhood— why people shut down instead of opening up when they feel hurt or threatened, and why power struggles and even violence seem normal. Like the air we breathe, the paradigm for war has enveloped how we talk to each other for so long that it's hard to see outside it and realize there is an alternative.

Excited by this new awareness, I began to consciously develop systematic descriptions of the traditional War Model for communication and of my own alternative model, Powerful Non-Defensive Communication(PNDC). While my descriptions are based on my own Euro-American experience, people from many racial and cultural backgrounds confirm that this traditional model, with some variations, is used in their families and communities as well.

Although this alternative way of communicating is new for most of us, to varying degrees, I don't see myself as having actually "created" it. Rather, I think I have been given the gift of articulating how we have misused our basic communication tools within a war-like system and how instead we can use them more constructively, according to their natural functions.

In this book, you have an opportunity to compare these two systems for yourself. In the first quarter of the book, I describe the War Model. You will learn exactly how we have translated the rules of war into conversation; how power struggle has the characteristics of an addiction; how the three passive and the three aggressive defensive modes equate to common personality types; and how we misuse each of our three basic forms of communication—questions, statements and predictions.

The remainder of the book walks you through the steps in learning the Powerful Non-Defensive Communication model. You will find two chapters are devoted to each of the three forms of communication. For example, the first chapter on questions explains how to ask questions in a fully non-defensive way. The second contains more than a dozen types of non-defensive questions and demonstrates how to use them in different situations at home, at work, and in the community.

Next, you will find a chapter on developing the non-defensive attitude crucial to these skills. This is followed by a chapter on how to practice them. I use in-depth examples, some of which I carry throughout the book, so readers can gain a deeper understanding of how to use the skills. You can use the numerous summary charts and the Index of Examples as a resource for dealing with current issues in your life.

We no longer have to be bound by the old rules for communication. We can choose new rules that empower us to be more open, spontaneous, vulnerable, and honest. They can help us protect ourselves while being more compassionate. They can guide us toward immediate solutions to conflicts that previously would have seemed irresolvable. The stories in this book demonstrate the power of listening and speaking non-defensively in ways that have gone beyond even my own expectations.

When I teach this process to third graders, they learn it rather quickly! For adults, the hard part is unlearning the old ways. Just like learning any new skill, it takes awareness, patience, and gradual development. On a personal level, I think of PNDC as a meditation practice in the sense that I know I will need to continue working on my own non-defensive skills for the rest of my life. At the same time, becoming increasingly non-defensive has already transformed me. Others who have learned this method consistently describe it as "freeing," "disarming," "contagious," and "revolutionary."

Human beings can interact in a limited number of ways. We can use our senses—sight, sound, taste, touch and smell. We can talk, listen and even interact on a telepathic level. In each case, we exchange and create certain types of energy. The energy created by the traditional dynamics of verbal communication causes people to suffer pain and violence. I still feel certain it doesn't have to be this way. I'm increasingly convinced that our communication methods determine our individual and global reality.

One hundred years ago we were traveling in horse-drawn buggies; today we travel in space and possess nuclear technology. This quantum leap demonstrates our capacity for phenomenal change. But unless we rid ourselves of defensiveness and power struggle, which lead to conflict and alienation, it is unlikely that we will have the wisdom to contain the destructive potential of our technology. Beyond the issue of finding intimacy and meaning in our own lives, I believe learning to communicate non-defensively is our next evolutionary step, an essential key to our survival.

Despite the level of strife on earth, I am inspired by the human capacity for transformation and compassion. I believe we can learn to speak in new ways that honor each person's full humanity. This book provides the fundamentals for those new ways. We can take the war out of our words.

PART I

THE
WAR MODEL

A Traditional System
for Communicating

1

Defensiveness

The Only Self-Protection We Know

The motto "To be open is to be vulnerable, and to be vulnerable is to be weak" underlies all the defensive maneuvers we use in war. We would be very unlikely to stand on an open battlefield with no protection unless we were on a suicide mission. Our openness would make us vulnerable to attack; we could be killed.

I believe we use this same rule of war as the basis for how we talk to each other; we think that being guarded and closed is our best protection. Unfortunately, rather than offering us safety, our reluctance to be open can actually harm us. This chapter will detail how this axiom of the battlefield works and show the devastating effect it has on all our relationships.

Defensive Barriers in War and Conversation

Dictionaries define "protection" as "defending from attack." By carrying these associations from the battlefield into our conversations, we bring a war model to our communication. We may become defensive any time we feel a need to protect ourselves.

Creating a barrier between ourselves and the other person is usually the first step in our defense. However, we protect different things when we talk to each other than we do in war. Rather than protecting our body, we seek to protect intangible things, such as feelings and beliefs, from being hurt or controlled. We try to protect our ego, our self-image.

It doesn't take much for us to feel threatened by what someone says to us. Often, all a person has to do is say something in a judgmental tone, such as "Isn't that report finished *yet?*" In our effort to protect ourselves from these keenly felt judgments, we automatically create an emotional barrier between ourselves and the other person. Many of us can actually physically sense a wall go up inside us. Emotionally, we go into the bunker.

During one of my workshops, I did a spontaneous role-play to demonstrate how quickly we can become defensive. Using a critical tone, I asked a woman named Akaya, "Do you *always* peel potatoes *that way?*" Startled, she pulled back a little, narrowed her eyes, and then responded, with subtle, playful defiance, "Yes." Her body language suggested that I should get out of her face. Everyone laughed, including Akaya. A few minutes later she raised her hand and said, "You know, Sharon, I didn't even have a potato in my hand, and still my walls came up so much it took me a minute or two to be able to refocus on what you were saying." Although Akaya is a brilliant diversity consultant, like most of us she became immediately defensive in response to a judgmental tone.

If we so quickly create walls of separation over how we peel a potato, whether in a workshop role-play or our own kitchen, imagine what happens when the stakes are higher—when we are worried about the welfare of our child, an important change taking place at work, or an ethical issue facing our community.

De-Facing The Enemy

When we initiate the defensive reaction of creating an emotional barrier, we simultaneously begin to perceive the other person as an adversary.

When Marcus and Sally first met they immediately felt like kindred spirits. Marcus was generally warm and open. But as their relationship continued, Sally noticed that sometimes when he was upset he had trouble talking. When she asked Marcus what was bothering him, he would reply that nothing was wrong. Only when she coaxed him would he eventually tell her what was troubling him. As time went on, his resistance to talking when he was upset increased. The more she probed, the more reluctant he was to reveal his feelings. During these interactions, neither of them felt an ounce of kinship; they didn't even like each other.

After ten years of this, when Marcus became upset about something, he would glower, fold his arms, and slump in a chair. His oppressive energy filled the living room, yet he refused to talk about what was upsetting him. As soon as Sally saw that posture and look she would freeze, knowing what was coming. She would force herself to start out gently, asking him what was wrong. "Nothing!" he would reply harshly. She would continue to coax, with a veneer of sweetness in her voice. "I can tell you're upset, honey. I'd really like to help. Won't you tell me what's the matter?" He'd say, "I told you! *Nothing is wrong!*" Sally would then move quickly into her own anger, which was, after all this time, lying close to the surface. "Look, I am not a stupid woman. I can tell when something is wrong!" Her anger then became his opportunity to blame her for the problem. "I was just fine before you started bugging me. Just lay off, would you?"

Increasingly, over the years, they played out this scenario, leaving both of them furious and emotionally shut down for hours, sometimes days. Marcus and Sally's scene is but one of the defensive scripts that millions of us perform over and over.

When we react defensively, treating even a loved one as an adversary, we stop seeing the complexity of the other person's motivations. We aren't focused on the loved one's experiences or insecurities. Our focus, instead, is on construing the other person as *intentionally* motivated to hurt, manipulate, or control us. This view allows us to slide easily into the dual belief that we are morally superior to our opponent in the conflict and that we are being victimized. Sally once complained, "I'm sick of this. He resists every time I try to help him talk about his problems. He's trying to drive me crazy!" While the other person may have a complex combination of motives, we see his reaction only in terms of how it is directed at us, the way we would see an enemy approaching in battle. We no longer see the face of someone we know, perhaps even love.

In war, this process is called "de-facing the enemy." During a lecture on the war tactics used by neo-Nazis and skinheads, Dr. Larry Dawkins, chair of the speech department at Mount Hood Community College in Gresham, Oregon, described his experience in boot camp. The cadence for marching, he said, was established by having the soldiers yell "Kill, kill, kill, kill" with every step. As he explained the motivation for this procedure, "The Marines want soldiers to see the enemy as evil, as someone dangerous and thus necessary to kill, so they do not want him to see the face of the enemy as another person who has a family and feels pain."

Such image-making stimulates many of us to react defensively to entire groups of people. Fearing them, we build emotional barriers that prevent us from understanding that most of *them*, like most of *us*, are regular human beings who just want to live their own lives. This defensiveness opens the door for any group to legitimize its assaults on another. No matter who does it, the process of de-facing the enemy allows us to see ourselves as morally superior victims who are justified in attacking others. This rationale creates a psychological process through which we deny our own responsibilities in conflict, project unethical motives onto others, and blame them for a wide range of problems, including our own behavior even as we attack them. I refer to any group or person who is functioning in this way as acting as a "superior-victim-attacker."

At a core level, the irony is that the way we talk to each other in our own homes is qualitatively the same as that used by hate groups and others who want to control our thinking. When we habitually protect ourselves defensively, we wall ourselves off from each other increasingly over time, acting like enemies even with the people we love most. We see this happen not only with other adults but with our own children as well.

Hiding Information

As we build emotional barriers, our second defensive reaction is to *hide* any thoughts, beliefs, feelings, behaviors that make us feel vulnerable. We assume that exposing information might give others power to hurt or control us. For example, Maria was having dinner with her friend Celeste, who spent the entire evening talking about how insecure she felt in her relationship with a man she had been with for several years. During their conversation, Maria was shocked to learn that Celeste had never told him she had an eating disorder.

Dismayed, Maria thought, Here is a woman who is a physician, well-respected in her field, and she spent the evening talking about how afraid she is to tell the man she loves about a critical issue in her life.

Celeste may have been afraid of rejection. She may also have been cautious about telling her partner[1] because, if their relationship ended on negative terms, he would possess damaging information about her. We can hypothesize that her fear was of being hurt or of the control he might have over her life. In addition, Maria hadn't shared her own feelings with Celeste. Not only was Celeste afraid to talk to her partner, Marie was afraid to tell Celeste how upsetting she found that information.

Most of us have a common bond with these two women. We are also afraid, in varying degrees, to tell our family, friends, co-workers, and others in our community vital information about what we think, feel, believe, and even do. Like Celeste, we often associate honesty with exposing ourselves in a way that might lead others to reject us or give them control over us.

We hide information for different reasons. We may hide certain information from our parents, even throughout our adulthood, because we fear their judgment or rejection. This might be anything: a belief in reincarnation, our reasons for quitting a job, our sexual orientation, our dislike for some gift. It is astonishing how many of us actually hide evidence of our way of life—religious artifacts, alcohol, books—before the visit of a family member.

Sometimes in business we don't give clients information because we're afraid it might displease them or result in their taking their business elsewhere. In trying to please our customers, we may abdicate our responsibility to give them our best professional advice. Don,

---

1. Out of respect for the variety of domestic relationships in our society, I will use the word "partner" to describe all persons in a committed intimate relationship, including husband and wife.

the owner of a small printing company, had a customer who wanted to order some business cards. The customer had been adamant about what she wanted. "I want this logo in these three colors, and I'm in a hurry. Can you get it done by Thursday?" Don immediately knew those three colors wouldn't look crisp or professional, but the client clearly didn't want his advice, so he withheld his opinion and simply said yes, he could do it.

Another kind of information we frequently hide is "flaw revelations"—feelings of inadequacy or some perceived weak point in our character that might make others disrespect us. We may not want a woman friend to know that we are terrified to stay home alone at night or are afraid of getting AIDS because she would see us as immature. We choose to be unknown rather than expose ourselves by opening the door to rejection or control.

Does Defensiveness Protect Us?

Following the tactics of combat, we assume we must build emotional barriers and hide many of our thoughts and feelings to protect ourselves in our interactions. Following are four basic questions to ask yourself in examining this assumption.

1. Do I feel safe when I am defensive? Sometimes people feel safer when they are defensive than when they are defenseless, which assumes an either/or condition. However, the vast majority of people in my workshops indicate that they do *not* actually feel safe when they are defensive; rather, they feel threatened and insecure and usually perceive others to have some kind of power over them.

The power we perceive others to have over us may be to fire us from a job, judge us harshly, reject us, or simply refuse to hear what we have to say. For teachers, that "power" may be a boy rolling his eyes during a lecture; it may be a co-worker who constantly interrupts us in meetings and ignores what we say. For a parent, it may be a child's accusation: "That's not fair!" It may be our own parent, who still treats us as if we were a child, or a partner who does not willingly participate in doing household tasks. When we focus on the other person's power over us, we are usually not focused on our own strength, or even on the other's vulnerability. Our psyche shifts instantaneously into the position of victim, clearly an unsafe place to be. The irony is that whenever two people are both defensive, *each* can simultaneously feel like the other's victim.

2. What happens to my confidence when I am defensive?

Some people get an adrenaline rush when they are defensive and feel more confident than when they are not defensive. Such people may thrive on adversity, sometimes losing confidence, perhaps becoming angry or depressed, if they are not in some competitive conflict. Most people, however, report that their level of confidence goes down as soon as they feel defensive. Even if we ultimately verify our point, having to defend ourselves can create insecurity and make us feel less confident, as if having to prove to some judge that we are telling the truth.

3. What happens to my sense of competence when I am defensive?

Most people say that having to defend their competence makes them feel less adequate. Dick, a physician, had thoroughly studied two options for performing knee surgery on a patient and selected the better one, based on the circumstances. Later, another doctor challenged Dick's decision. Dick said that although he never doubted he was right, the mere act of having to defend his decision seemed literally to drain some of his feelings of competence.

4. What happens to my ability to learn when I am defensive?

Almost everyone responds that their ability to learn is severely limited. They shut down, are unable to take in information, and are closed to learning. For example, one task of professionals in the employment and training business is to retrain workers who have seen their jobs evaporate, or who have become disabled, and thus feel very vulnerable. Instead of being open and appreciative, these clients sometimes act closed, even angry, toward the counselors and teachers who want to help with their transition. In many other professions, as well, staff members or employees increase stress and conflict by defensively resisting the efforts of others to teach them new processes and techniques.

In intimate and professional relationships, defensiveness on our part is more likely to make us feel unsafe, insecure, incompetent, and unwilling to learn than to fulfill its wartime function of protection. The irony is that in the name of self-protection we thwart not only the growth of our own self-esteem but also our actual competence. Instead of becoming connected through open interactions, we become isolated.

What effect does defensiveness have on your

- sense of security?
- confidence?
- sense of competence?
- ability to learn?

Finding Security

Although we act defensive when we want to protect ourselves, feelings of genuine security usually involve a sense of confidence and freedom from apprehension. This is in keeping with the ideal we may hold of healthy, safe, and well-adjusted children, who play without fear, are curious and delighted with themselves and others, and are in awe of the magic of every new discovery. These little human beings have not yet internalized the notion that openness is dangerous. For many people, the image of a secure adult is one who has retained this openness, along with confidence, warmth, spontaneity, and creativity.

Who Is Better Protected?

Most people describe their image of a secure person as someone who is respected and successful. They generalize that openness in secure people will increase the possibility that others will want to help them rather than harm them. Secure people are often seen as having "good luck" in life and are more likely to have the strength and wisdom to be effective leaders.

By contrast, the image of a defensive person brings to people's minds someone who is jaded, worn down, hostile, guarded, suspicious, untrusting, and full of conflict. Some examples are the naysayer who puts a wet blanket on creative ideas during the staff meeting, the person who would rather remain unattached than take a chance on an intimate relationship, or the person who runs into misfortune repeatedly. People most often express less desire to help a defensive person because of this perceived hostility.

While we may give way to defensive people in influential positions who have the power to harm us, professionally or personally, we generally respond better to leaders who are *not* defensive. Organizational studies clearly demonstrate that companies permeated (usually from the top down) with defensive executives and employees do not, over time, perform nearly as well financially as those with a corporate standard of openness among themselves and their customers.

When we add defensiveness to our interactions with each other, we create a reality that is completely different from the one we would have if we were non-defensive. We create hidden agendas, poor self-esteem, and incompetence. We build relationships that are rife with conflict and devoid of intimacy and respect.

The Making of a Power Struggle

Whenever we are defensive, not only do we build emotional barriers, see the other person as an adversary, and hide vital information, we also create a reality that revolves around a *power struggle*. A power struggle is essentially a fight in which we use our words, tone of voice, and body language as weapons of war in order to gain control over someone else. Unless our struggle has escalated to physical conflict, we are fighting primarily with psychic power in order to gain control of a relationship or of a particular situation or group. These struggles for power can include two or more people, each trying to gain influence over a family, classroom, business, community group, or cluster of friends.

Once we win a power struggle and gain psychic dominance, we may control other people's decisions and actions. For example, while serving on a committee, two people may struggle to determine which one can garner more support from other committee members to control the organization's budget, select a keynote speaker for a conference, or dictate work assignments. In an intimate relationship, the struggle may be over what to have for dinner, how to discipline the children, where to vacation, whether to have sex tonight, what house to buy, or what movie to see.

In some cases, our power struggles may involve gaining control over another person's feelings. We might want to demonstrate that we have superior knowledge and make the other person feel intellectually inferior. Or we may put someone down for a variety of other reasons. At one workshop, Elaina told a story about a co-worker, Susan, who had come up to her one day and said, "You look so beautiful in that dress." Feeling warm and open, Elaina smiled broadly and responded, "Thank you," whereupon Susan continued, "Isn't it nice that they are making better clothes for large women now?" Elaina was devastated, instantly sinking from feeling joy at looking great to feeling shame that she was overweight, and believed that Susan's comments were intended to make her feel bad. This incident had happened three years earlier, and their relationship had never been repaired. In fact, it had become progressively worse.

Like war, a power struggle can be ongoing, with many battles fought over time. From that one comment, Elaina and Susan's battles spread to other sniping remarks, as well as disagreements over how to perform procedures at work, operate within their company's budget, and purchase supplies.

Whether the power struggle involves one incident or has the ongoing character of a soap opera, once we engage in it, it holds us tight. Neither person wants to give in, admit error, or give in to the other, even if it would be in our mutual best interest.

Four Aspects of Defensive Behavior in Any Interaction

- Building emotional walls
- Hiding information about feelings, thoughts, beliefs, or actions
- Seeing the other person as working against our goals—an adversary
- Engaging in power struggle

Power: An Object to Fight Over

When engaged in a power struggle, we perceive power almost as if it were a material object, like a nugget of gold that we assume cannot be shared. Most of us take turns winning and losing in our struggles with others. Some people give in on a more permanent basis, losing the war and letting themselves be dominated.

Bound and Alienated

A very interesting emotional dichotomy occurs during our power struggles. We become simultaneously *bound to* and *alienated from* the other person. We become so compulsively locked into our conflict that we spend a great deal of energy thinking about the other person, complaining to others, rehashing our last battle, planning for the next one, and carrying it out—going the next round. It is as if we are locked into a tug-of-war, only instead of each hanging onto that chunk of gold, pulling and pushing to wrestle it away, we wrestle psychically, pulling and pushing against each other with our thoughts, feelings, and actions. In this way we become bound, inextricably tied to a person from whom we feel totally estranged.

This condition of being simultaneously bound and alienated explains why we can still be thinking—days, weeks, or years after one incident— about what we "could have said" to someone who upset us. Like Elaina, who brooded for years over how she could have responded to Susan's remark about her weight, we are still locked into the power struggle. This process applies as much to people we love, such as a spouse or a child, as it does to people we don't like or even despise. It is a terrible paradoxical trap to be in, regardless of whom we share it with.

Winning: The Primary Goal

Winning becomes the primary goal in a power struggle. Thus, in many relationships, we carry on perennial battles over politics, religion, or even who started the conflict that ruined the holiday dinner. Winning the argument becomes far more important than gaining understanding or resolution. A classic example of this behavior occurs in the film *Who's Afraid of Virginia Woolf?*, where two people who once were passionate become hell-bent on destroying each other with words. When our focus is on winning, rather than on what we are learning and how we are strengthening our own character, we lose integrity.

Acceleration of Conflict

When we are bound in a determined-to-win struggle over power, the conflict will naturally accelerate and intensify. After ten years, the minute Sally saw that Marcus was upset about *anything* she instantly felt extreme frustration and anger. As soon as she asked Marcus about what he was feeling, he felt attacked and equally angry. A level of intensity that had at one time been an *end* point in the conflict now became their *starting* point.

Fears of Loss and Failure

The intensity surrounding our power struggles is further amplified by the fear that, even if we win one battle, we might lose the next one. We often develop a deep-seated fear of loss of something tangible (money, house, job) or intangible (control, prestige, respect, love). These fears are not necessarily unrealistic, because, as many of us know, we *can* lose a lot in a power struggle. An ongoing power struggle in the workplace can result in someone's losing a job. At the very least, we may lose any intimacy we feel with another person the minute some cue prompts us to rejoin a particular battle.

While most of us might naturally experience fear of loss to some degree, the process of being in a power struggle can magnify this fear to the point that it dominates our lives. Our fear of loss can extend into a fear of failure, as well as becoming a generalized fear of not getting what we need unless we win any power struggle that comes our way. At its furthest point, our fear can lead us to the philosophical assumption that there is not enough for everyone to get what they need in life. Some psychologists and sociologists refer to this assumption as *poverty consciousness*. The phrase implies that we are focused on scarcity—what we don't have—rather than on abundance—what we do have. This way of seeing usually applies on several levels of existence: material, emotional, and spiritual.

Conflict Avoidance

I see another irony here. While we often feel compelled to try to win any power struggle we engage in, we may also be terrified of conflict (a fear that can also be strongly influenced by cultural background). Many of us see conflict and power struggle as practically synonymous. We often fear that even a minor argument could escalate rather than resolve differences, costing us more than we are prepared to pay. And, given our propensity for power struggle, escalation often does occur at a high price. Therefore, if we want to stay out of a power struggle, we avoid conflict as if it were a fatal disease.

The desire to avoid unwanted power struggles can be so extreme that in many cases, if we try to discuss a difference of opinion with someone, we may even be accused of *causing* conflict. Felicia's family talked passionately about their differences, but they came out of conflicts hugging each other and saying, "I love you." For years, therefore, she could not understand why friends and co-workers reacted so negatively to her when she raised an issue that was bothering her. "People treat me like I am causing a problem instead of trying to solve it," she said. "If I persist in trying to air out our differences, they start avoiding me."

Avoiding conflict usually does not help us to resolve it. We are left carrying a tremendous bag of "stuff"—old frustrations, angers, and hurts—around with us. Unfortunately, this bag is not one we can set down in order to take a rest. Unless we empty it by processing conflict effectively, it stays permanently—and heavily—on our backs.

Power Struggle as Addiction

A vast number of recovery resources now teach us that addiction to alcohol, drugs, smoking, or any other unhealthy pattern affects us in several similar ways. First, the addiction exerts control over our behavior. Second, the addiction frequently causes us to create the illusion that our involvement with it is essential to meeting our needs. Third, the object of our addiction becomes the most important thing in our lives, more important than anything or anyone else. Fourth, the process of addiction becomes progressively destructive. And finally, the addiction fails to give us what we need, leaving us feeling empty and craving something more. Thus we repeat the cycle, which exhausts our energy and renders us psychologically and spiritually—if not literally—lifeless.

I believe that power struggle functions as an addiction. When we are in a power struggle, we frequently exhibit these same tendencies and characteristics. We have a compulsion to win that can become more important than caring for another person or even our own ethics. The belief that winning is essential to our well-being blinds us to a progressively destructive process that leaves us with less than we started with.

People from a variety of cultural backgrounds describe an automatic tendency to respond defensively, creating power struggle. *Given the addictive character of power struggle, it may be the most pervasive addiction on earth.* But just as we can recover from other addictions, we can recover from this one. To do so, we must face the magnitude of its impact on our lives and its inability to give us fulfillment. Far from helping us to achieve our goals, power struggle blocks us from meeting two basic human needs: to feel connected with others in love and to maximize our capacity for individual growth.

When We Engage in Power Struggles, We

- treat power as if it were an external object to fight over
- become simultaneously bound to and alienated from the other person
- make winning our primary goal
- accelerate rather than reduce conflicts
- focus on fears of scarcity and loss
- often try to avoid conflict, and are left with unresolved feelings
- engage in a process that becomes an addictive cycle

Like Flies in a Jar

Deepak Chopra tells a story that paints a vivid picture of the situation in which I think we find ourselves: When flies are put in a jar and left there with the lid on for a certain length of time, 95 percent of the flies will never leave the jar once the lid is removed. The flies have come to accept the boundaries of the jar as their reality. It does not occur to them that another experience lies beyond its confines.

In a strikingly similar way, I believe we have lived in a power-struggle jar for centuries. We are so locked into using defensive reactions that most of us can't even envision other ways to react even to minor conflict, let alone to mistreatment. We do this so regularly that we have developed whole sets of defensive behavioral patterns that are common across various cultural, racial, and sexual lines.

Moshe Feldenkrais says, "Until you know what you do, you cannot choose to do otherwise." The following three chapters will present an array of our typical defensive reactions in order to provide an accurate understanding of them. While most of us can identify some of our own defensive reactions, we are often unaware of many of them. Even if we *are* aware, we may not fully understand the dynamics of the process we are using.

Ironically, whatever our degree of awareness, our defensiveness usually feels legitimate, even necessary. Yet most of us have a very different view of other people's defensiveness. We are more likely to see them as being deliberately manipulative, even in cases where the people are completely unaware of what they are doing. It is vital to remember how often we all react automatically and sincerely believe our reactions are justified. Defensiveness is a complex, deep trap, and many of us cannot see our way out of it. The more skilled we become in recognizing and understanding how we "defend" ourselves, the more easily we will be able to escape the power-struggle jar and move into a new realm in which we can communicate more effectively.

Basic Categories of Defense

Defensive reactions fall into three well-known categories: fight, flight, and surrender. These reactions have been adapted to psychology from a military context, in the order of the warrior's preference. According to the rules of warfare, if we think we have the strength to win, we should dig in and fight; if we don't think we can win, we should run like hell. Only if we can neither win nor escape would we sometimes choose to surrender as an alternative to death. Thus, these three defensive maneuvers are commonly seen as progressing on a continuum from passive surrender to aggressive fight. I have observed that each of these categories—surrender, withdrawal (flight), and counterattack (fight)—actually contains both a *passive* approach, undertaken primarily for self-protection, and an *aggressive* approach, undertaken for retaliation as well as self-protection. Ultimately, then, we have six modes of defensive reaction in which we can engage.

Defensive Modes as Personality Types

Most of us use all six defensive modes at various times or perhaps use different ones with different people. We may have a favorite one we use most often or one we fall back on when all else fails.

Our preferred defensive style is often such an integral part of our interaction with others that it is seen by those around us, and even ourselves, as our "personality," a significant part of our identity. Each of the six defensive modes therefore corresponds to a common label that describes a certain personality type. Having particular defensive reactions as part of our perceived identity can make it harder for us to give them up. As Scott, a workshop participant, said, "If I stop being defensive, I won't have any personality at all! My friends won't know who I am."

Many of us have legitimate reasons for fearing to give up our defensiveness. Lena Horne has described how she first wrapped isolation around herself, as the defense she felt was necessary to her survival. For her, like for so many of us, defensiveness was the best way she found to protect herself. This great singer eloquently describes her own later healing process, and how people were amazed by the sound of her voice, her spontaneity, her passion. They did not realize, she said, that for the first time they were seeing and hearing the "whole" Lena Horne. As we become less defensive, rather than losing our personality, we can be more open, free, and spontaneous.

2

Surrender

Although surrender may seem to be a simple act of giving up, I regard it as an actual defensive maneuver. In warfare, we allow the enemy to tell us what to do in exchange for agreeing not to kill us. In verbal interactions, we may exchange our compliance out of fear for our physical safety or for our emotional security. Thus, even as we surrender, we are attempting to influence the other person in order to prevent further conflict.

Surrender–Betray:
Co-Dependent Personality Type

Surrender–betray is a passive format for protecting ourselves. We betray ourselves by giving in to someone who is mistreating us and then go so far as to see our own behavior—instead of the other person's—as the cause of the problem. A good example is Gordon, who worked together with Selma on a variety of projects. When Selma asked Gordon to undertake a certain task necessary for their project, he always complied. However, when he would ask her to do a project-related task, she would usually respond by sighing, rolling her eyes, and shaking her head. Gordon was worried about the quality of their work and did not want to be in conflict with Selma, so he often did more than his share. He also decided that he was asking too much of Selma, particularly since she was recently divorced and trying to adjust to being a single parent. In addition, he thought, she had been at the company longer, so he needed to prove his willingness to go the extra mile.

Gordon surrendered to Selma when she acted irritated with him for asking her to do her share of project tasks. He not only gave in to her message that she didn't want to do her part, he also blamed himself for demanding too much of her. When we betray ourselves by this type of surrender, our primary purpose is usually some form of self-protection. But we may also be protecting another person, as Gordon was, even though Selma was taking advantage of him. Many of us make excuses for co-workers, friends, or family members who treat us rudely, rationalizing as to why they are in a "bad mood," as if we are doing them a favor by allowing them to treat us poorly.

Denial

Gordon didn't even realize he was surrendering. He simply thought he was making the choice to be a good team partner and making sure the job got done well. When we surrender totally, we usually aren't aware that we are doing so. We suppress our own capacity for critical thinking, adopt the other person's viewpoint as our own, and defend the other person's behavior, just as Gordon did. It is as if we have been taken as a prisoner of war and brainwashed into thinking that our captor is our ally.

When we surrender in this way, we often believe what other people tell us, even though their perspective is slanted toward their own advantage. People who dominate us may even think they have our best interests at heart. It may be a parent or minister who wants to influence everything—religious beliefs, choice of career, whom we marry. Unfortunately, in many cases, the more brainwashed we become, the more "normal" it seems. We may not realize until years later, if at all, the cost of allowing someone else to direct our course.

People who are making unfair demands or otherwise mistreating us may or may not consciously know they are being unreasonable. They can be in denial too, not actively aware that they are using another human being in a non-reciprocal way to meet their own needs. Regardless of their levels of consciousness, both parties engaging in this process ultimately suffer damage to their character and self-esteem.

Surrendering Out of Fear of Loss

We may use the defensive mode of surrender–betray because we sub-consciously fear some kind of devastating loss if we don't cooperate with the person who is treating us poorly. It could be loss of a job, loss of our child's custody, or loss of the person with whom we are in love. Or we might be trying to protect our children from conflict, giving in to another person as a way of attempting to keep peace among family members. When we surrender totally and refuse to acknowledge how we are being mistreated, we are less likely to experience the fear of loss consciously.

Surrendering Out of Guilt

Even in situations that do not threaten us with some drastic loss, we may still surrender completely. We may surrender to rude treatment when we feel guilty about our own behavior or take too much respon-sibility for someone we love. Our young son, for example, might speak harshly to us. When we ask the child to speak in a more respectful tone, he may blame us for his behavior, saying, "It's *your* fault. I'm *hungry.* You haven't fed me lunch yet!" We may look at the clock, see that it is past lunchtime, and take all the blame for our child's mood. "You're right; you must be hungry. It's almost twelve-thirty. I'll fix lunch right away."

In this case, we have surrendered to the boy and taken all respon-sibility for his abusive behavior. We may also apologize to a parent who is treating us disrespectfully or make excuses for mistreatment by our spouse because of guilt about our own past behavior. In each case, we voluntarily give up our right to be treated with kindness.

Surrendering Out of Habit

In the examples presented thus far, each person was surrendering in a situation where some mistreatment was actually occurring. However, we may also surrender in situations where the other person has no desire to dominate us. For example, one evening Damon asked his partner, Cynthia, what time she wanted to have dinner. She immediately answered, "Oh, I'm sorry, I should have started getting it ready sooner." Cynthia assumed he was justifiably upset by her not having begun to cook and willingly surrendered with an apology. Damon only wanted to plan together when to eat. He felt frustrated at how often her immediate surrendering interfered with simple decisions and also felt sad that Cynthia so easily assumed she was doing something wrong, based on old habits from childhood.

Betraying Others

In many cases, we wind up betraying others as well as ourselves. By accepting and rationalizing our own mistreatment, we often expose others to it. If we accept abusive behavior from a spouse, we are also jeopardizing the welfare of our children. If we succumb to a supervisor's demand for unreasonable work hours, it can adversely affect coworkers, who may be judged by the standard we set.

If we assimilate into a culture that demeans us because of our race, age, religion, or sex, we may pass the humiliation on to others close to us. Fran, a Native American woman, said that when she was a child her mother always made her wear a hat in the sun, or even use an umbrella, so her skin wouldn't get any "darker." Despite her desire to protect Fran, her mother's surrender to the predominant culture's bias against dark-skinned people actually taught Fran to be ashamed of the color of her own skin. Fran in turn became more susceptible to accepting the prejudice she received from others.

The Co-Dependent Personality

People who use this defensive mode are often labeled as having a "co-dependent" personality. While these people may surrender even when the other person has no desire to dominate, in extreme co-dependence they may even defend the actions of a partner or family member who is physically abusive.

Regardless of the degree of mistreatment, when we surrender completely to an abusive person, we bond with that person, often literally feeling "protected"—the opposite of what is actually happening. In essence, it is a process of assimilation wherein we relinquish the strength of our own reasoning and will—even our identity—and join

> ### Format for Surrender–Betray
>
> Betraying yourself by denying the validity of your own needs or viewpoint while defending another person's mistreatment of you.

symbiotically with someone who is mistreating us. We become a willing partner in our own abuse, colluding in our oppression. Whether the situation involves avoidance of responsibility, accusations, demands, criticism, or physical violence, the fog of denial clouds our own inner wisdom, leaving us unable to adequately protect ourselves and our loved ones.

Surrender–Sabotage: Passive-Aggressive Personality Type

The second and more aggressive form of surrender is surrender–sabotage. We give in to what the person wants, but we *are* aware on some level—consciously or semiconsciously—that we don't like how we are being treated (unlike surrender–betray). We therefore suppress our frustration and, instead of openly acknowledging our discomfort, employ rationales such as these:

"I don't dare complain; I don't want to lose my job."
"You can't fight city hall."
"I don't want to lose this relationship, it's good in so many ways."
"If I say anything, it will just make things worse."
"I don't want to rock the boat."

When we use surrender–sabotage, we are suppressing our own desire to rebel openly.

Since we have not fully surrendered, however, we are more motivated to fight back in some way. Here, the goal is actually twofold: to protect ourselves and to retaliate. We comply with the other person on some level and then use "hidden" aggression to get even, replacing open rebellion with sneak attacks. While others may clearly see our behavior as hostile, we may or may not be fully conscious either of our anger or of our efforts to retaliate. This type of defensive maneuver always contains some form of double message because we are overtly complying and covertly attacking. The following categories describe common methods of surrender–sabotage.

Reneging on a Commitment

One way in which we give double messages when we use surrender–sabotage is to make a commitment and then not fully keep it. We may break a commitment by not doing what we said or by having a negative (uncommitted) attitude that motivates us to undermine the other person or the project.

Maligner

We might respond to a person who has made an unreasonable demand by saying warmly, "Sure, I'll help out" (giving no obvious clue that the request has upset us), and then complain about the person to others. In this case we sabotage by maligning the person's reputation. While we may actually do the job, we will undermine the integrity of our commitment by verbally attacking our work partner.

Martyr

Martyrs may do what someone else needs or wants, but subtly or overtly demonstrate their resistance to the new burden. Our body language and tone of voice communicate that we are helping at great cost. We may slump our shoulders or sigh deeply in response to a request for help.

Even if we are motivated to help another person, we may believe that too much is being expected of us or that we are doing more than the person is doing for us. The relationship is no longer reciprocal. We help, and the other receives help. We are strong; the other person is weak. In the process, we become condescending and undermine our ability to have intimacy and genuine joy in the relationship. We also damage the respect we have for the other person—adult or child—which in turn undermines that person's strength. When we behave as a martyr, we sabotage more than the enjoyment of an outing or a work project. We sabotage our sense of reciprocity and equality.

Procrastinator

We may agree to do something we would rather not do and then procrastinate and fail to get it done by the designated time. We may not consciously decide not to keep our commitment, we just keep putting it off. The effect is still one of undermining both the other person and the project. When we make a habit of this, others often feel betrayed and lose trust in us. Procrastinators not only sabotage the person being let down, they also sabotage their own competence and self-esteem.

Careless Performer

Sometimes a person may agree to do a particular task and then perform it carelessly, commenting, "I did my best, I just didn't have time to do any more." Or, if the person is more clearly angry about having to do the job, "I did what you asked, what more do you want? You're never satisfied, no matter what I do."

Many relationships are damaged by sloppy work that is a thinly veiled if not an obviously outright form of sabotage. In these cases, the family member or co-worker who asks for the work to be redone is often accused of being a nit-picking perfectionist.

Each of these four types of surrender–sabotage involves making a commitment and then breaking it by not following through with 100 percent integrity in attitude and action. When we break commitments, we not only undermine the other person, we sabotage ourselves. Maligning another, acting like a burdened martyr, procrastinating, and doing careless work are all forms of sabotage that exact a great toll on our productivity and ability to work together in community.

Sequential Contradictory Statements

While the behaviors just described involve some type of contradictory message, they usually include one or more actions that contradict an original statement of commitment. The following types of surrender–

sabotage involve no commitment; the contradiction is strictly verbal. The sabotage, nonetheless, is patent and destructive.

Compliment–Insult

When we follow a supportive sentence with a subtle—or perhaps direct—put-down, we sabotage. Clara told a woman she met at a professional meeting about her artistically talented son. The woman responded, "How wonderful that he has such gifts. It is so nice that each person has special talents." Clara felt put down by the woman's switch from initial support of her pleasure in her son's ability to an apparent need to remind her that he was no more special than anyone else—compliment followed by insult. Or recall the example of Elaina's comment to Susan from chapter 1, "You look so beautiful in that dress," followed by, "It's so nice that they make better clothes for large women now."

Another commonly used form of sequential contradictory statements occurs in business situations, where managers have been taught to use positive feedback as a preface to negative feedback. This practice of preceding a discussion of the *real* reason for the meeting with a compliment is so common that many people simply wait for the other shoe to fall when they hear the positive comment. While receiving genuinely positive feedback about job performance is vitally important, using compliments as a technique to soften the blow of negative feedback can be destructive. I refer to this practice as "bonding with people before giving them the ax." It often creates a sense of betrayal instead of support.

"Yes–But . . ."

Frequently, we agree with someone and in the same breath disagree by raising an objection. We throw out a quick "yes" as a brief acknowledgment, then rush on to disprove what is being said. The person is set up by the "yes," only to be undercut by the "but." As a result, "yes" turns into "no."

Many of us have had the experience of inviting a friend to dinner and hearing in return, in a pleased tone, "Yeah, that sounds great. I'd love to come." Then the person pauses and continues in a changed voice, "But I have to prepare for a major meeting at work tomorrow, so I'd better not." When this happens, we are lifted up in expectation and then disappointed. Such a friend, attempting to be polite, is actually unkind by being unclear.

Sorry–Not Sorry

All too often we tell another person we are sorry, but we do so in a manner that invalidates the apology. This practice has become so common that we rarely hear people say "I'm sorry" in a way that takes genuine responsibility for doing something hurtful. Sorry–not sorry can take several forms. Here are three.

1. Sorry–blame. This form of sorry–not sorry starts with an apology followed by blame. Janet says, "I feel hurt because you haven't called for a long time." Bob replies, "I'm sorry. [*pause*] Have you been feeling insecure about our relationship lately?" Bob has followed his apology with the suggestion that Janet's own insecurity is the real problem.

2. Sorry–denial of intent. Here we indicate that we are sorry for having done or said something that was upsetting and then follow the initial apology with a denial of having intended to do anything hurtful. This kind of apology implies that the other person misunderstood our motives. We commonly use phrases such as "I'm sorry, I didn't mean it that way"; "I'm sorry you took it that way"; or "I'm sorry you felt that way." In each case, we are only sorry that the other person was so inept as to misunderstand our honorable intentions.

Politicians who have to backtrack after issuing a statement that has negative ramifications often make such "apologies" by saying, "I'm sorry if what I said offended [this person or that group]." Here the person is apologizing *in case* something was offensive without ever truly acknowledging that something said *was* actually offensive.

3. Sorry–excuse. We often say we are sorry and then give an excuse, as if the excuse should be grounds for a pardon. If our supervisor is concerned that our overdue report is holding up other team members from completing their project tasks, we might say, "I'm sorry I haven't finished it yet, but I've been so busy with three other projects." We may also commit to making some personal changes and then come back to our therapist or partner with an apology attached to a myriad of reasons for why we were unable to follow through. The message here is, "I'm sorry, but it wasn't my fault." It is hard for others to feel reassured or satisfied when we make an apology and then essentially erase it by describing circumstances beyond our control.

Attacking Humor

Several types of humor are common vehicles for contradictory passive-aggressive messages that often are not funny.

Sarcasm

Sarcasm is perhaps the most prevalent form of covert attack in the guise of humor. When someone asks us for assistance on a very hectic day, we might respond in a sarcastic tone, "Remind me to ask *you* for help sometime on the busiest day of *your* life." Or, in a meeting at work, we might respond with a sneer by saying, "How long did it take you to think *that one* up?" Often, if we express sensitivity to a sarcastic remark someone else makes, or ask for clarification, the person will say, "I was just kidding," and pretend that we are making a big deal out of nothing. Sarcasm is frequently inherently dishonest.

Prejudiced Jokes

Men and women from a wide variety of ethnic, religious, and professional groups report the painful effects of sabotaging joke-telling. Under the cover of humor, a person will disparage entire groups that listening friends are a part of. The joker then denies that this negation includes those present or that it should affect them.

Samuel, a Jewish man, related how Tony, a co-worker of his, would regularly come up to him, pat him on the back, smile warmly, and proceed to tell a joke that was insulting to Jewish people. If Samuel tried to object or suggest in any way that he didn't like the joke, Tony would laugh heartily and say, "Lighten up, it's just a joke," or, with a tone of slight irritation, "Don't get uptight, you know I don't mean anything by it." If Samuel didn't accept the joke, Tony would act increasingly irritated and make some comment like "I'm just trying to be friendly," implying that he might stop being "friendly" if Samuel didn't accept his insulting jokes.

Passive-Aggressive Personality Type

Sarcasm or prejudiced humor can be quite aggressive and may not seem to fit into the category of surrender. In each case, however, people who use these defensive modes do not feel comfortable or safe enough to express their true feelings directly. They therefore choose a covert form of aggression that enables them to deny any bad intent if questioned about what they said. People who use this defensive mode frequently are referred to as having a passive-aggressive personality type.

When we use any of these formats for surrender–sabotage, we act like prisoners of war, hiding our hostility in order to survive. We surrender, but we don't really give up. As we have seen, surrender–sabotage, unlike surrender–betray, has an aggressive component. While it may be quite subtle, such behavior can be very hurtful. Although the covert part of the message is usually denied, it can frequently be more blatant and harsh-sounding than a direct statement of our concerns would be.

Even when we successfully sabotage another, we usually still feel trapped because we are unable to deal with the other person clearly and directly. While the function of our sabotage is to undermine, it is we who are behaving in incompetent and divisive ways, whether we fail to accomplish assigned tasks or sarcastically attack another person. Using this defensive mode, we may become bitter, harboring deep-seated resentments of other people's expectations and control over us. Eventually, we undermine ourselves far more successfully than we undermine anyone else.

Formats for Surrender–Sabotage

RENEGING ON A COMMITMENT

Maligning
Agreeing with or giving in to a person and then gossiping about that person

Martyrdom
Following through on what you said you would do, but with an attitude of irritation or feeling burdened and thus not with full commitment

Procrastination
Making a commitment but not completing the task in the designated period

Carelessness
Carrying out your commitment in a sloppy or neglectful way

SEQUENTIAL CONTRADICTORY STATEMENTS

Compliment–Insult
Following a compliment with an insulting comment while acting as if you are only saying something positive

Yes–But
Briefly agreeing with or supporting someone and then proceeding with disagreement or criticism

Sorry–Not Sorry
Following an apology with a remark that takes back the apology (in one of three ways)

1. Sorry–Blame
Saying you are sorry and then implying that the other person really caused the problem

2. Sorry–Denial of Intent
Saying you are sorry, but denying that you intend
anything hurtful

3. Sorry–Excuse
Saying you are sorry and then offering a reason for
why you did what you did

ATTACKING HUMOR

Sarcasm
Saying something in a joking manner but covertly
criticizing through a judgmental tone

Prejudiced Jokes
Using humor to convey prejudice toward a group of
people, often in the presence of a person who belongs to
that group

3

Withdrawal

The second category of defense is withdrawal. When we withdraw during an interaction with another person, we pull back so our position can't be seen. Instead of surrendering, we take cover. We may hide certain thoughts, feelings, beliefs, and behaviors or even physically retreat from the scene.

Withdraw–Escape:
Passive Personality Type

The more passive type of withdrawal is withdraw–escape. Our motive here is to protect ourselves by escaping from some interaction. Some of us may not even regard this kind of withdrawal as defensive but, rather, just an unwillingness to engage in negative or unpleasant conversation. We suggest that we are above power struggle when we say to a third party, "Well, I wasn't going to fight over it. If he wants to think that way, let him." When we do not set clear boundaries or express our opinion in any way, we are often still reacting defensively.

We usually withdraw to avoid some kind of conflict, rejection, or loss. We may want to avoid exposing some inadequacy or piece of information about ourselves of which we're ashamed. Recall the example in chapter 1 where Celeste, probably to avoid his rejection, refrained from telling her partner that she had an eating disorder. Frustrated with her friend's insecurity, Maria subsequently withdrew from Celeste, without telling Celeste how *she* felt. We may also withdraw in order not to hurt another person's feelings or to avoid dealing with some demand or expectation someone has of us. Whatever our motivation, withdrawal is escaping from what feels like an unpleasant arena, a painful situation, or even a serious war zone.

Often a significant part of our motive is that we are afraid the other person will gain some kind of control over us if we expose our position. We may anticipate that if we speak up in a straightforward manner, the other person will judge us, argue with us, gossip about us, or do something else to hurt us personally or professionally.

Physical Withdrawal

Most of us can think of a time when we left a room to get out of an argument. We have also seen people get up and leave—be it the living room, the conference room, or the campfire circle—without responding to what someone has just said. Whatever the environment, these people have chosen to respond by leaving, rather than by sharing what they think or feel.

In extreme cases, our physical departure might involve literally moving house and home across country to escape ongoing interactions with a certain family member who can be emotionally dominating or is just an invasive nuisance. We may leave because of an unhealthy relationship with an intimate partner. Unfortunately, if we haven't resolved the issue within ourselves, it may haunt us and, in many cases, arise again in the next person who assumes the role of the one we left behind.

Mental/Emotional/Verbal Withdrawal

When we withdraw our attention rather than physically departing, we simply remove our focus from the other person and put it somewhere else. We may look away, or out the window, if we are bored with someone who is indulging in a monologue. We may withdraw in response to criticism of how we are doing some task. We may feel too tired to defend ourselves, and fear the argument that will ensue if we do. Or, if our partner says something that is emotionally upsetting to us, we may simply change the subject or begin another activity, such as mindlessly turning on the television or flipping through the pages of a magazine.

When we withdraw our attention from someone, that person will most likely be consciously aware that we are not fully present. Even though we may withdraw because we feel helpless to deal with the situation, the other person usually will not regard us as powerless; instead, our departure can have a powerful effect on the one left behind and often causes feelings of abandonment.

Withdrawal Behind a Veneer of Responsiveness

In each of the following forms of withdrawal, people who appear to be responsive to us actually disagree with our perspective. Although they create the impression of being supportive, or imply agreement with what we are saying, they are hiding their own feelings and opinions.

Asking Questions in Order to Avoid Self-Exposure

Some of us ask other people questions, not only as a means of drawing them out but as a way of hiding our own attitudes, feelings, and behavior. We may have a battery of continuous questions that allows us to avoid self-revelation because the other person is kept busy providing information. Many people feel appreciated when we ask a lot of questions and may not realize until later that we never exposed anything about our own life, feelings, or opinions.

We sometimes respond to a question with a question of our own instead of giving an answer. This can give the illusion of responsiveness in cases where we are intentionally avoiding an honest answer. Suppose that a woman and I are out walking and pass a store window displaying a flowered couch. When she asks, "Don't you just love that couch?" my swift reply may be, "Are you thinking of getting a new couch?" Far from indicating genuine curiosity, my question effectively redirects the conversation so I can avoid telling her I cannot think of one positive word to say about that couch. It is, in fact, the ugliest I have ever seen.

Active Listening as a Means of Withdrawal

Many of us use "active listening"—a process that became popular in the 1970s—as a form of withdrawal. Often now referred to as responsive listening, its purpose is to paraphrase what we think another person is trying to tell us. In this way we ensure that we understand correctly before we respond with our own reactions.

When we use responsive listening, instead, as a way to *avoid* expressing our own opinion, we violate its purpose. For example, if someone at a party expresses a political opinion with which we disagree and we want to sidestep discussing the issue in more depth, we might say, "It sounds like you are really upset about what the city council just did" and then quickly bite into an egg roll. Although we may convey this response in a tone of friendly agreement, we have completely avoided mentioning our own satisfaction with the action taken by the council. This misuse of responsive listening happens frequently.

While some may feel supported by a person who uses active listening in this way, many others see through the facade. When people clarify what they "hear" us saying without ever expressing their own opinion in response, those of us on the receiving end are likely to find it condescending, insincere, irritating, or even enraging. It is like talking to an echo, shouting into the void. No one is there.

Offering Encouragement While Hiding an Opinion

Let's say we are expressing something that we are upset about; the other person reaches out to us, smiling and nodding and making affirming sounds or comments. We assume this shows agreement with what we are saying, when in fact the person actually disagrees with us but is withholding this opinion. When Celeste described how hard it was to tell her intimate partner about her eating disorder, Maria expressed warmth and support while withholding her own frustration and disagreement about hiding such an important issue from a partner. When we try to give support to a friend without fully stating our own opinion, we often do so to avoid conflict, but we are being duplicitous. The person who later finds out what we were really thinking may feel betrayed. When confronted, we are likely to say, "I was just listening," or even, "I didn't know you wanted me to express my own opinion. I thought you just wanted support for *your* feelings."

A person can sometimes tell that our response does not feel completely sincere, but some of us have the ability to withdraw behind such a convincing veneer of warmth and apparent responsiveness that even the most astute observer might fail to see through it. We are in error if we assume that we can always tell when another person has withdrawn.

I witnessed an example of this when I went with my friend David on a visit to his parents' house. I knew he found them oppressive and didn't like their politics, which they served up in portions as ample as the meal, but I was hard put to see evidence of his discomfort. He radiated warmth and laughed infectiously. Only after he walked out the door and exclaimed, "Am I ever glad to be out of there!" did I witness his true feelings again. David did not say hurtful things or spend a lot of time complaining about his parents. Mostly, he just wanted to get through the visits and leave intact—to escape with as little damage to himself as possible. Far from appearing passive, a surprising number of people who exude great warmth use withdrawal as a primary defense. In many cases they do care a lot about others, but their fear of conflict costs them their honesty.

Passive Personality Type

When we withdraw defensively, whether by making an obvious withdrawal or by giving the illusion of responsiveness, we are actually hiding from what we perceive as another person's power to affect our lives negatively, either in the moment or over time. We are not taking a positive, assertive action; our focus is on avoiding, on letting someone else have control—of the conversation and perhaps of us. Although David acted outwardly responsive when his parents said things that offended him, his actions were still passively designed to prevent his parents from gaining control over him. He had learned at a young age that if he disagreed with them, his father would overwhelm him with arguments and his mother would emotionally withdraw. Hiding his own opinions behind his warmth and laughter was his defense against his father's verbal battering and his mother's rejection.

Ironically, as previously mentioned, when we do notice someone else's withdrawal, we usually experience it as an action that has a lot of power. Withdrawal by another commonly arouses our own feelings of rejection. We may feel lost, helpless, or even enraged when someone walks off, stops paying attention to what we are saying, or responds supportively in a way that clearly lacks sincerity. We often do

Formats for Withdraw–Escape

PHYSICAL WITHDRAWAL

Walking Out
Leaving the physical setting in order to avoid a conflict or some kind of stressful interaction

Quitting/Moving
Quitting a job or moving to a different location to avoid ongoing stressful interactions with someone

MENTAL OR EMOTIONAL WITHDRAWAL

Attention Withdrawal
Withdrawing your attention from someone who is talking to you by such things as daydreaming, looking out the window, or reading

Emotional Withdrawal
Emotionally withdrawing—hiding feelings or beliefs about what someone is saying—in order to avoid conflict

RESPONSIVE WITHDRAWAL

Asking Questions to Avoid Self-Exposure
Asking questions as a way to show interest in the other person while avoiding conflict by hiding your own disagreement with her or his perspective

Using Responsive Listening as a Means of Withdrawal
Paraphrasing what another person says in order to appear responsive but actually to avoid giving your own opinion

Offering Encouragement While Hiding Your Opinion
Demonstrating concern and emotional support for a person, thereby implying agreement, while hiding your actual disagreement with his or her perspective

not realize that the person who withdraws to escape does so purely for the purpose of self-protection, with no intention to do harm. Such a person is usually left to struggle alone—internally—with a Pandora's box of feelings.

Withdraw–Entrap: Vindictive Personality Type

Withdraw–entrap is the more aggressive form of withdrawal. In this case, we withhold either our reaction to what another person is saying or information that the person needs in order to draw the person into some kind of trap. The person may get nervous and say something inappropriate or may not do some job correctly because important data are missing.

This defensive mode is analogous to a hunter's "sport." Like the bandits in the old Westerns who take cover before the ambush, we withdraw and wait until the prey is lured into a trap or comes out in the open. Then we go in for the kill. We have trapped the person into talking too much or feeling insecure or looking incompetent. We criticize whatever error we enticed the person to make, or we simply sit by and watch the struggle.

This defensive mode is by nature punitive, and to use it is often very calculating and manipulative. Nonetheless, people can react this way and be only partially conscious, or even unconscious, of what they are doing. Our defensive reactions are habitual, often having been established in childhood. While withdraw–entrap has an offensive component, it is still rooted in self-defense; we don't feel secure enough to be open and direct, so we withdraw to gain power in some interaction.

The remainder of this chapter covers three basic ways we use withdraw–entrap: turning withdraw–escape behaviors into entrapping ones, staring the other person down, and withholding vital information.

Adding a Vindictive Motive to Withdraw–Escape Behaviors

The motive for withdraw–escape is self-protective retreat, without the aggressive intention of retaliating against the other person. However, the same behaviors used in withdraw–escape can also be used as withdraw–entrap—if the motive is to control, hurt, or punish the other person in some way.

Using Physical Withdrawal to Entrap

When we preemptively walk out of the room without answering, rather than just withdrawing to escape, we can be calculating to draw the other person into a state of frustration, helplessness, or anger. The action can also be calculated to make another person feel abandoned, especially at a time of expressed vulnerability.

Asking Questions to Acquire Damaging Information

In addition to using questions simply to avoid self-exposure, we may also use questions to entrap another person into exposing damaging information. Like an espionage agent, we may ask seemingly supportive questions, while hiding our ulterior motive of drawing out certain material that we can use against the person later. I frequently hear stories of employees who act as confidants to co-workers, only to report the confidential comments to others, perhaps even a supervisor. These people insidiously draw others into exposing information that can be used to weaken a position at work. The same kind of thing happens among family members and friends.

Entrapping in this way is a bit like the tattling we did as kids. I remember sometimes being jealous of my little sister, Candy, because she was always so "good," whereas I sometimes got into trouble, usually from being rambunctious or talking back. One day when Candy was taking her turn at washing the dishes, I asked her, in a conspiratorial, friendly whisper, "Do you *always* rinse every dish?" For a while she insisted she did, but finally, in response to my friendly coaxing, she admitted that she fudged once in a while, whereupon I ran to Mom, gleefully shouting, "Mom, Candy doesn't *always* rinse every dish *either!*" Somehow, I must have thought that Candy's imperfection would vindicate me. Ultimately, it didn't help my cause with my mother, and my sister felt hurt that I had turned a moment of confidence against her.

The Stare-Down

A surprisingly common and very powerful category of withdrawal is refusing to give another person any visual or verbal response during a face-to-face interaction. We may simply stare intently and adopt a tense body posture, like a cat waiting to pounce. Sometimes our facial expression is laced with smugness or boredom, other times with coldness or anger. Our motive is to wait, to set the other person up to react in a way that plays into our hands.

The classic routine of the two vaudeville comedians depicts how this process works. When we withdraw to entrap someone else into reacting in certain ways, we essentially set the person up to become the straight man for our punch line. Unlike a comedy team, however, we do not have this person's willing cooperation. Here are examples of some common scenarios.

Blaming Our Own Mood on Another

Recall from chapter 1 how Marcus steadfastly refused to respond to Sally's probing as to why he was upset. Marcus would scowl, stare, and wait until Sally asked what was wrong, at which point he would say tersely, "Nothing." Knowing something obviously *was* wrong, Sally would protest the lie, at which point Marcus would attack her verbally, claiming he was in a fine mood until she started bugging him. His scowling and staring drew Sally in; his denial that he was upset laid the trap enticing her to protest and argue with him. At that point he would come out of his withdrawal and blame her for causing his mood. Both at home and at work, many of us all too often use some form of sullenness—intense, silent negativity—as a trap designed to set someone else up to take the blame for our own bad temper.

Avoiding Accountability

Sometimes a person will purposefully withdraw in order to get another person to back off, to avoid being accountable for a specific behavior. For example, if a team member at work has not followed through on completing her part of a project by the deadline, we, as co-worker or manager, may ask the woman, "When are you going to be finished with your part of the project?" She may sit there with a frozen stare, saying nothing. Nervous because of the silence, we may surrender by dropping the request for information and adding, "Well, just get it done as quickly as possible." We then walk away to escape the interaction, leaving the unresponsive person off the hook and unaccountable, at least for the moment.

If we are already frustrated with this person for her lack of follow-through and correctly interpret the stare as hostile, we may up the ante and express our frustration more directly, saying, "Well, can't you even *answer?*" or "You are holding up the entire team effort!" Now the person can shift quickly to the position of innocent victim and accuse us of attacking her. She might reply, "You don't have to attack me. I was just trying to think carefully about when I will be finished so I can give you an accurate answer." Often we feel trapped into apologizing at this point, "Sorry, I was just frustrated—I didn't mean to attack you." Either way, we walk away feeling zapped. The team member who withdraws in this way may be moving into her silent stare unconsciously, from the force of an old habit of avoiding accountability, or she may feel consciously angry at us for "pressuring" her.

Getting the Upper Hand in Negotiations

In various kinds of negotiations among parties in conflict—be they union negotiations, divorce proceedings, or business deals—a representative on one side will remain silent and unresponsive to a proposal from the other side. The purpose is to wait for his adversary to become nervous and say something that might be damaging to the adversary's position. An old saying about negotiating business deals goes, "Whoever speaks first loses"—analogous to being the first to show one's hand in poker, and suggesting that the one who holds out longer will get the upper hand. Put another way, the implication is that whoever speaks first has the weaker bluff and is more likely to back down and demand less.

Creating Psychological Insecurity

Some people gain power in intimate relationships by maintaining a kind of stoic silence in order to stimulate nervousness and insecurity in the partner or date. Sheri, for example, said when a male friend did that, she would find herself behaving in ingratiating ways just to get a response. She would talk too much and then, fearing rejection, become upset with herself.

This manner of withdraw–entrap fits traditional male-female scripts, in which the man is cast as the strong, silent type and the woman as flighty, with less personal strength. Both men and women, however, entrap in this way. The person who becomes insecure will often devalue herself or himself, trying harder to please the other and often becoming more clingy or "needy." Many of my clients have experienced this kind of withholding; it has great power to stimulate loss of confidence and can dramatically shift the power differential in the relationship.

People also use this defensive maneuver to establish psychological dominance in the workplace. Typical examples are the blatant ignoring of what another person says in a meeting or failing to respond to a simple greeting. It is common for people to know someone at work who regularly stares at them and strides on past without returning a hello. The withholder may be motivated by a particular anger or may just generally devalue a person who does not hold an important position in the company. The withholder might also be expressing prejudice based on gender, race, or sexual orientation. Such withholding can effectively undermine another's confidence in a professional setting.

Coercing a Commitment

When Carla called Regina to see about getting together during the week, Regina responded that she had a "week from hell" and didn't have time to do one more thing. Instead of asking Regina what had happened or expressing some empathy ("OK, maybe another time," or even, "That's too bad, I was hoping to see you"), Carla remained dead silent at the other end of the line. Regina, feeling pressured, sighed and said, "Well, maybe we could have an early morning break-fast on Tuesday," knowing even as the words came out of her mouth that getting up earlier would be distracting and tiring before an im-portant meeting at work. Carla quickly replied, "OK, that would be great." Regina hung up, furious. Although this had happened with Carla before, she swore it would be the last time she slipped into the trap and made an extra commitment she couldn't afford.

Withholding Information

The third category of withdraw–entrap centers around withholding information that is important to the other person. When Wayne, for example, came into a corporation as a young middle manager, he changed procedures and issued directives without adequately con-sulting long-standing employees. Phoebe, a member of his depart-ment, attempted several times to tell him that a precise change he was making had been tried several years earlier and had been abandoned when serious production problems resulted. After Wayne ignored her advice to reconsider his decision, Phoebe remarked to herself and a few co-workers, "I'm not going to say anything more. I'll just wait until he runs into problems. When production is down and we have a mess to clean up, it will be on his head." From that point on she would simply look at Wayne stony-faced any time he gave her in-structions, often walking away without a word. Although the stony stare indicated that she had resorted to withdraw–entrap, the most crucial aspect of her withdrawal was that she withheld information.

When production problems begin to arise, Phoebe still said noth-ing to Wayne. "Why should I warn him?" she told a co-worker. "He wouldn't listen anyway. Let him find out on his own." Phoebe let her manager hang himself. While she could not control whether he lis-tened to her or not, her personal reaction to his closed mind was to pull back and wait—with angry pleasure—for his fall.

In this case, Wayne initiated the problem by refusing to listen to someone with more experience. However, in many instances some-one reacts out of jealousy or insecurity, even when another employee has committed no offense. A new man may see a co-worker as stand-ing in the way of what he needs and assumes that he has to fight for what he wants. A person angry at being overlooked for advancement may take it out on the person who got the position.

Vindictive Personality Type

In both our professional and personal lives, we can find people who behave in this way, perhaps carrying childhood jealousy and competition into adulthood, wanting to pay others back for real or perceived injustices. Whatever our motive, when we vindictively use withdrawal to entrap others, we become self-appointed judges meting out punishment. Even if, like Phoebe, we originally intend to be helpful, when we withdraw with the goal of watching another person fail, we are being vindictive. Phoebe maintained silence even after the problems she had predicted began to occur and until it was too late for Wayne to recoup. When he was fired, she thought he definitely had it coming. Yet her reaction had as much impact on her own life as it did on his. When we react vindictively, we create a mood and an attitude within ourselves that *we* have to live with.

Formats for Withdraw–Entrap

WITHDRAW–ESCAPE FORMATS
WITH A MOTIVE OF ENTRAPMENT

Physical Withdrawal
Leaving a setting to entrap the other person into certain reactions, such as feeling angry, helpless, or abandoned

Asking Questions
Asking questions while hiding your own opinion or motives, in order to acquire damaging information

THE STARE-DOWN

Blaming Your Mood on Another
Acting upset, then denying it, so if the other person objects to your denial you can blame the "probing" for your mood

Avoiding Accountability
Refusing to answer a question, hoping the person will give up trying or will become more aggressive, and subject to accusations of attacking you

Getting the Upper Hand in Negotiations
Maintaining silence during a negotiation in the hopes that the other person will give in to your demands

Creating Psychological Insecurity
Using silence to make someone feel insecure and less equal in the relationship

Coercing a Commitment
Remaining silent to pressure someone into making a commitment

WITHHOLDING INFORMATION

Withholding needed information to entrap someone into looking incompetent

4

Counterattack

The third and final category of defense is counterattack. When we counterattack, we engage in open conflict rather than surrendering or withdrawing. We know we feel attacked, and we fight back. Unlike surrender and withdrawal, there is not much variety in the formats for counterattack. We simply either justify our own position or attack the other person's.

Counterattack–Justify: Defensive Personality Type

In the more passive form, counterattack–justify, we verbally defend ourselves against another's criticism or judgment. This defense is definitely more assertive and aboveboard than surrender–betray or withdraw–escape, because we stand up for ourselves directly. Nonetheless, we are still only trying only to protect our own position rather than attempting aggressively to hurt the other person.

Many of us have an automatic tendency to defend ourselves when we are "accused" of something. If our partner says, "You just don't care," because we failed to do what was wanted or expected of us, we are likely to respond with, "Yes, I do!" We frequently spend a great deal of energy justifying and explaining how much we do care, often to no avail. We can try to defend anything, from what we believe to how we spend money.

Lisa and Sawyer often had arguments over how much Lisa spent on the groceries. Sawyer did not like to shop or cook, so Lisa often did both. She was frustrated because Sawyer liked to have wonderful meals, especially when they had friends or family over, but he didn't seem to understand what kinds of ingredients were necessary to make those meals or how much it all cost. Sawyer, who paid the bills and felt the financial pressures, accused Lisa of not being mindful of budgetary restrictions.

Sawyer fell into the habit of confronting Lisa about the cost of the groceries as soon as she returned from shopping. She usually felt defensive before she even walked in the door, and almost invariably he would be upset about the amount. "What? You spent one hundred and fifty dollars? We don't need nearly that much!"

Often Lisa would respond gently, "Honey, I was really careful. I just tried to get enough so I wouldn't have to keep running back to the store all week. I think it ends up being cheaper this way. And your folks will be here all weekend. I knew you'd want to serve nice meals. The wine for dinner really adds to the cost." Lisa was defending both her behavior and her rationale regarding her grocery purchases.

Sometimes, frazzled from the stress of being criticized, Lisa would go on a tirade. "I don't want to have to run to the store ten times this week! Do you want me to feed your parents turkey-neck soup? Sawyer, groceries cost a lot these days. What am I supposed to do?"

Implication: A Covert Weapon

We justify our behavior in this way out of a desire for self-protection, but we are still engaging in a covert form of counterattack. When Lisa countered Sawyer's position that she had spent too much, she did it only by *implying* that his judgment about the cost of the groceries was off base. She never said to him directly, "Your expectations about grocery expenses are totally absurd!" Instead, by saying, "I had to spend this much," she implied that he was being unreasonable to expect her to spend less.

With our children, we often use our energy defensively to justify our own requests. Corey had ongoing arguments with her daughter, Beth, who resisted doing housework. Beth would tell her mom she didn't have time to do the dishes, or agree to do them and then not, or get angry and say Corey was unfair and expected too much. In response, Corey, trying to control her tone, would plead through gritted teeth, "I think I have a right to expect some help with the household chores. I can't work all day and do everything around here too. I'm not being unreasonable, I just want us to cooperate."

Sometimes Corey would express her frustration more aggressively, saying, "I don't think it is too much to ask for some help doing the dishes when I work all day and buy the groceries and *fix the meals!*" Whether her anger was suppressed or overt, Corey was putting her energy into justifying her own request for help.

When we justify our behavior, we often are not aware that we are making implications that cast blame on the other person, who feels attacked. Even though Corey's approach was to defend herself, all Beth heard was a nagging mother. Sawyer thought Lisa was attacking him for what he believed were legitimate financial concerns.

Even in cases where the person doing the defending is being emotionally abused by the other person, the defense is very likely to be felt as an attack by the abuser. For example, if a father humiliates a son about making a mistake and calls him stupid, the child being accused may quietly reply, "I am not stupid" or "I didn't mean to make a mistake." In these cases, the child is still fighting back, no matter how timidly, because he is defending himself and implying that the parent is wrong. Even such timid statements of self-defense, however, as we know from increasingly frequent accounts of abuse cases, often stimulate the attacker to intensify the attack.

Countering the Attack

When we justify our behavior, we put more energy into countering the other person's position than in clearly establishing our own. Jason arrived home from work late one night to be angrily greeted by his partner, Trina.

TRINA: Where have you been? You said you'd take responsibility for dinner tonight!

JASON: I didn't say I'd do dinner.

TRINA: Yes, you did. We talked about it yesterday.

JASON: I only said I wouldn't *mind* doing dinner tonight.

TRINA: Well, you didn't let me know you had changed your mind!

JASON: I still haven't said I'm not going to. Just because I didn't come home right at five o'clock to make dinner doesn't mean I'm not going to make it!

Whereupon Jason turned heel and stormed into the kitchen, slamming doors and pans in his apparent meal preparation.

In his effort to defend himself, Jason simply shifted his defense to counter each specific accusation. He began by denying having said he would make dinner, then indicated he wouldn't "mind" making dinner, then implied he had intended to make dinner all along. Finally, he went off to do it.

What frustrated Jason the most was that he knew he had fully intended to make dinner and believed he was responsible about keeping commitments. He was upset that Trina did not trust him to follow through, but the more he argued against her accusations, the less able he was to state his own position.

Giving the Other Person Ammunition

When we justify our reactions, we often merely supply the other person with ammunition to use against us. Maggie, a social worker in a state welfare department, had a problem in dealing with her supervisor, Claudia, who accused her of being too emotional and of overreacting about a client in a difficult situation. Although this did not happen frequently, Maggie was upset at being told to be more objective and to refrain from expressing compassion for people in desperate circumstances. When accused of reacting emotionally, she would sometimes vehemently reply, "*I am not!*" She denied her own feelings and inadvertently implied that such emotion would be inappropriate. At other times she would say, "Well, maybe I *am* emotional, but I have a good reason to be upset about what is happening to this person," implying that feeling emotion for a client is usually inadvisable, but this case was an exception to the rule.

Many of us—when accused of overreacting—issue denials or plead extenuating circumstances. Maggie sensed that she was betraying her own feelings when she used these defenses but didn't know how else to respond. She walked away infuriated, knowing she had somehow confirmed the supervisor's accusations. Her attempts to defend herself had backfired.

Justification: A Sign of Weakness

When people defend themselves by using excuses to avoid responsibility, they may simply justify the status quo—persistent tardiness, sloppy work, jealous rages, or a host of other reactions. Although we often use counterattack–justify to explain legitimate reasons for our feelings or behavior, we risk being lumped in the same category with people who are making excuses to rationalize their failure to meet obligations.

It may be true that we were so busy this week that we barely had time to breathe, much less call a friend, but when we say that to defend ourselves, it still sounds like an excuse. When we insist to our partner that we *did* have to spend so much on groceries, we let the other person's attack define the terms of the argument. We come across as needing to prove our point or rationalize our experience, and in the process we lose our strength.

When we defend a legitimate position, we can appear to be trying to build up a weak position. Others often interpret verbal self-defense as an indicator of guilt. By defending himself, Jason weakened what started out to be a legitimate position, one that did *not* involve breaking a commitment. Likewise, Corey hurt rather than strengthened her position when she continued to reassert the legitimacy of her expectation that Beth help with housework.

Defensive Personality Type

In strategic war terms, counterattack–justify is one of the passive defenses because we are simply trying to ward off a real or perceived attack. If we frequently justify our beliefs, feelings, or actions, we may be referred to as "a defensive person." But no matter how loudly we

---

Format for Counterattack–Justify

Explaining or justifying your own beliefs, feelings, reasoning, behavior, and experience in order to prove the other person wrong

defend ourselves, we still feel backed into a corner, always having to prove ourselves or verify our own legitimacy. Ultimately, we hurt our credibility and lose respect rather than gain it.

Counterattack–Blame: Aggressive Personality Type

The motive in counterattack–blame is to retaliate with overt aggression. Here, we attack the other person's position, rather than simply defend our own. An example of this defensive mode is depicted in an old Andy Capp cartoon. Andy stumbles into his house in a drunken stupor, apparently in the wee hours of the morning, to be greeted by his wife: hands on her hips, hair wound up on curlers. Andy peers up at her and bellows, "Is that any way to greet yer 'usband when he comes home?" As he staggers past her, he comments under his breath, "A good offense is the best defense."

When we counterattack by verbally assaulting someone else, we hope to get ourselves off the hot seat by putting the other person on the defensive. Andy's criticism of his wife's late-night appearance is a calculated attempt to distract her from focusing on his drunkenness. We can counter a criticism by immediately throwing one of our own back without directly responding to what the other person has said. Conflict-causing differences repeatedly result in a set of accusations by one person becoming entwined with an opposing set leveled by the partner. For example, when Trina accused Jason of reneging on his commitment to make dinner because he arrived home late, he might have countered with an accusation: "You are so rigid! If I'm a minute late you go into spasm."

Disguising Blame

Even when our tone is gentle, we can still be issuing accusations. Lisa might tell Sawyer, "You've seen me shop, honey. You know I always look for the bargains and don't buy things we don't need." Here, cloaked under a sweet tone, Lisa accuses Sawyer of knowing better than to think she would spend money extravagantly.

Accelerating from Defending to Attacking

We can be especially prone to verbal assault when our frustration tolerance is low. In many cases, we may have been defending ourselves regarding some legitimate feeling or expectation and then escalate to heaping criticism on the other person. When Corey was completely overwhelmed and exhausted by managing a full-time job and a household, instead of defending her need for help she would sometimes attack Beth directly. "You *never* cooperate around here! You expect me to do everything while you just lie around and watch TV!"

Lisa too had sometimes reacted angrily to Sawyer's judgment of her grocery expenditures. "You are so quick to criticize when you never shop for groceries and you have no idea what they cost! Yet, you'd have a fit if I served your parents anything less than gourmet fare. You expect me to create meals fit for royalty without spending a dime!"

Many people fluctuate back and forth between defending themselves and attacking others, sometimes within the same conversation. Others have longer fuses and defend themselves for months or even years before they reach the limit of their frustration tolerance and blow up.

Blaming to Defend One's Own Desires or Intentions

Sometimes we attack others when we want to defend and promote our own desires or intentions. We may say to a spouse who thinks we can't afford something we want to buy, "You are just so controlling. You don't give me any freedom!" These attacks are designed to get the other person to give in and agree with what we want. The person being blamed may legitimately regard the other person as being strictly on the offensive. However, the blamer often feels a need to defend his or her desires in order to gain approval for them before taking action.

Blaming to Control Another's Behavior

We may also use counterattack–blame as a way to control other people's behavior. Parents who continually criticize everything from their son's haircut to his friends are often attacking as an attempt to control his behavior. Even if the parents' motives spring from concern for the child, this method—played out in milder form as the traditional lecture—only serves to alienate the offspring. I have consistently found that most critical parents do not experience their behavior as "offensive"; rather, they feel defensive about wanting to "protect" a child and uphold their own standards and expectations. Far from feeling powerful, they often feel helpless.

Conversely, in parent-child relationships, children often find verbal attacks effective for getting their own way. Children can become masters at pointing out everything parents do wrong, using that information to blackmail their parents into lowering their expectations regarding the child's behavior or giving in to demands for privileges that have not been earned. Unfortunately, when we respond to our children's accusations by lowering our expectations and awarding unearned privileges, we impair their potential for emotional and intellectual growth.

In an intimate adult relationship, an abusive person frequently has a symbiotic relationship with the other partner, and so feels betrayed and upset if the partner does not do what the abuser wants. Thus, the abuser feels justified in attacking everything, from who the partner's friends are to what the partner eats or wears.

The format for the attacks might consist of interrogating questions or a series of judgmental or accusatory statements. Often the abuser might repeat the same question or statement over and over, using it like a whip to break the other person down. In this classic situation, verbal assault is often a forerunner to physical assault.

A Cultural Epidemic of Abusiveness

I believe that we have created a social environment that has reinforced the development of abusive character in a growing segment of our population. Clients and participants in my workshops regularly tell stories about experiences with people, even strangers, who react to not getting what they want with a level of anger that is on the edge of violence. In families, businesses, and institutions, we have oiled the squeaky wheel, giving people who use aggressive, blaming behavior what they want. Blaming others, even to the point of filing frivolous lawsuits, has become a way of life for many.

Aggressive Personality Type

The behavior of aggressive personality types who misuse power and act belligerently can still be defensive at its core. In the majority of cases, abusive people feel they are fighting for their own survival and are not conscious that they are attacking or manipulating someone else. The daughter who has learned to get her way with aggressive accusations *believes* it when she tells her father, "You don't love me," as a way to avoid being punished for kicking her little brother. A lack of clear boundaries that require her to respect others has left her actually feeling like the victim. Feeling powerless and victimized—even when one's behavior is offensive and self-serving—is a trait many persons carry from childhood into adulthood.

A bullying way of life based on counterattack–blame often grows out of a dog-eat-dog view of the world. Even those who physically abuse others, including mass murderers, usually present themselves as victims and blame someone else for their crimes. It is possible that all aggression inherently emanates out of defensiveness, a knife that arises out of the anguish of old wounds to pass on the pain and suffering.

Format for Counterattack–Blame

Criticizing or blaming another person's beliefs, feelings, reasoning, behavior, and experience in order to justify your own position

Six Defensive Reactions

SURRENDER

Surrender–Betray: *Co-dependent personality type*
　　Giving in to someone who treats you poorly, blaming
　　yourself, and making excuses for the person

Surrender–Sabotage: *Passive-aggressive personality type*
　　Pretending to agree with someone who you think is
　　treating you poorly and then doing something to
　　undermine the person

WITHDRAW

Withdraw–Escape: *Passive personality type*
　　Avoiding talking about something you don't want to
　　discuss in order to avoid conflict

Withdraw–Entrap: *Vindictive personality type*
　　Refusing to respond to someone in order to draw
　　that person into a situation where he or she may feel
　　uncomfortable or act inappropriately

COUNTERATTACK

Counterattack–Justify: *Defensive personality type*
　　Responding to criticism by explaining your own
　　behavior or making excuses

Counterattack–Blame: *Aggressive personality type*
　　Attacking the other person's position in an attempt
　　to defend yourself

5

Common Misuses
of Our Basic
Communication Tools

If we tried to build a house by pounding nails with a saw and sawing boards with a hammer, we would find it a thankless task. We would damage our tools and construction materials and probably hurt ourselves in the process. Thinking we were using the tools properly, we would quickly feel helpless, frustrated, defeated, and angry. We might blame the "damn saw" or the "stupid hammer" for not working right, never realizing we were using the tools incorrectly. And for all our trying and blaming, we would continue to feel inadequate. We'd waste an incredible amount of time and energy and certainly wouldn't end up with a place we wanted to live in. If everyone tried to build houses in this fashion, most of us would be homeless.

I believe it is just as impossible to build the kind of human environment we want when we misuse our basic tools of communication, which have been shaped by our focus on defensive self-protection and power struggle. Because we use them as weapons instead of constructive tools, we often communicate in a way that increases conflict instead of resolving it. This can happen even when we want to communicate respectfully, because the misuse of these tools has become institutionalized.

In this chapter I will describe specific ways in which I believe we misuse each of three basic forms of verbal communication: questions, statements, and predictions.

Questions: Villains in Disguise

At a family reunion several years ago, Sylvia asked her great-aunt Mabel,
whom she had not seen for many years, about Mabel's two daughters
who lived far away and were unable to attend. When Sylvia innocently asked, "How are your daughters?" Mabel replied gruffly, "So
who are you, the FBI?" Made almost speechless by her aunt's reaction,
Sylvia mumbled something innocuous and changed the subject. While
Mabel's response to a genuine question may seem extreme, it is very
understandable in light of how questions are often used.

Dictionaries, which reflect our common usage, focus on words like
"interrogate" when offering a definition for the verb "question." Here
is a list of other verbs used:

ask	doubt
challenge	examine
cross-examine	inquire
debate	mistrust
disbelieve	object
discredit	probe
dispute	pry

These definitions reflect a tendency to use the question as part of an adversarial process.

When Sylvia asked her a simple question, Mabel felt "interrogated," hence her reference to the FBI. We have no idea what Mabel was afraid of. Perhaps one of her daughters was an alcoholic, and the question caused her to fear exposure of a family secret. Like Mabel, we may sometimes be reluctant to answer a question because our answers can be used against us. Further, we also frequently resist *asking* questions for fear of being seen as invasive and prying.

The use of questions as tools of interrogation is so common that when workshop participants practice asking questions non-defensively—regardless of how much communication training they have had—they are continually amazed at how hard it is to refrain from adopting an accusatory tone of voice or body language.

Using Questions in an Adversarial Way

Using a Question to Make a Statement

We have two primary formats for using questions adversarially. The first is to use questions as statements in disguise; the second is to use *entrapping* questions to put a person in a compromising position.

Whether we do it consciously or unconsciously, any time we use a question to give information rather than gather information, we violate its natural function. Mabel's response—"So who are you, the FBI?"—was a statement in the guise of a question. She used the retort to express her own feelings of discomfort with Sylvia's question about her daughters' well-being. Obviously, Mabel wasn't really asking Sylvia about the FBI. She was telling her she didn't like the question and felt put on the spot.

Many of our questions function as statements. We may ask a file clerk, "Do you always sort the mail that way?" Rather than openly stating whatever problem we see with how he is sorting mail, we hide our judgment behind the shield of a question. Whatever the circumstances, the other person usually hears the criticisms loud and clear. He knows we have not made a sincere bid for information. He may even accuse us of being critical, but since we did not openly express criticism, we can deny it and say, "I was just wondering."

Here are just a few examples of how we mask statements as questions.

Question	Underlying Message
"What did you do *that* for?"	I am irritated.
"Do you want to go to a movie tonight?"	I would like to go to a movie.
"Since when do you care what he thinks anyway?"	I don't want to deal with your feelings of anxiety.

We have three basic ways of turning a question into a statement of our own opinions and feelings: *tone of voice, body language,* and *adding words.*

Tone of voice. In each of the examples just given, the speaker's tone of voice passed on a certain message. The tone of our question often conveys a specific attitude or feeling; it can sound accusatory or judgmental, warm or caring. Even a tone laced with warmth carries a message about our own feelings and will turn a question into a statement.

Along with infusing feeling into the question, another method is to speak rapidly and clip our words. We also often punch certain words out harder to give them more emphasis: "Do you *always* have to *shout* when you are *upset?*"

Moreover, many of us were actually taught to ask a question with additional emphasis on the last word and a tone that rises in pitch. "What did she *say?*" This is contrary to a statement, where the tone comes down in pitch to a place of rest. A rise in pitch frequently gives the question a tone of increased urgency, expectation, and even insecurity and is very likely to block the listener from answering sincerely.

We are so accustomed to using our tone of voice in these ways that we are often not aware of it. We may even get irritated when someone else tells us that our question sounded accusatory or judgmental. In such cases, if we examine our own thoughts and feelings closely, we may well discover that we were indeed sending a message.

Voice Tones That Can Make a Question Defensive

- Sounding harsh or accusatory
- Accenting key words: "Why did you do *that?*"

- Sounding singsong or overly melodic in tone
- Speaking rapidly or clipping the words
- Raising the pitch at the end of the question

Body Language. When we ask a question but really want to convey what we think or feel, our body automatically expresses itself defensively. Its language falls into a number of patterns, many of which are common across cultural lines. Most of us shake our head from side to side to convey judgment or disbelief—a practice so ingrained that I call it "the defensive shimmy." When this motion is pointed out, the person practicing a non-defensive question will attempt to self-correct and then, almost invariably, nod up and down, as if the head were a forefinger we can point and wag to get our view across. Typically, in this situation, when we attempt to suppress one motion another one pops up.

As I give workshop participants feedback about the ways in which their body language infiltrates their questions, they try harder and harder to control it, becoming more and more incredulous at how their own opinions seem to leak out of their bodies in yet another way to contaminate their questions. When our intentions are different from our words, our body acts effectively as a lie detector.

Body Language That Can Make a Question Defensive

- Shaking the head from side to side, as if saying no
- Nodding the head up and down, as if saying yes
- Shrugging the shoulders, as if the answer is unimportant
- Pushing the head and neck forward
- Condescendingly tilting the head to the right or left
- Frowning intensely, squinting, opening eyes wide, raising eyebrows, or wrinkling the forehead

Adding words for emphasis. We commonly add certain words to our questions, turning them into statements. We may ask, for example, "Do you *really* feel that way?" The word "really" suggests we don't believe the person or we disapprove, or both. We also add superlatives such as "always," "ever," "never," "only," and "all."

"Do you *ever* listen to what I say?"

"Are you *only* going to paint one side of the house today?"

"Is that *all* you are going to do?"

We also use the negative contraction of certain verbs ("do," "did," "have," and "are") in order to transform a question into a statement.

"*Didn't* you think that movie was awful?"

"*Aren't* you going to the meeting today?"

Rather than asking for information, such added words usually suggest our surprise, shock, or disapproval.

Words That Can Make a Question Defensive

EXTRA EMPHASIS
- "Do you *ever* . . . ?"
- "Are you *just* . . . ?"
- "Are you *only* . . . ?"
- "Do you *always* . . . ?"
- "Is that *all* . . . ?"
- "Do you *really* . . . ?"

CONTRADICTIONS
- "*Didn't* you go . . . ?"
- "*Haven't* you done . . . ?"
- "*Can't* you do . . . ?"
- "*Aren't* you going to . . . ?"

Using a Question to Entrap Others

The second adversarial format uses questions to entrap other people into exposing damaging information. Inherent in the use of the entrapping question is the expression of our own disapproval.

Gotcha! Multiple choices with no right answer. Lynette was greeted one morning by her law partner, Walter, who asked her, "Are you an attorney or a social worker?" Knowing he was irritated with her for volunteering at Legal Aid and sensing the trap in the question, she responded, "A little of each, I guess," and walked away. Moments later, she realized that she had just confessed to being only "a little bit" of an attorney and became furious, not only with Walter but also with herself. Often, when we are asked entrapping questions, we are aware of the ploy but can't think fast enough to respond without compromising ourselves.

Many entrapping questions are phrased in the context of having only two possible answers—in this case, social worker or attorney.

Either answer carries certain implications. If Lynette responds by saying she is an attorney, the implication is that she should be focusing on billable hours for the firm; she shouldn't be doing volunteer work, even at Legal Aid. If Lynette responds by saying she is a social worker, the implication might be that she should change careers. Either way she chooses to answer, she has walked into the trap set by her colleague, who believes her work as a volunteer is inappropriate.

Questions seeking a self-incriminating yes or no. "Just answer the question, yes or no!" is a line we might associate with a Perry Mason courtroom scene. We typically use this method at home and at work to entrap someone into either a lie or a confession. We ask our children, "Have you done your homework yet?" when we know they have been playing Nintendo since they arrived home from school.

Another common entrapping question is, "Do you want to know a better way to do that?" or, more subtly, "Do you want to know another way to do that?" If we say yes, we are acknowledging that the other person's way is better even before we know what it is. If we say no, we are indicating that we are unwilling to learn new things. Employees have told me they feel entrapped and patronized when either a co-worker or a supervisor asks such a question instead of discussing the situation openly.

The leading question. We also entrap someone by phrasing questions in a way that is likely to lead to the answer we want to hear. We may use an if–then format: "If you love me, then why shouldn't we just go ahead and get married [or make love]?" Or, "If you love me, then why don't you trust me?" and so on. Most of us feel manipulated when others ask us questions intended to lead us to *their* conclusions.

Formats for Entrapping Questions

- Multiple choice with no right answer
- Questions to which both a yes and a no answer are self-incriminating
- Leading questions

Even when we are trying to be sincere or are genuinely wanting to resolve some conflict, our culturally encoded habits lead us unintentionally to ask questions using tones and phrasing that express our own reactions or entrap others. Because we often remain unaware that the manner of our delivery is adversarial and contributes to another's defensive response, we tend to lose faith in the question as an effective tool for gathering information.

Statements: Lords of Truth

Our second communication tool is the statement. Instead of using statements as tools for clarity and understanding, we often use them to control other people's opinions and feelings. This practice is deeply embedded in Western culture and in other cultures as well.

Making Adversarial Statements

Twenty-three hundred years ago, Aristotle observed three environments on which he based his model for communication: opposing attorneys in the courtroom, partisan politicians in the legislature, and vendors in the marketplace. In the first two cases, he witnessed interactions that were overtly adversarial in nature. In the third case, he observed craftspeople and artisans trying to persuade others to buy their goods. In all three situations, the goal was to convince or persuade another.

Aristotle's model is still taught today to students in English composition courses in European and American universities. Classes are offered in "Argument," the assumption being that learning the principles of argument will help students communicate effectively and powerfully.

I believe this deeply ingrained and pervasive model leads us to express ourselves in consistently polarizing ways. We misleadingly *objectify*, stating our opinion as fact (Aristotelian logic), or we ardently *convince* (Aristotelian rhetoric), trying to persuade or coerce others into agreeing with us.

Objectifying

Stating our opinions as fact has long been advocated as a way of communicating thoughts and beliefs. According to its historic interpretation and use, Aristotle's principle of logic is based on the idea that the speaker holds *the truth*, which is transmitted to others. When we objectify our statements we act as lords of truth; we perceive our own thoughts, feelings, and experience to be superior. If I speak the truth, then you are misguided any time you disagree with me. As a result, we have learned to discredit anyone who does not think, believe, or even feel as we do.

Subjective experience elevated to objective truth. Many of us hear and make statements every day that turn our own personal experience and beliefs into a generalized truth:

> Running is good for you.
> Women are manipulative.
> Men are insensitive.
> The only person you can really depend on is yourself.
> Love is the most important thing there is.
> You have to be cutthroat to succeed in business.

The list of statements presenting opinion as fact would make a paper trail that might reach to the moon.

Dictating reality. Whenever we state our opinion as fact, we state our own belief, feeling, or observation as if it applies equally to all people in one particular group, or even all people in general. When I say "Rain is depressing," I elevate my statement from the realm of personal experience to universal truth, maintaining it is so for every person. Rain can't be depressing for me and rejuvenating for you. My statement does not leave room for you to have a different experience.

Polarization. If you do not agree with me, you will automatically be in an adversarial position. If you make your disagreement known, the subsequent interaction could easily turn into a right/wrong verbal battle. You might say, "Rain is not depressing. It rejuvenates life. It is a great time to light a fire and settle in with a good book!" I could respond, "No, it isn't. Rain makes everything closed in and oppressive. It chills you to the bone and makes it so you can't even go for a walk."

Such argument is the staple of bickering spouses. It reflects, sadly enough, an everyday reality for many of us.

The mechanics of turning opinion into truth. In any argument, the way we use nouns (or pronouns) and verbs transforms a statement from an expression of subjective viewpoints and experiences into a declaration that sounds like objective fact. When we use inclusive nouns such as "you," "we," and "it" to represent everyone or every situation, we generalize our own experience. We might say, "It isn't possible to do that," making our statement absolute when, in fact, others might envision how to do whatever "it" is with ease.

We also objectify our personal experience by using state-of-being verbs—such as "is"—that effectively turn opinion into fact. In the sentence "Running *is* good for *you*," both "is" and "you" generalize the statement as applicable to everyone.

Words That Turn Subjective Opinions into Statements of Fact

- Inclusive nouns such as *you, we, they,* and *it:*
  "*You* just have to . . ." ; "*We* had better . . ."
  "*It* won't work . . ." ; "*They* are so . . ."
- State-of-being verbs that suggest an absolute or objective condition :
  "Movies *are* . . ." ; "Rain *is* . . ."
- Generalizations used with a state-of-being verb:
  "Men *have* . . ." ; "Teenagers *are* . . ."

We have models all around us for stating our opinions, beliefs, and feelings as fact. Young children begin to do so at an early age. As we grow older, we are taught in our schools and universities that we should make "objective" statements because they are less subject to "bias." I believe every statement we make is inherently grounded in personal experience, which is subjective. In the name of objectivity, we have learned to lie, bluffing about the strength of our own viewpoint in order to sound more authoritative. The myth of objectivity creates arrogance and makes us closed to learning from others.

The essential dishonesty of presenting our own perspective as truth leads to a host of psychological and interpersonal problems.

When we presume that we can be objective, I think we not only try to force our viewpoint on others, we also project our own feelings and biases onto them. We risk reinforcing our prejudices and alienating ourselves to varying degrees from many of the people in our lives.

Ironically, we can create such adversity even when we are working to help a friend or family member. Suppose a young man, frustrated with learning a new task, declares, "I can't do it." If we, as the helper, counter with an objective statement of our own—"Yes, you can"— the frustrated learner might reply, more resolutely, "No, I *can't*," and increasingly lock into his own resistance.

While there is a growing movement toward validating subjective expression, I believe it is hard to move away from our history. Even those of us who are trying not to objectify our own thoughts and feelings may do it consistently, often unconsciously.

Convincing

If we are in a conversation with someone who disagrees with us, the ingrained reaction for many of us is to try to convince the person to agree. When I ask people to imagine communicating without ever trying to convince anyone to agree with them, they usually look incredulous. But I do believe that whenever we try to convince others to agree with us, we misuse statements in an effort to control others, which is likely to create resistance and power struggle.

Adding emotional appeal. According to Aristotle's model, when someone resists the "truth" of our message we must switch to what he calls rhetoric, the "art of persuasion." This sort of persuasion is to be used with those people considered to be inferior, who don't get it— that is, agree with us—when we tell them what is true. Rhetoric often involves using emotional appeal to convince others to agree with what we say or want.

The kind of emotional tone we use in our effort to persuade can vary a great deal. If we are negotiating a business deal, we may add a tone of nonchalant confidence in order to display a superior level of competence. If we are trying to get a child to do homework, our tone may sound authoritative and stern.

In many cases, our tone—at least initially—may be more like

honey than vinegar. Suppose, for example, that a young wife has already spent the allotted amount in her monthly entertainment budget, but she wants to go out to dinner and a movie. She may say to her partner, who loves Thai food, "Honey, I just read in the paper about this great new Thai restaurant, and it's right by the theater where that movie we wanted to see is playing." Her voice might be soft, a little hesitant. She might even follow up her initial statement with a disappointed sigh. "It's too bad we don't have any money left for entertainment this month." She is enticing her partner to want to go out, hoping he will suggest that it wouldn't hurt to spend a little extra. She isn't hitting him over the head—yet.

The more skilled she is at the art of persuasion, the more likely it is that the other person may walk away thinking that whatever she wanted him to do was actually his own idea. From this perspective, it is better to seduce than badger.

Shifting from coaxing to coercion. If her partner resists her efforts to persuade him to go out, she may coax a little harder. "Well, it wouldn't hurt to go over the budget just this once!" If he seems determined to stay home, she might become more intense, using verbal coercion. "Every time you want to go over budget, I go along with it. Remember the 'Niners game? You never budge when I want to! You're satisfied just sitting around the house unless it's something *you* want to do." Now she is hitting him over the head—her efforts to convince have progressed to a direct attack. In the process, she presents her view as superior and labels her partner as a couch potato or just plain selfish.

When we use persuasion with anyone, even someone we love and respect, we reduce that person to the status of someone who needs to be manipulated.

It is quite common in certain kinds of professional and personal relationships to use attacking statements as a means of coercing others. The coach who makes humiliating statements to a player who has made a mistake wants to "convince" the player to hold onto the ball. In abusive intimate relationships, it is common for the abusive partner to make debasing statements about the other in an effort to "prove" that the partner is unworthy of respect and deserves to be abused.

In varying degrees, most of us may at times go beyond gentle persuasion when trying to convince others. In homes, offices, stores, restaurants, and schools, we argue in an attempt to get our point across, often disrespecting the other person's ability to make an informed decision. In many cases, the more a person resists, the harder we try, intensifying the struggle. When we try to persuade others and fail, we are likely to feel frustrated and angry. In many cases, the other person gains power over us simply by resisting our efforts.

Predictions: Foretellers of Doom

The battlefield prediction "Surrender or we'll fire" offers the enemy soldier a choice between becoming a prisoner or a casualty. In our own lives, we use predictions primarily to threaten or coax others in an effort to dictate their choices. Rather than using the prediction as a constructive tool, once again we misuse it as a weapon and try to force others to comply with our wishes. We commonly do this in one of two ways: making threatening predictions or offering rewards.

Using Predictions in an Adversarial Way

Threatening Predictions

People commonly make threatening predictions in one of two ways. They make predictions designed to punish others who do not submit to their control, or they threaten punishment they do not intend to follow through on, simply to scare others into doing what they want.

Punitive predictions. Marsha, the mild-mannered mother of a friend of mine, had been married for many years to Johnson, a well-known potter. Upon finding out that Johnson was intending to leave her for another woman, Marsha cried, "If you do, I will break every piece of your pottery I can get my hands on." "You wouldn't dare," he responded, and stormed out anyway, apparently confident that his work was safe. When Johnson didn't come home that night, Marsha destroyed all the pottery in the house. When she made her prediction, she moved entirely away from caring about how Johnson felt about her to wanting to control him, to *force* him into staying with her. Her prediction also let him know she intended to make him suffer if he left, and she followed through on it.

Whenever we are invested in punishing the person who resists our efforts at control, we are using predictions punitively. As we all know from the evening news, people threaten to kill and sometimes do kill a partner who leaves them. When we make such extreme predictions, the desire to control the other person is matched by a desire to inflict punishment if the person does not act according to our desires.

Most of us could cite situations in which people predict and carry out severe consequences. Following are some common examples.

PARENT TO TEENAGER: If you walk out that door, don't ever come back.

SUPERVISOR TO EMPLOYEE: If you don't like it around here, look for another job.

TOURIST TO HOTEL CLERK: I don't care if the hotel is full, I belong to your discount club, and if you can't upgrade my room I'll go elsewhere.

Regardless of its magnitude, a punishing prediction is destructive to relationships. The other person—adult or child—usually correctly senses our vindictiveness and realizes that we want to hurt anyone who doesn't do what we want.

Falsely threatening predictions. We may make falsely threatening predictions when we feel desperate about trying to control another person's behavior. The consequence we predict is usually one that we have no intention of following through on. We use an empty threat in the hope that the other person will believe our bluff and do what we want. We huff and we puff, but we don't blow the house down. In some cases, we make the threat in anger, deluding ourselves in the moment that we mean what we say. After ten years of marriage, whenever Marcus would clam up and she couldn't get him to talk about whatever was bothering him, in frustration, Sally sometimes threatened him with divorce, knowing she didn't intend to carry out her threat. She only wanted to pressure him into talking.

Parents might warn a teenage son that he can't go on the Saturday ski trip if he doesn't do the dinner dishes Friday evening. After coming home from an evening out, they may find the dishes crusting up on the counter and their son sound asleep in bed. Although they may argue the next morning, they renege on their threat to keep him home. The new admonition that follows him out the door—"All right, you may go, but you are going to have to do dishes twice next week"—will probably not hold enough water to wash a teacup.

The main difference between these two types of prediction is that falsely threatening ones are less punitive. We care more about the actual effect of the predicted consequence on others and ourselves. We really don't want to deprive our son of the ski trip. In an effort to coerce, we want to instill the *fear* of punishment, but we are not driven to punish or retaliate if our warnings go unheeded. In most cases, when we overplay empty predictions, the targeted person ignores the threats but feels our punitive attitude. Consequently, it's a double loss. We are perceived as punishing, yet still feel powerless to control the other person's temperament or behavior.

Predicting Rewards

I used to have a friend whose grandmother would say to the children who visited her, "Give Grandma a kiss and you can have a cookie." Even as a child, my skin would crawl when she said that. I knew I was being offered a present to do something I might not otherwise want to do. In fact, I usually made an excuse to avoid the kiss, even if I had to give up the cookie.

While we would now generally view that kind of bribe as inappropriate, I believe we often do essentially the same thing when we offer our child a reward for doing a routine task. We don't want to resort to punishment, so we offer the bribe to try to get control in a positive way.

If your three-year-old daughter gets into a kitchen cupboard and makes a clamor with the pans, you might try to divert her by saying, "If you come into the playroom, I'll get out your finger paints and your clay." While you are offering her a creative alternative, advocated by some child psychologists as "diversion," you are hiding the fact that you don't like what she is doing and that your goal is to get her to stop.

If and when the child figures out that the offer of finger paints is a ruse to get her away from the kitchen, she is likely to feel at least some mistrust of you, even if she accepts the offer. Or, suspicious of your motives, she might resist and continue to bang her wooden spoon on the metal pan. She might also begin to resist painting and working with clay, some of her favorite activities, because she associates them with being controlled. When children sense the manipulation inherent in a bribe, they frequently will adamantly refuse to participate in activities they might otherwise enjoy.

Because the bribe is really, at its core, our attempt to control someone else's will, we may often resort to threats if the bribe is turned down. We may start out with an offer to take our son and his friends to a movie if he cleans his room. Days later, if he has made no effort to do so, we may switch tactics and threaten: "If you don't clean your room, you can't go to the baseball game on Friday!" When we start out offering a movie and end up threatening to take away a sports activity—possibly one he already had permission to attend—the relationship suffers a breach of trust.

I believe that all our institutionally prescribed ways of using questions, statements, and predictions break our trust with each other. They not only fail to help us resolve conflict, they literally *cause* defensiveness. To attempt to get out of an addictive power struggle by communicating in these ways is like a junkie going to a dealer for a cure.

The Current "Real World"

Having been taught that habitual ways of using questions, statements, and predictions can meet our needs and influence others, it is no wonder that so many of us become manipulative. Our ways of speaking have affected our character.

With our grasp of the true power of communication so skewed, it's as though we were in a dream state; we've gone down the hole with Alice into a land where everything is distorted. Unfortunately, it is not a dream at all; it is a reality we have created—a world teeming with power struggles among angry people. We believe this power-struggle world is the only real one. I have never once heard someone use the term "real world" to refer to the love and courage many people demonstrate every day. Instead, the "real world" connotes a harsh, pitiless place where cruelty is truer to our nature than kindness.

Even though pain and sorrow are an integral part of our experience, I do believe we can create a world—one person and one relationship at a time—in which we greatly diminish needless hurt and suffering.

Process Determines the Outcome

When we engage in any physical activity, we usually trust that the process determines the outcome, that the means determines the end result. If I told you that I could cut a basketball in half and dribble it down the court, you'd probably think I had a bizarre sense of humor or some trick up my sleeve. If I seriously insisted that I could do so, you'd probably think I was crazy. Yet we defend ways of talking to each other that consistently block us from reaching our goals.

We have failed to pay close attention to the direct relationship between how we speak and the pervasive conflict it causes. We lack inner clarity about what we are doing. Nothing is exactly as it seems. A question may not really be a question. A statement may really be a threat. A prediction may be merely a bluff.

Sometimes we mix questions, statements, and predictions in a way that accomplishes less than any one could alone. For example, a supervisor may say to an administrative assistant, "Please get this report done by Friday." This sentence could be interpreted in any one of three ways:

As a question: "Can you get this report done by Friday?"
As a statement: "I'd like to have this report done by Friday."
As a prediction: "If you don't get this report done by Friday, I will be very upset."

I believe that blending forms of communication in this way can confuse not only the listener but also the speaker. Simply put, we get mixed up—and our muddle makes it all the easier to deny that we are communicating in divisive ways.

Recently I saw a bumper sticker that stopped me in my tracks: FIGHTING FOR PEACE IS LIKE SCREWING FOR VIRGINITY. When we talk about "fighting for peace," our very language reflects our attempt to reach a goal with a process that moves us in the opposite direction.

Likewise, our predominant ways of talking to each other move us toward conflict instead of resolution, judgment instead of learning, resistance instead of openness, anger instead of love.

The War Model: An Airtight System

Despite its destructiveness, the war model for communicating has such internal consistency that we don't seem to have other "realistic" options. To most, it can seem incomprehensible that there could be another "real world." Even if our hearts are initially open, we can become defensive just by using traditional conventions for questions, statements, and predictions. Our strong pull toward defensiveness, combined with how we commonly speak, puts the locks in place, enclosing us in an airtight system of conflict. As long as we remain tied to these concepts of how to protect ourselves and how to communicate, we have no more chance of escaping the power struggle jar than do those trapped flies.

I have presented a detailed picture of this war model in order that we may thoroughly understand dominant communication patterns. Now I think we can begin to create a different "real world" by examining and learning a new, non-defensive way of speaking.

Misuses of Our Three Basic Forms of Communication

QUESTIONS

Using a Question to Make a Statement
Expressing your own opinions, feelings, and beliefs under the cover or guise of a question

Using a Question to Entrap Someone
Using a question to draw someone into exposing information that is self-incriminating and makes the person look bad

STATEMENTS

Stating Personal Opinion as Fact
Stating your own personal opinion, feelings, and beliefs as "universal truth"

Using a Statement to Convince Others to Agree
Using statements about your own thoughts, feelings, and beliefs to try to persuade someone to agree with you

PREDICTIONS

Threatening Predictions
Predicting negative consequences in order to try to force someone into doing what you want done

Coaxing Predictions
Predicting appealing consequences to someone in order to try to coax the person into doing what you want done

THE NON-DEFENSIVE MODEL

Tools Instead of Weapons

Introduction to Part II: A New Real World

The film *Babe* became an unexpected worldwide hit. The movie takes its name from its star, an appealing, innocent pig who was raised among sheepdogs. But unlike his canine family, Babe does not view sheep as inferior, dumb creatures who are capable of responding only out of fear. And so he does something different. He talks to them respectfully—asking them questions, expressing his opinions, and predicting the consequences he believes will result depending upon what they choose to do. He does not nip at their heels to get them to move, or attempt to frighten or coerce them in any way. To the amazement of the sheepdogs and farmers alike, the sheep respond cooperatively.

Babe creates a whole new model for interspecies communication. While the movie is popularly viewed as fantasy, it is also a projection of an alternate image of community. Just as for decades science fiction has projected images of our technological future, I believe *Babe* envisions a social future.

People used to be incredulous at the technological "advances" depicted in science fiction, but not anymore. If the story of Babe had taken place on another planet, we might be more willing to consider that such communication would someday be feasible. But here, on this planet, such change is harder to envision. I have heard *Babe* described as heartwarming, moving, humane, delightful, and sweet, but I haven't heard many call it realistic.

Yet, in a strikingly similar way, people now train horses by talking to them. A recent television program showed a person talking to a horse that had never been saddled; within an hour or so, it voluntarily took the saddle. How intelligent and humane this technique is compared to the age-old method of force and domination, with a rider sitting astride an angry, bucking animal until its will is broken.

The methods of communication used by these horse trainers and Babe are indicative of a major paradigm shift that has already begun. I think the film realistically portrays the potential power of different ways of interacting in society at large. A growing core of people is already seeking to speak and listen in these new ways.

Part II of this book presents a step-by-step guide to using Powerful, Non-Defensive Communication so we can make a radical shift in how we interact with each other. I will demonstrate how to use questions, statements, and predictions non-defensively; describe the nature, function, and effect of each; and give detailed instructions for using different formats of all three tools skillfully.

Just as Babe's conversations with the sheep were straightforward, the basic steps for using this process are simple. We ask sincere questions to gather information. We make open, honest statements to clarify our thoughts and feelings. And we predict for others how we will respond to various choices they make—all without trying to convince them to agree with us or control how they respond. At first, these steps may even seem so simple as to lack power. However, just as Babe's conversations with the sheep had far-reaching effects, this new way of talking and listening can produce dramatic results.

Some Attitudes and Behaviors Fostered by Non-Defensive Communication

Accountability	Humor
Assertiveness	Kindness
Clarity	Knowledgeablility
Compassion	Receptiveness
Consistency	Respectfulness
Directness	Responsiblity
Firmness	Responsiveness
Flexibility	Self-motivation
Friendliness	Sincerity
Honesty	Thoroughness

6

The Question

Curiosity Didn't Kill the Cat— It Won the Peace Prize

Since dictionary definitions mirror common usage of a word, the fact that the word "question" is almost entirely defined as interrogation, or, if inquisitive, is seen as prying, reflects a troubling common belief. Many people think those who ask questions based simply on curiosity are "sticking their nose where it doesn't belong"—an offensive, inappropriate, and possibly dangerous thing to do. The message is that only those who are authorized to interrogate have the right to ask questions. So it isn't hard to see why we often hesitate to ask questions for fear of being rude or invasive. And when we do ask questions, it is easy to slip into interrogation mode—frowning, looking intense, and sounding accusatory.

Sincere curiosity is often the missing piece in our questions. Many of us were even actively taught to fear it. Parents who wanted to teach their children not to ask inappropriate questions repeated the old adage, "Curiosity killed the cat." Curiosity is actually at the heart of any genuine question. I believe we would have a decidedly different and healthier world if the saying went, "Ask all the questions you can think of—curiosity wins the peace prize."

Nature: Curious and Innocent

The character of a non-defensive question is never harsh, accusatory, or interrogating. It is gentle, respectfully offering others an invitation to speak.

Innocent

Essentially, a non-defensive question is innocently curious—reflecting the purity of the child who asks how a flower grows or what makes an airplane fly. By curious I mean eager to learn, know, or understand without any negative connotations. We ask a question solely for the purpose of discovery. We have no hidden agenda, no goal beyond wanting to clarify our understanding. Accordingly, I think the character of the purely curious question is inherently innocent, untainted with ulterior motives.

Open

While we can easily envision this innocence in a child, it is hard for many of us to imagine asking a genuinely innocent question during a fight with our partner or in response to someone criticizing an idea we just proposed. Children want to know the answers to their questions; we often do not. In fact, when I ask people to think about asking totally non-defensive questions, someone periodically says, "Well, if I ask a really sincere question, then I would have to want to hear the answer." That is very true. The following story illustrates how hard it can be to ask genuine questions when we are afraid to make ourselves vulnerable by finding out the answer.

Mena had arrived at an ongoing evening workshop in tears. She was a full-time homemaker with no income of her own. Her husband, Todd, had just told her he had come close to taking everything out of their bank accounts and leaving her and their children. Devastated, she had come to the workshop that night hoping to figure out what to do, how to talk to Todd about this crisis. We worked together, helping her practice asking, and wanting to hear the answer to, one single question: "What made you want to take the money and leave us?"

The idea of asking that question in a sincere, open way—after learning that her partner had almost left her with total responsibility for the family and no money—was initially incomprehensible, not only to Mena but to everyone else at the workshop. Mena practiced asking the question again and again, but feelings of rage, despair, and pain radiated through her words. The actual question got lost in the messages conveyed by her emotions: "I can't imagine what I would do" and "I feel so angry, so hurt, so betrayed."

While it was hard for Mena and the others to imagine being able to ask the question without emotion, each person in the room began to see clearly that her husband would not be able to respond openly to the question as long as her feelings permeated it. When her question was asked defensively, with her feelings soaking up any genuine curiosity, Mena sounded accusatory and closed to receiving information. Everyone felt empathy for her pain but could see that, under the circumstances, Todd might respond with guilt or anger to the emotional message leaching through her question. The actual question would remain unheard.

Mena's situation exemplifies how hard it can be to take our feelings out of a question. When we hear something that feels offensive or hurtful, we often reveal our immediate emotions in our faces. (Psychological and anthropological studies have shown that people in a variety of cultures, even isolated societies, use the same facial expressions to show hurt, anger, fear, happiness, and joy.) Any question we ask at that moment is likely to be contaminated by our gut response. The task of asking an innocent question at this point can be daunting, to say the least, but whenever we inject feelings like hurt or anger, the "question" turns into a statement.

Mena was able, with arduous effort, to come to terms with a genuine desire to ask Todd the question and sincerely seek to know his answer—to be open to understanding. While it was incredibly painful to do, Mena could respectfully ask Todd what had brought him to the point of wanting to abandon his family, rather than use the question to accuse him of it.

Neutral

As Mena worked to become open by taking her own feelings out of her question, her tone became more neutral, vital to a non-defensive question. Others sense this neutrality and are more inclined to respond sincerely. In response to questions asked in a more neutral tone, people typically say:

> "I felt like you wanted to know how I felt instead of just telling me your own reaction."
> "I didn't feel pressured, as if you expected a certain kind of answer from me, so I could tell you how I really felt."
> "The question felt very calm to me, so it seemed safe to answer it."
> "My defenses dropped, and I felt compelled to answer the question sincerely."

Most English speakers have been taught to come up in tone at the end of a question and down in tone at the end of a statement. I find that coming up in tone at the end of a question, however, often conveys more defensiveness, urgency, or expectation than if we come down at the end. Most people tell me that when they hear a question asked in the tone of a statement, it sounds more neutral and they feel freer to answer truthfully.

Because a neutral question lacks emotional intensity, people sometimes initially describe it as monotonous, even insincere. This may be because people sometimes initially get a little tight when they try to ask a neutral question. They will stare blankly or intently. Or their voices will become flat in tone, sometimes even cold, which can mistakenly convey a lack of interest or even hostility.

One way to avoid sounding cold and to eliminate tension is to imagine yourself as calm and relaxed. The picture that comes to mind is of a group of people sitting contentedly on the porch of an old cabin on a summer evening as the heat of the day begins to wane. Watching some clouds begin to move in, one of them asks lazily, "Do you think it's going to rain tomorrow?"—not caring much whether it does or not.

Inviting

Our question should be a genuine invitation for the other person to speak. An inviting question, asked in a gentle tone, seems to create a feeling of safety in the recipient and a desire to respond. I don't think our question can be a *genuine* invitation unless we give up trying to dictate or manipulate how the other person responds.

Sometimes people fear asking a non-defensive question because they see it as giving someone permission to dump on them. Mena might have been afraid that Todd would take her question as an opportunity to attack her verbally. I want to emphasize that inviting someone to speak does not give the other person license to abuse us. If the response is a cruel one, we can set appropriate boundaries. However, in a surprising number of cases, even in difficult circumstances, I find that the other person is more likely to respond honestly and without malice to neutral, genuine questions. Mena did go home and ask her one sincere question. She returned the next week to say that she and Todd had the best talk they had ever had in twelve years of marriage.

Function: Gathering Up Information

The natural function of a non-defensive question is simply to draw people out so they will be willing to provide accurate information. The question is a data collection tool. A non-defensive question helps people crystallize what they think, feel, and believe. It enables them to clarify their position to themselves and to us.

We ask, I think, far too few questions. We often react to what people say without ever understanding their precise meaning, their feelings, or their motivations. In a theoretical armchair fashion, we may know we have to find out what another person means before we respond. But in the moment we bypass most of our opportunities to ask questions, either because we fear being invasive or because we assume that the other person's meaning is obvious.

Our Assumptions Prevent Us from Asking Questions

Once when I was speaking to an audience of businesspeople, a woman named Rhonda raised her hand and asked, "Well, isn't what you are teaching us kind of like what we would learn in . . . um . . .

charm school?" Despite my effort to freeze my expression into a cari-
cature of receptivity, a flash of anger probably showed in my face momentarily. My automatic assumption was that Rhonda was insulting
me, using an outdated expression such as "charm school" to make
what I was teaching seem shallow or superficial—like a class in man-
ners. I automatically assumed that "charm school" had the same associations for Rhonda as it did for me.

Somehow I found the presence of mind to ask, simply and calmly,
"What do you mean by charm school?"

Rhonda replied, "Well, in charm school they taught us to memo-
rize things, and I don't know if I could ever remember all this without memorizing it." I was stunned by her answer. The tension in the
room settled like yesterday's dust.

When a person speaks to us, the meaning of the sentence is based
on thoughts, feelings, beliefs, or assumptions that are far less self-
evident than we often think. When we respond with an inaccurate or
limited understanding of another's meaning, we are often, without
even knowing it, carrying on two parallel conversations; the twain
never meet. Our erroneous assumptions create much of the drama in
our miscommunication.

If I had responded according to my initial urge, I would still probably have restrained my anger. I would have politely defended my
work. Smiling through slightly gritted teeth, I might have said,
"Well, I don't really think it's like charm school. I think using non-
defensive communication can add a lot of meaning and depth to our
lives."

My comments would have addressed what I assumed Rhonda
meant—that the process I was teaching lacked depth, instead of what
she actually meant—that she was afraid she wouldn't remember it.
Depth versus memory. Had I responded defensively, I would never
have understood or addressed her concern. That exchange might
have affected the tone of the entire workshop and upset me each time
I thought about it in retrospect.

Any Information Is Important Information

When we ask non-defensive questions, we are, in essence, seeking
to find out, What am I dealing with here? Regardless of the content
of the person's response, we are receiving important information.

First, we are learning what the other person is willing or not willing to tell us.

We gain important information, even if a person avoids giving us an honest answer by denying some covert message. When Sally asked Marcus if he was upset and he said, "No," he continued to display body language to the contrary by slouching, scowling, and staying in an obvious funk. Unfortunately, Sally dismissed his reply. Her most important piece of information at that moment was that Marcus was upset and for some reason was unwilling to admit it.

Sally might instead have focused on the information she *did* receive as her starting place in dealing with the issue. She might have begun by asking herself, Why would Marcus deny being upset? What is his purpose in refusing to talk?

She might have asked him, "Are you saying you are not upset because you believe that nothing is wrong, or because for some reason you don't want to talk to me about it?"

Had she asked herself—or him—such questions, she could have been on the path of genuine curiosity.

Instead, Sally got bogged down in her own issues: needing to control whether Marcus talked or not, defending her own intelligence, and insisting she could tell when he was in a bad mood. While it can be hard not to get caught up like Sally did when someone we love is upset and won't talk to us, our traditional approaches make the problem worse rather than solve it.

A sincere question can stimulate the person asking it to become more curious and open to new understanding. If the other person's answer substantiates our worst suspicions, we are still in a better position to respond. Even if the person continues to deny having a problem, that is crucial information.

I believe that by making open, curious questions the foundation of a conversation, we gain as much clarity as another is willing to offer *before* we respond with our own thoughts, feelings, and beliefs. Were we to ask someone like Marcus a question, I imagine that we are trying to see the shape, size, and texture of the landscape of his position. Our position may look like Kansas, with lots of flat land and rich soil. His may look like California, with a different shape and more varied terrain. Whatever we learn gives us the basis for responding as accurately, realistically, and meaningfully as possible to his current state of being.

Mental preparation

- Am I feeling sincere, calm, and relaxed?
- Have I given up the need to control how the other person answers?
- Am I willing to hear the answer?
- Is my question curious? innocent? open? neutral? inviting?

Questions Take Us to New Depths

Although I have focused here primarily on situations involving conflict, because they are often of greatest concern to people, questions can be highly effective in almost any circumstance. Many of the conversations we pass over lightly have—beneath the surface—a wealth of information that is easy to access when both people feel open and cooperative. Even a few questions can bring us great benefit, whether we are at home planning to remodel the house or at work discussing approaches to marketing a new product. We can learn much more than we might imagine about people we know and love by asking more questions in peaceful moments.

Effect: Disarming—and More

To many, the idea of asking a sincere, open question seems pleasant, safe, and somewhat innocuous, but not necessarily powerful. Yet the impact of Mena's question about why Todd wanted to leave her and their children went far beyond anything she could have anticipated. In innumerable situations, amazing shifts can happen for both persons involved.

Keeping Ourselves Open to Receiving More Information

The mechanics of a non-defensive question require us to shift our focus momentarily from ourselves to the other person. That shift helps to move us out of our own feelings long enough to be receptive to what the other person has to say. When Mena shifted away from her own pain enough to ask Todd about why he had almost left, she learned that his immediate impetus had nothing to do with her—a crucial piece of information. An incident where he worked had sent him over the edge regarding his long-held feelings of being trapped in a dead-end job. He was only thirty-five and couldn't imagine staying there all his life, but he didn't believe that he could change careers while he had a family to support.

Mena felt overwhelming relief when Todd gave her more information, and at the same time, she learned about ways in which she had contributed to the problem. Even though Mena managed money exceedingly well, she had many fears about financial security, in part due to a poverty-stricken childhood. Over the years, any time Todd had mentioned his job dissatisfaction, she had balked, saying they couldn't afford to make changes. As a result, he felt shut off from coming to her with one of the most significant issues of his life. Her question finally opened that door.

From what I have seen, most of us continue to swim around in our own reactions, reluctant to come up for breath long enough to find out what the other person actually means. Even when we are already caught up in our own emotions, we can begin to pull ourselves out by opening up enough to ask a sincere question.

A few years ago, I went to buy tires from a man I'll call George. Every time I asked George a question about the tires, he replied, "You don't need to know that." I felt he was insulting me as an intelligent woman, and I was furious. I walked around outside, waiting for my new tires to be put on, fuming all the while. "I can't believe what he said to me!" I said to a friend who was with me. "If I had more time, I would just take my car somewhere else. What is he, some arrogant jerk who thinks only men have a brain fit to understand tires?"

This was not a genuine question.

Then, abruptly, I stopped in my tracks and said to my friend, "Well, I guess I'd better practice what I teach." I thought about what question I could ask him and decided on this one: "Do you believe that I have no need to know about the tires I'm buying?" I practiced it a few times, breathing deeply each time before I started until I could begin to feel calm and sincere.

Sometimes when I think of a non-defensive question, I have to work hard not to turn it into an entrapping one. It would have been easy, both with Rhonda and with George, to have been so sure that I was right about their intention that I could have asked my question hoping to catch them red-faced. In both cases, I would have been wrong.

When I asked George if he thought I didn't need to know about the tires I was buying, he stared at me blankly for a few seconds and then said, "Oh, no, it's just that I used to teach mechanics at the community college, and the guys I taught always challenged me and never thought I knew what I was talking about." When I asked questions to gather information about my purchase, he apparently thought I was like those students, not respectful of his knowledge and perhaps even challenging his level of expertise. Once more, the information I received was not at all what I had expected.

The Disarming Effect

People often comment on the "disarming" effect of a non-defensive question. Apparently the openness and sincerity of the question enables the recipients to answer freely, without fear. And so they "disarm," laying down their own defensiveness because they no longer need it within a safe environment.

Recall that George's first reaction—when I asked him if he thought I had no need to know about the tires I was buying—was to stop and look blank for a moment. This is common, just before people drop their defensiveness. The subsequent transformation is often shocking. Sid, who has been practicing non-defensive communication for several years now, said to me once, "When a guy drops his defensiveness, it's as though he doesn't have to take the time to take off his suit of armor. It disappears instantly, the way the sun can evaporate a wisp of cloud."

As George answered my question, his entire demeanor and attitude changed. He was open, happy, almost exuberant. He literally followed me out of the store and down the sidewalk, giving me his business card, shaking my hand, smiling broadly, and saying, "Please, if you ever need tires again, come back." As often as I see this kind of transformation, I am still amazed. We are often accustomed to thinking that people will continue to be true to our past experience with them. This reflects our tendency to see a person's defensiveness as "personality," which we all will carry with us throughout life, and prevents us from recognizing that people have the capacity for instantaneous change.

Sometimes a single non-defensive question can be effectively used in situations that recur again and again. Mihn, a Vietnamese refugee, had come to the United States and gone to work for a large urban university. Mihn described the first time she encountered an upset student who was swearing because of problems with a loan application. She broke down in tears after she hung up the phone, thinking she must have caused the problem. After encountering a few more angry students, Mihn realized she hadn't done anything to cause their behavior. The next time a caller screamed and swore at her, she retorted, "Same to you!" and hung up. But while she was asserting herself more, she was still not happy with her own reactions, and the level of anger and abuse she received continued to make many workdays unpleasant.

After Mihn took a PNDC workshop at her university, the next time someone called and started shouting at her, she asked, honestly, "Are you angry at me for some reason, or are you just upset about your financial aid?"

She reported that the person calmed down immediately and replied, "I'm not angry at you. I'm just upset because I won't be able to go to school this term if I don't get my financial aid worked out." The student went on to talk to her very respectfully. Whenever Mihn asked this question, or some variation of it, the caller usually stopped treating Mihn as an adversary—a cog in a bureaucratic machine—and shifted to seeing Mihn as an ally and stopped dumping anger on her. Any of us who work with the public can use non-defensive questions to give people an opportunity to disarm and work with us toward constructive solutions.

Non-defensive questions can even be disarming in heated debates over political issues. One woman told of an incident that occurred when she was handing out information on a controversial ballot initiative. A man had walked up and begun to argue angrily. He leaned over the booth and waved his arms, looking as if he might actually assault her. At first she felt panicky and thought she might have to call security, but after a few deep breaths, she looked at him as gently as she could and asked in a mild tone, "Do you think we will be able to agree on this?" She said he looked as if all the air had been let out of him. He sighed deeply, shrugged, said softly, "No, I guess not," turned, and walked off. She was stunned.

A sincere question from a parent can stop an ongoing power struggle with children and teens. As Corey began to practice non-defensive communication, she sat down with Beth when she was *not* seeking Beth's help and ask her some genuine questions.

"Do you believe I should do all the housework?"
"When you say I am being unfair to ask you to help, do you say it because you are angry or because you think you should not have to help at all?"
"Do you have any desire to help me around the house?"

Previously, any question Corey had asked Beth had been designed to coerce Beth into helping. In response to genuine questions, Beth—underneath her defensiveness—showed more concern and desire to share the work than Corey would have ever imagined. While it was still an uphill trek, this conversation laid the groundwork for some significant changes in how they resolved issues about housework.

Children and teens can also learn to ask non-defensive questions to diffuse potential conflicts. A high school student had been murdered in a fight that ensued after someone had made an insulting remark about his mother. After a class in non-defensive communication, another student reported how he had handled a similar situation by asking, "Why are you saying that about my mom?"

The other boy shrugged and said, "I don't know. I just wanted to piss you off, I guess," and walked away.

Some of the startling success stories I hear involve issues such as sexual harassment. Nancy, a young woman who had just graduated from college, was hired by a large corporation. She had not been employed very long before her immediate supervisor, Frank, began putting his arm around her and calling her "honey" and "sweetie." Nancy said nothing because she didn't want to appear uptight and she needed the job. Yet she was surprised by such treatment in a time of so much awareness of sexual harassment, not to mention its legal consequences. One day, Frank grabbed her bottom as she bent over to pick up a box. That evening, traumatized, she called her mother, who helped Nancy figure out a non-defensive question to pose to her supervisor.

The next day, Nancy privately asked Frank, "Do you believe that I wanted you to touch me in that way?"

He paused and then replied, "No, I don't think you did. I can see I have humiliated you, and I will never do it again." Posing a genuinely curious question in such situations can be exceedingly difficult because we feel violated or betrayed. Yet Frank's response is a testament to the power of a question to create trust and resolve a potentially hazardous issue.

Establishing Separateness

When I reacted angrily to George's negation of my request for information about the tires I was buying, I was defending against his right to dictate what I did or didn't need to know. I was like a child rebelling against a parent's authority, and in the process I gave him power over me.

A non-defensive question helps to establish the subjectivity of each person's viewpoint and thus can assist us in remaining separate from someone else's judgment, even if the person's answer doesn't please us. Instead of continuing to react as if George had the authority to decide what I did or didn't need to know about the tires, I asked him directly for his personal opinion about my desire for information.

My question made it clear that his comment was his own subjective opinion; I was no longer bound by, or struggling against, his viewpoint. Then I could express my own opinions and needs more confidently.

When anyone states opinion as fact, as George did, the person is applying a personal opinion generally to another person or group without their consent. Any time that happens, we can genuinely ask, "Are you stating that as your own opinion, or are you stating that as a fact?"

This question asks the person to stop and think. Much of the time, he or she will shift and acknowledge the statement as a personal opinion and accept that we may have a different one. Even if the person still claims the opinion as fact, we can now express a different viewpoint without feeling defensive.

The process of establishing this separateness can be freeing. Maggie decided to see if she could avoid being caught up in the judgments of Claudia, her social work supervisor. When one of her clients lost his welfare money due to a technicality, she became concerned. Claudia, remaining true to form, criticized her for being "too emotional."

This time, rather than trying to defend herself against Claudia's judgment, Maggie simply asked, "Do you feel emotion when you know someone is going to become destitute?"

Claudia paused and frowned, then sighed as she answered. "Well, I do—but it doesn't do any good." Her tone changed completely, sounding almost defeated. After one question, Claudia had moved from accusing Maggie of being too emotional to expressing her own emotions.

If, on the other hand, Claudia had responded by saying, "No, I don't feel emotion for clients. My job as a professional is to remain objective," Maggie would then have been free to respond with *her* opinion without coming across as defensive. Maggie successfully separated herself from Claudia's judgment by shifting her focus from self-defense to information-gathering. Upon describing the experience, she reflected that she had never before felt so free of Claudia's judgments.

A sincere question often has the effect of equalizing a conversation, even in cases where there is a power differential. It enables us to separate ourselves from someone else's judgments so that we can walk away with our confidence and self-esteem intact, no matter how the other person responds. By asking the question she did, Maggie was able to move from feeling defensive to feeling confidence in her own level of compassion.

Asking for Clarification

Many of us frequently phrase things in a such a way that we don't say what we mean. Let's take the example of the friend or family member who says, "You haven't called for so long that I thought you didn't care anymore." We might react intensely to this implication if we have supported this person over the years. Rather that just going with our initial reaction, we can first ask, "Do you believe that if I haven't called you recently, it means that I don't care about you?"

Here, we ask our friend to confirm, deny, or qualify the statement. The immediate reply may be, "Well . . . I do know you *care*. . . . I was just missing you a lot and wishing you would call." This clarification causes a huge shift to occur. One moment ago we were talking to a friend who thought we didn't care; now we are talking to one who has been missing us. We have moved from blame and alienation to caring and connection in a few seconds.

Sometimes one question can clarify and resolve a serious misunderstanding that might go completely unnoticed for years. Molly told me a story about a conversation she had with her four-year-old daughter, who was attending preschool in the country. She usually encouraged Alison to wear pants to school, while her husband, Stan—to her surprise and frustration—encouraged the child to wear a dress, sometimes even a long skirt. When they argued over it, Molly would say, "Alison plays on a jungle gym and sometimes rides a horse at preschool. How do you expect her to be active like that in a long skirt?" Her question was designed to convince him to agree but never produced an answer that satisfied her.

In the car on the way to school one day, Alison frowned and said, "You always want me to wear pants and Daddy wants me to wear a skirt." Instead of following her urge to defend her reasons, Molly asked Alison, "Why do you think Daddy wants you to wear a skirt and I want you to wear pants?"

Alison's answer—"He wants me to be a girl and you want me to be a boy"—left Molly speechless. She was delighted at having a daughter and had simply thought Alison would have more freedom of movement in jeans. She proceeded to talk to Alison about her difference in opinion with Stan in a way that satisfied Alison that her mom was glad she was a girl. Molly said, "Thank God I asked her that question! She might have ended up spending a fortune on therapy some day because of some vague feeling that I wanted her to be a boy."

On the morning of the second day of a workshop, Toni announced she had a story for us. After learning about non-defensive questions, she had gone right home and called her partner, Geraldo, who was living in New York. They had talked about his moving to Illinois, where she resided, because his job skills were more portable than hers. Not wanting him to feel pressured to move, she had told him during a recent call, "You don't have to move out here if you don't want to." He met her comment with dead silence, changed the subject, and seemed withdrawn during the rest of the conversation. She didn't ask him anything more because she assumed from his reaction that he really *didn't* want to move. Ever since that conversation, she had been struggling with her own sadness.

After the first session of the workshop, Toni decided to ask Geraldo to clarify his reaction. He explained, "When my first wife got a job in another city, she told me, 'You don't have to move if you don't want to.' Shortly afterward, she asked me for a divorce." Toni burst out laughing from relief as she told us the story. Had she not asked that single clarifying question, Toni might have backed off and not talked about plans for the move as much. Geraldo might have subsequently confirmed in his mind that she didn't want him to come and backed off as well. The assumptions they each made could have led them to become increasingly strained and distant from each other, resulting in a self-fulfilling prophecy that manifested both their fears.

Holding Others Accountable

We can directly ask a person to address issues regarding individual responsibility and motivation. After Gordon realized that he was taking on too much of Selma's share of the workload—and his exhaustion was causing problems at home—he decided to talk to her. The next time they met, he asked, "Do you believe I am doing more than my share on the projects we have worked on?"

Selma took a deep breath and replied, "Yes, and I've been feeling very guilty about it." Gordon said his eyes almost popped out. He fully expected her to retort, "No. What *is* your problem?" Because of the irritation she had shown whenever he talked with her about project tasks, he did not believe she would admit—or even care—that he was doing more work. Having been asked a direct question in a non-threatening way, she took more responsibility for her behavior. In asking her to address this issue directly, Gordon also demonstrated more willingness to hold her accountable for not sharing the workload equally. If Gordon's question had been intended to get Selma to admit that he was doing more work than she was, it would have been entrapping. Instead, the sincerity of his question drew out Selma's honest answer.

I find that most people are much more careful about answering a respectful question that leaves them accountable for their response. Sally had begun to work on her own defensiveness, and one day when Marcus seemed upset, she asked him very gently, "Are you going to refuse to talk to me if I ask you what is wrong?"

Sally reported that Marcus sat stone-silent for a while, and then "it was as if the stone melted, and tears streamed down his face. We had the best talk we have ever had." That one question prompted him to give serious consideration to his own willingness to talk and accomplished what all her coaxing and angry tirades over a decade could not.

Non-defensive questions can also be effective in cases where a person suspects he is being treated with prejudice. Floyd, a Native American who had recently graduated with a master's degree in social work, had gone to a district school office in a suit and tie to apply for a job in a local high school as a counselor to gangs. After giving him a bare glance, the woman behind the counter announced, "We aren't taking applications for bus drivers right now." Floyd felt angry and humiliated that she would assume he was applying for a job that did not require a college degree. When he tersely told her what job he was applying for and took the application, she acted cool and unapologetic. Feeling that he would make things worse by showing anger, he walked away furious.

To hold the woman more accountable for her own assumption, Floyd might have respectfully requested that she clarify her meaning. He might have asked, "Why do you assume I am here to apply for a job as a bus driver?"

She now has the responsibility for clarification. She can either expose—and struggle with—a prejudice, or she can explain some other reason for her remark. By holding people accountable for what they say, we can keep our own dignity, regardless of how they respond.

Taking Quantum Leaps

We have seen how people can make quantum leaps in personal growth when they ask non-defensive questions. The rest of this chapter will also discuss the types of changes that typically occur in the person answering the question.

The Person Answering the Question

When we ask non-defensive questions, the person answering the question frequently takes quantum leaps in one of two ways.

1. Increased self-awareness. The person answering the question often voluntarily reveals the reason underlying the defensiveness, even if not asked. George, a stranger to me, immediately confided that the students at the community college "never respected" his knowledge. Alison, even at the age of four, could explain that she had been upset because she thought her mom was rejecting her as a girl. Rhonda expressed her fear of not being able to remember the material she was learning.

People who expose their reasons for defensiveness have the opportunity to increase their own self-awareness spontaneously. For example, George may have often felt offended and reacted defensively when people asked him questions about the tires they were buying without consciously realizing why. When he answered my question, he brought the reasons for his defensiveness into his own consciousness.

2. Changes in attitude and behavior. We may change how we speak to others, our attitude, how much responsibility we take for our own behavior, or how we actually behave. When Mena asked Todd why he wanted to leave her and their children, he suddenly became able to talk about everything he was feeling without letting Mena's fears inhibit him.

Frank also took a major step when he promised to stop sexually harassing Nancy. Not only did George's whole demeanor toward me change, but I suspect he changed his response to the tire customers who followed me. After Rhonda clarified the relationship she saw between "charm school" and remembering how to communicate non-defensively, there was a noticeable difference in how quickly she assimilated the information, to the point that she inspired other group members.

Changes with wide ramifications can take place—changes that, with continued effort, can have lasting effects. Todd was able to shift toward making his work more meaningful because of his open conversation with Mena. He decided that he would go back to school and take classes to begin to prepare for a new career, some of which his company paid for.

The Person Asking the Question

The person asking the question can also experience dramatic shifts in self-awareness, attitude, and behavior, simply by gaining new information and by learning to understand false assumptions.

1. Increased self-awareness. Sally learned that Marcus wasn't withdrawing just to torment her; he was feeling extreme conflict between wanting to talk and following his father's dictates against exposing any vulnerability. This revelation not only made sense to Sally, it reinforced her confidence in herself—she hadn't been wrong in believing that Marcus was a sensitive person. She had begun to think that, in the beginning of their relationship, he had just duped her into thinking he had a tender spirit. Now she had far less desire to badger him and was increasingly able to let him be more accountable for whether he talked or not. Gradually, the cycle that had polarized them reversed itself and they moved instead toward the spirit of companionship they had started out with, only with deeper understanding.

2. Changes in attitude and behavior. Nancy's confidence and trust in her ability to protect herself became much stronger because she had been able to ask Frank a straightforward question about his inappropriate sexual advances. Corey found that something shifted inside of her when she sincerely asked Beth about her attitudes toward housework. She felt more comfortable and secure about expecting Beth to contribute; her need to defend her right to expect help dissipated.

Mena had falsely assumed that Todd wanted to leave because he didn't love her anymore. Based on the information she received from him, she too made changes. She began to deal with her anxieties about financial security, took bookkeeping classes, and acquired her own clientele. Having her own career also eased Mena's fears, some of which had been based on being totally dependent on Todd's income. She no longer worried so much.

I also grew significantly in my interaction with George. I had automatically attributed the motivation for his behavior to a sexist attitude. Men have had dominion over tires; I was a woman. However, I now feel confident that my assumption was in error. He was interpreting my questions as similar to those of his students in mechanics who did not show respect for his expertise. Ironically, I think he was reacting to me just as he had to his male students.

I learned on a much deeper level how easily we reinforce and build on prejudice. When someone does something offensive, I think it is insidiously easy to pin the cause on the most obvious difference between us, rather than take the time to find out if our assumptions are accurate.

This increased understanding leads the way to another major shift: both people can experience an instantaneous increase in rapport. Asking George one question created a level of trust that went far deeper than simply dissipating my anger. We developed a new relationship, entirely different from the one we had moments earlier. I don't believe we have to know someone for a long time to care about him. If a person opens his heart and shows his vulnerability, I can feel love, even for someone I have only briefly encountered. I can still feel the connection George and I experienced as we stood together on that sidewalk. Curiosity really did win the peace prize.

7

Formats for Asking
Non-Defensive Questions

The words we use hold within them a world of information that we often ignore. Part of what gives them great power is that each word we hear or say is like a blueprint for what we experience. Every word we have learned is associated with our own life. Filled with those associations, a single word can push our buttons, profoundly impacting on how we feel and react. Just hearing "It's going to rain today" may cast a feeling of depression or a feeling of anticipation—of being lonely in a cold house or curled up beside the fire with a good book. We may or may not be aware of what caused our change of mood, yet it is as if we have entered our own virtual reality. The sound of a word can control us, putting us into the trance of a habitual response that comes from deep within our psyche.

The Blueprint Hidden in the Words

During one workshop, Anthony, a big teddy bear of a man, described his difficulties with losing weight. Whenever he visited his mother, which was fairly often, she would fix a big meal. And Anthony, who was forty-two, would oblige by eating a lot—as much as did when he was a teenager. People in the workshop started suggesting solutions to his problem, mostly based on theories revolving around the idea that his Italian mother's cooking was a symbol of nurturing he couldn't resist.

I began to ask Anthony some questions, one of which was, "Do you feel nurtured when you eat your mom's food?" Puzzled, he shrugged his shoulders and replied, "Yeah, I guess so." He didn't sound sure, so I asked some more questions, including, "What does eating a lot mean to you?" He sat for a minute, with that telltale blank look people often get before they take a quantum leap in understanding; then he opened his eyes wide and lifted his arms in an expansive gesture. "Macho!" he said. "Macho . . . whichever one of us four boys ate the most was considered the biggest and strongest!"

Everyone in the room was surprised at his answer, including me, for I too was attached to the stereotype of the nurturing Italian mother. But *competition*, rather than nurturing, was the part of the blueprint for eating that kept Anthony overindulging. He would slip into his own virtual reality around eating every time he went home, without any conscious awareness of why until he answered my question. His blueprint for eating was associated with male strength.

Anthony then realized that participants in weight-loss programs he had joined had all also assumed his habits were associated with maternal nurturing. While it had never quite clicked, he hadn't really thought about why. Now, in response to a single question, he had more accurate information to use as a basis for resolving his issues with food. By asking sincere questions to fill in the picture of his eating blueprint, we were able to support him in a way that provided genuine help.

Generalizations: Conventions for Misunderstanding

Too much of the time, I believe, we react to others based on generalizations, even when the person speaking is sharing a subjective experience. When we generalize, we apply one word, phrase, or image indiscriminately to many different situations. Most of us in the workshop automatically—without seeking additional information—attributed the cause of Anthony's overeating to the single image of a nurturing Italian mother.

If we do ask questions about a statement someone makes, we often ask about the whole idea, rather than the particular words. If someone says, "Italian women are very nurturing," we might say, "What do you mean?" asking the person to clarify the overall statement.

Rather than asking a general question, we could ask about each word, beginning with the words "Italian" and "women": Does the person mean all Italian women, or just those who are mothers? Young women? Old women? Both? Does the person mean that they are inherently nurturing or that they have learned it from modeling? What about "nurturing"? Does it have to do with cooking or with how much affection the mother shows? Are Italian women more nurturing than women who aren't Italian? When we ask questions about individual words and phrases, we often become more curious and gain much more accurate information.

There is an irony here. Asking questions about smaller bites from the statement can give us a great deal *more* information. It is like using a microscope to bring small details into focus, which gives us more knowledge of the structure and content of the whole. When we generalize, we are often lazy in our expression and sloppy in our understanding. By looking for the significance of individual words and phrases, we can quickly find deeper meaning.

The Tower of Babel: Many People, Many Languages

If the same word can mean something different to each of us, it might seem impossible for us *ever* to communicate effectively. We may fear we are destined forever to reenact the biblical story in which the building of the tower of Babel is interrupted by the confusion of people speaking in many different tongues.

While it takes some practice to do it consistently, once we learn to concentrate on individual words and phrases, I think we can make changes in our question-asking and understand each other's "language" rather quickly.

Margaret took my workshop shortly before she went to meet her husband, who was working out of state, for their twentieth anniversary. Later, she wrote to me:

> I briefly told Jack about the ideas behind this new kind of communication.
>
> He responded, "I think it's great. As long as you don't try to change me."
>
> It was a great opportunity to ask non-defensive questions. We had a long and heartfelt talk about what "change me" means to

him, and although I wasn't able to keep my facial expressions or hand gestures neutral, I did succeed in keeping my voice calm and asking honest questions so that he felt very willing to talk about his feelings. I can't tell you what a difference this is. I felt deeply honored by his trust and vulnerability with me.

By focusing her curiosity on what her partner meant by the words "change me," Margaret saved time and energy, avoided a needless conflict, and gained understanding and intimacy.

Content Questions: Getting the Story Straight

People sometimes express frustration about initially being unable to think of non-defensive questions quickly. The remainder of the chapter will present ways to formulate non-defensive questions more easily.

Rather than set scripts, the formats will suggest guidelines, so you can come up with questions that feel natural. With increasing familiarization and practice, using the various formats will become more intuitive. As you read, it may be helpful to practice saying some of the sample questions aloud, making sure your tone is neutral and the modulation in your voice falls, rather than rises, at the end of each one.

We have two basic formats for asking questions: One is to ask about content (the topic under discussion); the other is to ask about process (the interaction going on between people), which can include any feelings or attitudes that are affecting the discussion. Using each of these two formats, we can then ask many types of questions. Content questions gather information or clarify meaning about the topic under discussion.

Who, What, When, Where, How, and Why

Sometimes a simple way to start asking non-defensive questions is to use the standard questions reporters use to gain a basic picture of a given situation: who, what, when, where, how, and why. Such questions ask for specific pieces of information, an essential first step in gaining clarity in communication.

I could have asked Anthony questions beginning with these six words, such as *what* was mealtime at home like when he was young, *who* was at the dinner table, *how* did they behave, *why* did he think they acted that way, and *what* did the adults say or do in response to their behavior? As he answered, I would have learned the story of his childhood mealtime experience and probably would have heard about how he and his rowdy brothers laughed and joked and tried to see who could eat the most. I might have learned which adults or children commented on the biggest eater, all of which would shed light not only on Anthony's blueprint for eating but on the entire family structure as well.

Often we don't take time to get a clear picture of a situation before we react to it. A friend of mine, Rod, told me a story about reacting to a situation without enough information. His partner, Cynthia, had wanted to leave the house to go to an appointment, but a city truck was parked in the street, blocking their driveway. From the kitchen window, Rod saw Cynthia approach the truck.

A few minutes later, Cynthia came back in the house and announced angrily, "He won't move the truck." Rod was furious. "What do you mean, he won't move it?!" His question was angry too, definitely not an effort to find out specifically what had happened.

Without waiting for her to respond, he went outside, stormed down the driveway, and said to the man in the truck, "What's going on here? Why wouldn't you move your truck so my wife could get out of the driveway?"

The man in the truck looked blank, then irritated. "What the hell are you talking about? Nobody asked me to move."

Rod was stunned. "Didn't my wife just come down here and ask you to move the truck?"

"Nope," the driver responded, with a shrug and scowl.

Rod mumbled, "Sorry . . . would you move the truck, please?" and went back to the house.

"That guy says you never asked him to move. What did you say to him anyway?" This time he did want an answer, though his tone was still angry. "Well, I didn't *say* anything," Cynthia said. "I just walked down the driveway and looked at him so he'd know I wanted to get out. He never budged."

"What? You never *said* anything to him?" Rod sputtered.

"Well, no," Cynthia retorted, "but I *know* he saw me *looking* at him."

Rod blew up. "You made me look like an idiot, ranting at that guy!"

Cynthia replied, "Well, I never said I *spoke* to him, I only said he wouldn't move."

After a bit, they both laughed at the ridiculousness of the whole situation. Cynthia had provided very misleading information. But had Rod asked, "What did you say when you talked to him?" or "How did he react when you asked him to move?" or even "What happened when you went down there?" he would have known that Cynthia had never spoken to the driver at all.

More on Asking "Why?"

Because a "why" question often feels interrogating, I suggest several practices to help ensure a non-defensive approach. In chapter 5, I discussed how asking a question with a contracted word can make it sound defensive. Frequently, "why" questions sound interrogating because we habitually follow "why" with a contracted active verb, such as "didn't." Here are two ways to use a more non-defensive phrasing.

Follow the "why" with a verb that is not contracted.

Contracted: "Why didn't you do that?"
Uncontracted: "Why did you choose (decide) not to do that?"

The contracted question sounds accusatory. The uncontracted question has a more positive-sounding tone. This one practice can help the question sound clear, gentle, and non-judgmental.

Consider asking "what" instead of "why." Many people seem to experience "what" as sounding less interrogating than "why." Consider the difference in the ways Jason could have responded to Trina when she assumed he was breaking his commitment to make dinner because he arrived home later than usual.

Sounds more interrogating: "Why don't you think I would keep my commitment to make dinner?"
Sounds less interrogating: "What made you think I would not keep my commitment to make dinner?"

Any or all of the reporter's six questions can give us valuable information about the story of the other person's experience. This format is often also used in conjunction with many of the others that follow.

Inverting the Essence of a Statement into a Question

One way to clarify meaning is to invert a statement into a question, asking the other person to affirm, deny, or clarify the main point of the sentence. When I was buying my tires, I essentially inverted George's statement into a question.

> George's statement: "You don't need to know [information about the tires]."
> Inversion of his statement: "Do you think I have no need to know about the tires I am buying?"

Although inverting a statement in this way might seem like a simplistic bid to gain obvious information, many of us say things that are a far cry from what we actually mean or feel. For example:

> What George said: "You don't need to know."
> What George meant: "You don't have to challenge my knowledge like my mechanics students did because I know what I'm talking about."

"What Do You Mean?" Questions

In order to gain more accurate information before we react, we can ask directly about what a person means by virtually any word that is used. If someone negates our idea by saying, "It won't work," we may ask, "What do you mean when you say, 'It won't work'?"

This requires the person to be more precise instead of generally panning an idea. Whenever we ask a person who has made such a comment to clarify the specific meaning of the words, we make the person responsibile for explaining the remark rather than defending it.

Asking questions about the meaning of a specific word can also transform interactions in ongoing, intimate relationships. For example, if Margaret had not asked Jack, "What do you mean by 'change me'?" she might have resorted to an accusation such as "You never want to change!" Rather than making counteraccusations, we can just ask what the person means by certain words used to label us or our actions.

When your partner says, "You always defend your family, no matter what," you might ask: "What do you mean by 'defend'?" or "What [or who] do you mean when you refer to my 'family'?"

Your partner might be referring to particular family members, not all of them. He might mean I defend all my family members with regard to certain topics. Or he might be referring to my unwillingness to talk about hurtful things one or more members of my family have done to me.

The wealth of information that can come from asking questions about two or three words can be amazing, even in cases where we assume we already know what the other person means. As Sally and Marcus increased their own ability to deescalate their ongoing conflict around his moody withdrawal, Sally gradually asked more curious questions. One day when Marcus was seemingly in a bad mood, the following interaction took place:

> SALLY: Is something bothering you?
> MARCUS: I'm fine!
> SALLY: What do you mean by "fine"?
> MARCUS: I mean I can take care of myself.

All those years, Sally had thought that Marcus said "fine" to dishonestly indicate he was in a good mood. Now she realized he wasn't trying to deny that he was upset. To him, "fine" primarily meant he wanted to handle his problem by himself. His response was based on the messages he had received—from his father, his peers, and the overall culture—about men not needing emotional support.

Asking about Our Own Assumptions

In many cases, we may assume we know what another person means, only to find later that a misunderstanding has arisen because of our misinterpretation. We can ask directly about our own assumptions about another person's meaning, beginning with various phrases, such as, "Do you mean . . . ?" "Are you saying . . . ?" or "When you say . . . ?"

For example, we might ask the person to confirm or deny our own assumption about what is meant in the following cases:

> "When you say 'doctors are cold,' do you mean that you think they act superior?"
> "Do you mean that you believe professional women act cold as a way to command more respect?"

"Are you saying that men are cold because you think they have a hard time talking about their emotions?"

In each case, we ask directly about what we think the other person means by certain key words. We ask to find out if we understand what the other person is saying. It does not imply that we agree.

I am sometimes asked about the fact that such questions are not open-ended. The concern is that we are "leading"—not allowing the person to respond as freely as he or she might otherwise. If our assumptions are inaccurate, the other person will usually correct us. And if we don't question our own assumptions, we will hold them to be true. We thereby create possible misunderstanding or even solidify our assumptions into judgments.

Questions about Quantity

We can ask questions about quantity when someone makes a generalization about us personally or about a particular group.

If my partner says, "You always interrupt me," I can ask, "By 'always,' do you mean that I interrupt you every time you speak?" If he says "Yes," I have very different information than I would if he said, "Well, not every time, but usually whenever we discuss our plans— taking our summer vacation or putting in the hot tub—I think you get excited and don't wait for me to finish."

We can also phrase this kind of question differently. If a person says, "Teenagers are demanding and lazy," we might ask, "Do you mean all teenagers, most of them, or just a few?"

People often gain new insights from answering a simple question about quantity or degree. Such questions are surprisingly effective in stimulating others to consider more carefully the accuracy of their statement, the degree to which they mean it, and what prompted them to make it.

Questions That Compare and Contrast

Questions that address the opposite side of the coin often help people to expose more facets of their viewpoint and may spontaneously stimulate them to gain a more balanced perspective.

When a friend says, "You haven't called for so long, I thought you didn't care about me anymore," we might ask, "Do you believe that it's possible that I might not call and still care about you?" The friend can now consider a viewpoint that is opposite to the one just expressed and decide what to think. Often when we are feeling one way about an issue or a person, we forget the other side of the picture.

Sometimes we can ask several questions about opposites based on one sentence a person says. In response to the comment, "Some men are cold and unemotional," we might ask, "Do you think some men are warm?" and "Do you think some women are cold?"

Asking about Contradictions

We can also ask the other person to explain the relationship between two factors that seem contradictory to us. There are two primary ways to ask this kind of question: (1) "What is the relationship between [A] and [B]?" and (2) "Given [this] . . . why [that]?"

This is especially effective when people want to hedge and respond in a way that does not answer our question. If we ask a political candidate how a proposed bill will affect Social Security, the reply may be a platitude about "owing a great debt to our senior citizens and doing all we can to help them." Since this answer does not address our question, we could ask, "How does your comment about appreciating senior citizens relate to my question about the effect of your proposal on Social Security?" This question brings the focus back to the issue we originally raised.

Not only can we hold people accountable for what they say or do, we can also gain valuable information that is often lodged in the cracks of contradictions and might otherwise stay hidden. While Sylviaette worked on her thesis all weekend long, Cliff had helped by taking care of the meals and even doing some editing. The following week, when he asked her to take a break for dinner, she replied that she wanted to eat at her desk and keep working. Irritated, Cliff said, "You never take a break." "You never support my work on my thesis," Sylviaette snapped back. Cliff was stunned by this response; he had helped her in many ways over a period of months. He silently withdrew and tried to think of how he could effectively ask Sylviaette about what she had said. Later in the evening, the following conversation took place:

CLIFF: Given that I helped edit your thesis all weekend, what made you say that I never support you?

SYLVIAETTE: Well, you did help me, but every time I asked you to go over another section, you said "OK" in a tone that would make Eeyore seem happy by comparison.

CLIFF: Oh. *(thinking about her answer)* I guess it would have looked that way to you. I don't like to edit, even though I'm good at it. The funny part is, I volunteered to edit it because of how much I *do* want to support you.

Instead of feeling alienated, they began to feel much closer, which eased their work on the thesis.

A word of caution: I suggest that anyone who tends toward aggressiveness be very careful in using this "given A, why B" format, or possibly choose a different one. If not asked in a way that is clearly, authentically curious, this format can sound very accusatory or become entrapping. Because the question goes to the heart of any discrepancy, we can easily use this format to prove our own point instead of to gather information. It would have been easy for Cliff to have put a lot of emotion and judgment into his question: "Given that I *helped you all weekend*, why are you saying I *don't support you?*"

Used carefully, this format can help people examine discrepancies of which they were unaware, an exploration that can result in personal growth. Brad was considering taking an excellent job in a city about fifty miles from where his father lived. But he felt ambivalent because he didn't want his father to be alone. A close friend finally asked him, "Given that your dad never sees you unless you make it happen, what is making you so worried that he will feel alone?"

Brad knew his father hardly ever called or initiated getting together. They talked only when Brad phoned or arranged for them to visit, which he could do as easily from fifty miles away as from across town. As he wondered why he had worried about his father being alone under these circumstances, Brad realized that he was bothered by his own fear of becoming disconnected and was projecting that fear onto his dad. With this information, he was able to begin some inner work he had previously avoided—dealing with the loss he felt because of having an absentee father.

Questions about Past, Present, and Future

We may ask people about their childhood experiences, present ideas, or future plans.

"How long have you felt that way?"
"When did you decide that?"
"How are you feeling now?"
"When do you think you will do that?"

These questions can often shed light on what motivates people to change how they feel, decide on a certain course of action, or develop a certain attitude. For example, when someone expresses a "philosophy of life," we tend to simply agree or disagree rather than gathering information about what brought about this attitude.

Using First, Second, and Third Person

By asking basically the same question with a focus on different grammatical "subjects"—first, second, and third person—we can gain an enlightening perspective on what someone is saying from varying angles. If your partner generalizes about people "being manipulative," you could ask questions in any of the following forms:

THIRD PERSON: Do you think all people are manipulative? (*asking about the generalization*)

FIRST PERSON: Do you see me as manipulative? (*asking about yourself*)

SECOND PERSON: Do you think you are manipulative? (*asking about the speaker*)

When we talk in generalities, we often hesitate to bring the question home to ourselves, the two people in conversation. People also frequently talk in the abstract without being consciously aware of the effect it is having on someone who is present. During a retreat I facilitated for women over sixty-five, I was sharing a meal with two women: Clarice, who was thin and agile, and Emma, who was quite heavy and had serious problems with her knees. Clarice remarked, "I think that how people eat and exercise is important as preventive medicine—to keep in shape and avoid health problems." She had given no apparent thought to the impact that her words about people keeping in shape might have on Emma.

I asked Clarice, "Do you believe that if Emma ate properly and exercised, she would be in better shape and would have prevented some of the problems she is having with her knees?" Asking about how a generalization applies to someone who is present is often difficult. I had to think for a minute about whether I wanted to risk it, and I took a deep breath before I asked the question.

Clarice was horrified. "Oh, no!" she said. "I wasn't talking about *her*, I just meant 'in general.'"

I asked Emma how she had felt about Clarice's comment. Emma began to cry and replied, "I felt so humiliated. And I felt angry, too, that she would make that judgment without knowing how many different kinds of problems people can have. It's just not that simple. I eat very carefully and ride an exercise bike for one hour and swim every day, but I have a metabolic disease and it is hard even to maintain the weight I am at now."

Not only did Clarice realize how much she had hurt Emma, she was surprised to learn about Emma's regimen with diet and exercise. She recognized that she *had* been making a judgment about Emma without knowing it. Emma was relieved to talk about Clarice's comment. Although she had often previously felt such judgments from others, she had just closed in around her pain in silence.

After Clarice sincerely apologized for how deeply she had hurt Emma, she had a spontaneous awareness—one of those quantum leaps. Clarice had always felt superior to her sister, who typically ate a lot and did not exercise. Clarice's own habits of eating and exercising had become a way to compete with this sister—something she had never realized in all her seventy-two years.

Clarice commented that, although she was shocked at first when I asked her directly about the effect of her statement upon Emma, twenty minutes later, she realized it enabled a healing to take place. My *not* asking the question wouldn't have prevented Emma's being hurt. Asking, it brought her feelings out into the open so they could be resolved.

Questions About Value, Emotion, Reason, and Behavior

When we ask questions about what a word or phrase means, we uncover the person's blueprint for the structure of that word—how it subsequently both dictates and reflects that person's reality. Much of a word's meaning, and how we experience life in relationship to that word, comes from the elements we have attached to it. These include what I call VERB elements: values, emotions, reasoning, and behavior.

Element	Focus of Question
Value	What someone *believes*
Emotion	What someone *feels*
Reasoning	What someone *thinks*
Behavior	What someone *does*

Asking about a single VERB element. We can ask one question focusing on what a person believes, feels, thinks, or does and gain valuable information that may transform the conversation. The following questions are based on examples previously discussed.

VALUE: Do you *believe* it means I don't care about you if I don't call?

EMOTION: How do you *feel* when I come home late on a night when it's my turn to make dinner?

REASONING: Do you *think* I do not need to know about the tires I am buying?

BEHAVIOR: What *did you say* to the man who was blocking the driveway?

Even when people are arguing a point, if asked directly and nondefensively about what they think, believe, or feel they may stop arguing, shift their position, and answer more genuinely. Once when I was working with a classroom full of teenagers, one boy talked about getting picked up by the police and being harassed by other people "for no reason." A girl in the class (knowing his clothes identified him as a gang member) insisted, "If you're gonna wear those clothes, man, you're gonna get hassled. I used to. Then I changed how I dress and now I don't." The young man replied, "That doesn't have anything to do with it," and they argued for a minute.

I then requested that the girl ask the boy what he *believed,* instead of just trying to convince him to agree with her.

She asked, "Do you believe what you wear makes a difference in how you get treated?"

He responded, "Yes."

His response was immediate and straightforward—surpassing even a reluctant "Well, maybe." At fourteen years of age, before an audience of thirty peers, he was willing to shift his position dramatically and give an honest answer when asked a question about what he believed.

Applying all four VERB questions to the same issue. When we ask about a person's values, emotions, reasoning, and behavior regarding the same issue, we can acquire an even greater wealth of information. Jamilla, who was divorced, had an ongoing argument with her father, who was a minister. He kept insisting that she needed to find a second husband. A professor at the university that Jamilla attended had taken a PNDC workshop and helped her think of some questions to ask her father. Her first question was; "Dad, why do you believe that I should get married again?"

"So Mahogany (her three-year-old daughter) can have a daddy." he replied. His *belief* was that his granddaughter needed a father.

Then she asked, "What are you afraid will happen if I don't get married?"

He was *fearful* that Mahogany wouldn't have a good role model if Jamilla didn't get married.

Jamilla asked him, "Do you think that I have to be married for her to have a good male role model?"

"Yes," he said, "especially since you are so far away from me and your brothers." His *reasoning* was that Jamilla must get married to provide this for her daughter if she lived away from her hometown.

Then she asked, "Would you like to know what I do to make sure she has good role models?"

Surprised, he answered that he would.

Jamilla then shared with him that she had close male and female friends who spent a lot of time with her and Mahogany. She had been careful to make sure her daughter had not only good male role models but an extended "family." Father and daughter had never gotten to that point of discussion in the two years since her divorce because they had been stuck at point one: arguing about whether she should get married again. Furthermore, she had always assumed that his refrain about marriage was simply a tired moral argument with no genuine concern behind it. As an outgrowth of her questions, she understood more of his concerns and fears, he understood more of her way of life, and their relationship changed. Both father and daughter developed increasing acceptance and respect for each other's views.

Content Questions

1. **Who, what, when, where, how, and why:** Getting the details regarding a situation or a person's reactions
2. **Inverting:** Turning the other person's statement into a question
3. **"What do you mean. . . ?":** Asking for clarification about the meaning of a particular word or phrase
4. **Assumptions:** Asking the other person directly about your own assumptions regarding what he or she means
5. **Quantity:** Asking for clarification about words that describe amounts, percentages, or degrees
6. **Compare and contrast:** Asking questions about opposites, variations, and exceptions
7. **Contradictions:** Asking about any contradictions in what a person has said or done
8. **Past, present, and future:** Asking questions related to time factors
9. **First, second, and third person:** Asking basically the same question with a focus on different "subjects" (me, you, them) in order to gain perspective from different angles
10. **Value, emotion, reason, and behavior:** Asking about what a person believes, feels, thinks, and does

Process Questions:
Looking Behind the Scenes

All the types of questions presented thus far have been questions about the *content* of the topic under discussion. A *process* question focuses on some reaction either person is having apart from the topic. The reaction might be any attitude (sarcasm, superiority) or emotion (irritation, hurt) that seems beyond the scope of the topic being discussed. It might involve an unrelated side comment. It might be some behavioral trait, such as interrupting frequently.

A reaction might be triggered by the topic or involve an ongoing dynamic between the respective parties. For example, when Trina got upset with Jason for getting home late on his night to fix dinner, he felt hurt that she didn't trust him to follow through on his commitment. It was this feeling of hurt that accelerated his defensiveness, not just her assumption that he had forgotten. Often a matter at hand would not become so intense if it didn't prompt other reactions, such as trust issues or hurt feelings.

My own rule of thumb is, if the conversation is getting bogged down because either person resists talking cooperatively or senses tension, to switch from questions about content to questions about the process going on between the people involved.

Questions about Involuntary Reactions

I previously mentioned that automatic facial reactions can sometimes make it hard to ask sincere questions. On the other hand, they can also provide poignant clues for when to switch to a process question, whether we feel the reactions in ourselves or see them in another.

Suppose you ask your woman friend to go for a run on a cold day. If she moans and grimaces and finally says, "Oh, all right, let's go," you can ask, "Why did you grimace when you said OK?" She might respond, "The thought of going out now sounds terrible, but I know it will be good for me." Having answered the question and acknowledged her reaction, she may feel less resistant and become more committed to going.

I find this happens often when we ask about someone's reaction. After acknowledging it, the person's attitude may well shift and become more positive. On the other hand, she might have responded, "You know, I think I was hesitant to go because I am so tired and I've been fighting a cold." Given this information, she may decide, with your full support, not to risk becoming ill by running and sweating in the cold air.

Questions about Attitude

Many people over forty still get advice from their parents in a we-know-what-is-best tone. "Honey, you should put the giblets in the dressing instead of the gravy," or, "You really should send Jimmy to bed now." We typically react defensively, perhaps arguing, perhaps stifling our irritation.

In such situations, I think you can ask directly about the person's attitude in a way that maintains respect. For example: "Mom, do you think your way of making gravy is better than mine?" Or, "Dad, do you think I am not being responsible about when I put Jimmy to bed?" Likewise, you can ask a co-worker who gives constant advice, "Do you believe you know how to do this process better than I do?"

These questions draw the issue of the person's attitude out into the open where it can be addressed. We can ask about any reaction—submissiveness, pessimism, skepticism, hostility. Although most people could list dozens of attitudes that drive them crazy, usually they do not ask direct questions of the person exhibiting them.

When we don't openly ask about a person's attitude, it's as though we are fighting ghosts whose strong, invisible presence can affect our whole experience. Perhaps you are talking about vacation plans and your partner keeps making comments, such as:

"Well, we may not get to go if your mom gets sick again."
"Florida might be kind of expensive."
"Sarah is getting married next year, so maybe we should just stay home and save the money."

Instead of responding to these statements and trying to continue your conversation, I think it is much more effective to ask a question, such as: "Are you feeling pessimistic about taking a vacation?"

We can also ask another person for an interpretation of our own attitude: "Do you think I sounded judgmental when I told you my opinion?" Or: "Do you think I reacted defensively when you told me you were too tired to go to a movie?"

Questions about Motivation and Intention

Questions about motivation and intention could naturally apply to the majority of the examples in this book. By motivation I mean whatever causes a person to say or do something, or speak in a certain tone of voice, whereas intention involves a person's goal or objective.

I will deal with motivation and intention together because they often overlap. We frequently think we know exactly why someone said something, but we never discuss the motivation directly. We go away fuming, feeling manipulated or negated, when we could easily have brought the issue of the person's motivation out in the open.

Consider the following seven kinds of situations that call for questions regarding motivation and intention.

1. When we want to check out our own assumptions. Polly turned in her resignation to join another insurance company, where she would be able to advance, and the agent she worked for remarked, "You'll never make it." She could have asked him about the motivation for his comment: "Are you saying that because you want to keep me here?"

Checking out our assumption about someone's motive can have a powerful effect, even if the other person doesn't admit its truth. And in a surprising number of cases, people will acknowledge their motivation if asked directly.

2. When someone is acting inappropriately. Bill, the custodian at a high school, witnessed a woman teacher watching a student throw garbage on the hallway floor. She then turned to Bill and said, "Can you take care of that mess?" Bill wasn't comfortable challenging the teacher. He mumbled "OK" and cleaned up the mess, furious all the while. Later, in a workshop, he asked how he might have handled this situation.

He could have asked the teacher, "When you saw the student throw that garbage on the floor, what made you ask me to pick it up instead of asking the student to do it?"

It is possible that the teacher felt more intimidated asking the student to pick it up than asking the custodial person. Even if the teacher didn't admit that, she might examine her own behavior and behave differently in the future.

3. When we are puzzled by someone's behavior. In some cases, we are puzzled by a person's motivation or frustrated because we think we are receiving double messages about the person's intentions. A woman from a rape crisis agency was called to a small town by a sheriff who had requested advice on questioning rape victims. As the woman spoke with the sheriff, he looked away from her, chewed gum loudly, and played with a paper clip.

Finding herself getting irritated at his seeming lack of interest after she had come some distance to talk with him, she thought of a non-defensive question and asked him, simply, "Are you interested in what I am talking about?"

He put down the paper clip, glanced at her, and said, "Yeah, it's just a little hard."

The woman had asked the sheriff about his intentions—about whether he wanted to hear what she had to say. If his answer had shown a genuine lack of interest, or even hostility, she could have asked about his motivation for having called her. In that case, she might have found out he had mishandled a situation involving a rape victim, at which time another official had "recommended" he get some training. If so, the woman would know what she was dealing with and could respond more effectively than if she had never addressed the sheriff's seeming lack of interest.

In this case, both people's attitudes shifted, and the sheriff's comment became the basis for a valuable conversation. The woman learned that the sheriff was uncomfortable talking about rape. But he believed his job required that he develop some skill in dealing with violence toward women. The consultant left their meeting believing that their talk had genuinely helped the sheriff to deal with his own discomfort and so be more gentle with any victim of violence. Had she not asked that single question about his level of interest in the conversation, she would have continued to resent (her own interpretation of) his attitude, and the outcome would have been very different.

4. When we want to ask permission to approach a topic. Sometimes we hesitate to approach a topic at all, thinking the person might resent our question or that the timing might not be right for a discussion. In such cases, we can ask for permission to ask the question. "Is it all right if I ask you a question about what you just said?" Here we seek to find out if the person feels motivated to engage in discussion. We can also ask directly about how willing a person feels to do anything: listen to us, answer us, or make some kind of commitment.

We may also ask someone who seems determined that his opinion is the only one with merit, "Are you willing to hear what my reasoning is about this issue?" If the answer is "no," we no longer have to waste our time offering our viewpoint. If it is "yes," the person will usually be more committed to hearing what we have to say.

5. When we want to ask about any of the VERB elements. We can ask about any thought, feeling, belief, or behavior we think might be motivating the person. For example, "Did you feel hurt when I said that?"

6. When we want to ask about any defensive reaction. In order to understand motives or intentions, we can ask about a person's misuse of questions, statements, predictions, or any other defensive reaction. Corey might say to Beth, "Are you attacking me and telling me I am unfair as a way to get out of doing the dishes?"

To a person who is misusing a statement to try to persuade us to agree, we might say, "Are to trying to get me to agree with you?" Here, instead of just defending our own viewpoint, we are bringing the person's efforts to convince us into the open for direct discussion. So much of the time, our conflicts are related to reactions outside the context of the conversation.

7. When we want to see how someone perceives us. We can also apply this whole process in reverse—to learn how someone else perceives *our* motivation and intention. In cases where the person seems suspicious or defensive, we might ask, "What did you think my motive was in asking you that question [making that comment]?"

Hearing another person's reactions helps us examine ourselves.

Sometimes we may discover underlying motives we weren't aware of. Our friends, family, and co-workers often have valuable gems of information. Even if they are inaccurate, we will gain important information about how they perceive us.

Process Questions

1. **Questions about involuntary reactions:** Asking about tone of voice and body language
2. **Questions about attitude:** Asking about a specific attitude such as superiority or pessimism
3. **Questions about motivation and intention:** Asking about what caused a person to react in a certain way or what the person is seeking to accomplish in the interaction

---

Varying the Question Formats in One Conversation

In all likelihood, a single conversation will involve several different formats. Recall Lynette and her law partner, Walter, who asked her if she was a social worker or an attorney because she was doing volunteer work at Legal Aid. She allowed herself to be entrapped by saying, "A little of each, I guess." Later, she went back to him and asked him why he had said that. She used several types of questions to gather as much accurate information as possible.

LYNETTE: What made you ask if I was a social worker or an attorney?

WALTER: It seems like you're spending a lot of time working at Legal Aid.

LYNETTE: Do you believe the time I spend doing volunteer work takes away from the work I do here at the office?

WALTER: No, I think you do a fine job here.

LYNETTE: Given that I do my volunteer work at Legal Aid, why does it seem to you to be more in the realm of social work than legal work?

WALTER: Because you don't get paid.

LYNETTE: Do you believe that, as an attorney, I should always be
paid?

WALTER: Yes, we all put in a lot of years to get our degree, and we
should get paid for what we do. If we want others to respect us and know we are successful, we can't be giving
ourselves away.

Walter was actually concerned that doing so much "free work"
would affect her reputation as a "good attorney," which, in his mind,
would affect the firm and him as well. In this conversation, Lynette
used four types of question formats:

A question about Walter's motivation (process)
A question about what he believed (content)
A question using a "given A, why B" (content)
A question about her own assumption. (content)

You can use the formats for content and process questions alone or
in combination. Their varied contexts offer you a wide range of
choices. What is most important is to gradually become more comfortable asking questions rather than pressuring yourself to think of
several questions at any given moment.

If 50 percent of our conversations were comprised of questions,
most of us would finally feel we were communicating. Asking sincere,
thorough questions helps us fill in the picture of another person's experience. Just one question can often give us a panoramic view of
what is really going on inside someone. When we stop rushing to
thrust our own opinion into conversations and ask questions, we can
more clearly see another person's "real world."

8

The Statement

Vulnerability and Power Join Hands

When we make statements, that old war motto—"To be open is to be vulnerable, and to be vulnerable is to be weak"—comes into play with a vengeance. Just as curiosity is often missing in our questions, vulnerability is often absent from our statements. While we might make vulnerable statements to a partner during safe, intimate moments, most of us would rarely choose to expose all our thoughts and feelings during conflict. Complete openness would show that the "case" we are trying to prove is not as airtight as we would have the other person think; it would make us vulnerable to attack.

Recall Jason and Trina's quarrel about whether he broke his commitment to make dinner. If Jason is intent on proving that Trina is overreacting to his late arrival home, he is not likely to want to admit that he should have called when he was detained. He would see that as handing her ammunition. Likewise, if Lisa admitted to Sawyer that she did question the necessity of one or two items on the grocery list, she would anticipate Sawyer's replying, "See, I told you—you spend too much! You even know it yourself." In either case, any admission would be uttered begrudgingly, like that of a hostile witness.

For the same reasons, we generally don't choose to make statements that expose our vulnerability in the boardroom, at an office staff meeting, or with a political opponent. If we want to appear powerful to others, we usually consider that showing doubt or concurring with a point made by an opponent is equivalent to planting a land mine in our own territory. It will blow up our agenda and goals.

In a wide range of personal and professional situations, I think the

126

majority of us believe that such acknowledgment will weaken our position. One workshop participant commented that when we are open and vulnerable "we wind up as roadkill."

I believe this deeply ingrained habit of guarding against emotional vulnerability causes us far more problems than it solves. Regardless of the issue, when we hide information we lose, in bits and pieces, our honesty, our integrity, and our ability to work creatively with others to resolve problems.

An odd reversal happens when we put up a strong front and avoid saying anything that makes us vulnerable: we *compromise* what we say. We sift and sort to decide what is appropriate to help us achieve our goals at any moment, paralleling the classic story of the politician who begins his career inspired to do good, and winds up compromising his way into hell.

Nature: Open and Direct

The character of a non-defensive statement is not suspicious, guarded, or dominating. It is straightforward and clear.

Vulnerable

A fully open statement is vulnerable and unguarded and has no hidden facets. We express our weaknesses as well as our strengths, our fears as well as our hopes, our doubt as well as our certainty. We communicate our thoughts, beliefs, and feelings in a thorough way. Most important, rather than weakening a statement, I think vulnerability can strengthen it.

If we perceive something as a weakness, we may experience it that way even if it could in fact give us increased strength. Recently I was visiting my friend Vicki and overheard a message she was playing back on her answering machine. What I heard was, "Thanks for the shooter. The universe *does* provide for us, doesn't it? I took a walk yesterday and was able to go for blocks."

"What's a shooter?" I asked.

Vicki laughed. "A scooter," she said, correcting me.

"A scooter?" I repeated, still puzzled.

"Yes. Patricia has multiple sclerosis and has been walking with a cane for a long time. Recently she realized that the cane was no longer adequate to support her and she would have to begin using a walker. This was very hard for her. It made her feel so weak, vulnerable, and old; she couldn't stand the thought of people on the street watching her use it. So I asked her, 'How would it feel to you to use it if you were five years old instead of forty-two?' Patricia said, 'Well, it has wheels, so I'd like it.' So then I suggested that she think of her walker as a scooter."

Patricia had gone on a long walk with her "scooter" instead of sitting at home, feeling disabled and old whenever she looked at her new walker. In the beginning, she had seen it as a symbol of her disability, so it made her feel vulnerable and weak. Ultimately, the only thing she changed was her attitude. Now she saw the walker as giving her strength. In the same fashion, I believe we need to change how we see vulnerability. We need to begin to see it as a source of strength in our communication.

Just as innocence lies at the core of curiosity, I think openness lies at the core of vulnerability. Being an "open book" brings the same kind of purity to our statements that innocent curiosity brings to our questions. When we speak openly and vulnerably, we do not have hidden motives.

Direct

Directness is a another characteristic of an open, vulnerable, non-defensive statement. Having no ulterior motives means that we state our needs, desires, and goals directly. It seems ironic that we fear vulnerability, when it allows us to be far more direct than when we are closed and defensive. In classic warfare, soldiers hid behind shields and threw lances at enemy soldiers, hiding and attacking at the same time. Similarly, when we defensively hide significant portions of what we think, feel, and believe, while presenting a good argument or attacking others, we are also simultaneously hiding and attacking— we are not being straightforward. Being willing to expose our truth allows us to be vulnerable and direct at the same time, a more powerful combination than hide and attack.

Sometimes we avoid being direct because we are afraid we will offend someone and put ourselves in a bad light. Or we fear our honesty will hurt others. Wendy lived for a short time in a mountain cabin and had left some special river rocks there. When she returned to the cabin to get them, she visited briefly with Donna, the current resident. Donna knew Wendy slightly and asked if she would like to take a walk in the woods before she left. Wendy hesitated. She feared that Donna would want to take a much longer walk than she would. She also feared getting drawn into a lengthy conversation with a woman who was probably lonely. So she lied and said she had to get back to town for an appointment.

As Wendy walked back to the car, her mind was racing. She was trying to practice non-defensive communication, and here she had just lied to this woman. She could feel the sense inside herself that so many of us feel when we make an excuse and suspect the other person knows it for just what it is. She wondered, Could I possibly tell Donna the truth? While she feared hurting Donna's feelings, she decided on an impulse to turn around and see what would happen. "I lied to you," she blurted out. "I don't have an appointment. I was afraid you might want to walk longer than I did. And I know that when I lived here I got lonely sometimes, and I was afraid you might be lonely and would want to talk for a long time." Even as she said the words, she felt relief—and a genuine closeness to Donna, whose eyes sparkled with the gentleness of her smile. "I'd love to take a short walk," she responded. They took a pleasant walk and engaged in a brief but delightful conversation.

When Wendy opened up and expressed all of what she was thinking—even her lie—she made herself vulnerable. She was clear about her needs. Instead of the truth hurting Donna, it fostered a deeper connection, not to mention a good walk in the woods.

I still don't always say everything I think and feel openly and directly. Sometimes fear predominates—fear that my vulnerability will cause me some harm or that my directness will hurt someone else. I believe each of us needs to determine the degree of vulnerability and directness we choose in any given situation. As we practice, however, in an ever-increasing variety of situations, our vulnerability and our directness combined can have a powerful and constructive effect.

Subjective

Closely tied to the open and direct character of a non-defensive statement is its subjective quality. When we are more fully open, we can present what we say as our own personal experience rather than dressing it up as truth. It is true for us, no more and no less. Geneva, a woman in her seventies, had divorced Clyde a few years before. Clyde now always wanted her to invite him to any holiday meals she had with their adult children at her home; she preferred that they spend alternate holidays with the children rather than spending them together. But when she didn't invite him to her Thanksgiving dinner, he delayed sending her alimony check—her only source of income.

I suggested to Geneva that she consider telling him all of her reactions, including her fears about his withholding her alimony. Her eyes widened, and she said, "If that old coot knew how much it upsets me, he'd hold up that check till the ink faded." She added she'd be more likely to tell him she'd sic the Feds on him if he didn't pay up—which is what people often do: try to add *more* clout to what they are saying than they really believe they have. Geneva initially felt that expressing her vulnerability would give Clyde a weapon to use against her. She feared being financially helpless if she asserted her need.

Ultimately, she decided to try "the direct and vulnerable approach," as she tagged it. Before the next holiday, she said, "I would like for us to take turns having holidays with the kids and not have them with each other anymore. I don't want to invite you to my house, but I am afraid, if I don't invite you, you will hold up my alimony check like you have in the past."

She didn't invite him to dinner, and for the first time he did *not* hold up her check.

Geneva's statement was subjective. She expressed her needs and feelings in a way that carried its own energy. I think non-defensive statements often carry passion well because they express *our* thoughts, *our* feelings, *our* beliefs, without trying to counter what someone else has said. Others can get a clearer picture of our experience, and the vulnerability and directness provide a unique blend of softness and strength to the statement.

Descriptive

Geneva's statement to Clyde was descriptive. In a few sentences, it portrayed her experience regarding family holidays in the context of a particular issue, her relationship to her ex-husband. Our story in relationship to any issue can have many facets, some of which may be, or seem to be, contradictory. For example, part of Geneva's story was, "I don't want you to come to holidays at my house, and I invite you anyway."

When we describe our experience directly, we have more opportunity to foster understanding. We can do it briefly or in greater depth, as long as we cover the essential information relevant to the issue. When Geneva described her experience to Clyde, he was better able to understand her perspective and feelings; he may have previously thought she didn't invite him to holiday meals just to punish him in some way and so retaliated by holding up her check.

If Geneva had made her statement with the *motive* of getting Clyde to stay away and still pay her on time, it would have simply exacerbated the power struggle. Using a statement descriptively, we offer other people thorough information instead of gearing our words toward convincing them to react in a certain way. When we describe our own experience with sincerity and integrity, others are more likely to respond with increased openness and respect.

Function: Laying It All Out on the Table

A card player who shows a hand can lose the game, so the player who wants to win will hide most cards and just put out certain ones when they are called for. Many people live their lives this way, holding back information and playing their cards when they think they can gain the most. I think living this way is a gamble—in both the short and long run—and the odds of losing are much higher than the odds of winning. `

Expressing ourselves through non-defensive statements is a very different way of living from concealing information as if we were holding back a trump card. With non-defensive statements we gain power by providing as much information as possible.

In each of her previous long-term relationships, Debbie felt that the other person had been emotionally withholding and had often pulled back from genuine intimacy with her. Each time she had become insecure, losing her own strength and feeling increasingly dependent on the other person, who subsequently withdrew even more. At the end of the last relationship, she decided she would never again become so dependent on someone that she would lose her self-esteem. She spent many months learning to feel more secure in her independence. She knew from past experience that she did quite well on her own but seemed to lose herself when in partnership.

She finally met Paula, who did not seem to be emotionally withholding and with whom she felt a wonderful bond. At first, Debbie felt proud of her ability to keep her independence, but after a few weeks she sensed things beginning to shift into the old scenario. One Saturday, after they returned from a trip to the beach, Paula announced, "I'm feeling like I need some more space, so I think I'd like to go home instead of staying until tomorrow."

I don't know how to do this, Debbie thought. I see the same old thing happening all over again. Tears came despite her efforts to hold them back. Paula looked very worried and asked her what was wrong. "I don't want you to go," was all she could get out at first. "Well, if you need me to stay, I will," Paula responded. When she heard the words, Debbie knew that if Paula stayed, it would be for her sake, not because Paula wanted to.

Finally Debbie realized that she needed to say it all. She cried freely as she told Paula how each person she had been with had withdrawn. She told her how hard she had worked to not have it happen again, and how this relationship seemed different. But recently she had begun to notice Paula withdrawing more. She even said she thought Paula often seemed to feel the need for space during the times that they were the closest.

Debbie concluded, "When you decided to go home, I felt an almost unbearable wave of loss and hurt. And at the same time I knew I never again wanted anyone here who didn't want to be." She told Paula she did not feel angry and sincerely preferred that she go home. Debbie said later that she felt great being so clear about not wanting Paula to stay if she wanted to leave.

Debbie gave Paula all the relevant information she had. She described how she perceived both Paula's desire to go home and her reaction to it, including data from her own life history. She expressed the contradictions: she thought their relationship was different, she saw the same old thing happening; she wanted her to stay, she wanted her to go. Her goal was not to make Paula feel guilty or manipulate her into staying. She gave Paula a multifaceted picture of her state of being with regard to the issue of Paula's leaving in the middle of a weekend together.

Paula had enough wisdom to leave without trying to persuade Debbie to let her stay, but something important shifted in that conversation. Paula felt moved by the experience. She did not feel guilty, she felt free to go—and anxious to come back. Each of them had remaining work to do with regard to issues such as abandonment and fear of intimacy, and they did it, creating a very strong relationship in the process.

Often, in this kind of situation, we would not tell both halves of the story, only the half that fit with what we wanted most. If our biggest need was to have the person stay, we might talk about our feelings of abandonment and hope the other person would remain to console us. If we wanted to avoid having her feel pressured to stay, we would keep a stiff upper lip and tell her we wanted her to do whatever was best for her. Telling both halves—the whole story—in a non-manipulative way, and then expressing what we want most, can have a profound effect on both the person making the statement and the one hearing it.

Brandon was dating Camille, who would come back to him in between the other men she was dating. He felt used but couldn't bring himself to say no to her. Sometimes, when he was angry, he accused her of "just using him for a good time when no one else is around," which caused arguments.

Finally, Brandon learned how to tell Camille what he was experiencing in a more open way. The next time she came back, he said directly, "I think you came back because you are between boyfriends, and you take it for granted that I will be here. And I have been, at least so far. Even though I wish I could tell you no, I don't have the strength right now. I partly blame you for it, and I also know that it is my choice."

Brandon was telling both halves of the story in a situation where his need for Camille to stay was stronger than his will for her to go— the opposite of Debbie's situation.

Brandon discovered that his self-esteem had been more damaged when he either remained silent, pretending Camille had changed her mind and really wanted to be with him, or when he accused and blamed her. Telling the whole story actually made him feel stronger— and changed their relationship. He saw Camille more realistically, and she began to feel more respect for him, though her basic pattern did not change. Some months later, he was able to make the final break, something he hadn't been sure he could ever do. When it happened, it felt a little bittersweet, but easy.

When we express ourselves thoroughly without trying to convince the other person to listen to us, we can effect long-lasting changes. After a speech I had given, a woman approached me and introduced herself as Riassah. She was a psychologist who had trained in the United States as a young woman, living here for twenty years before returning to her native Iran. "While you were speaking, I had a rush of memories," she said. "I'd like to talk with you about them."

She told me about a conversation she had had with her brother when she was ten and he was nine. She described how he used to chase her and hit her, and how she would chase him and fight back in response. One day, when he was about to hit her, she said to him, "I don't like it when you hit me. It is not in my nature. I don't like for you to hit me, and I don't like to hit you."

She repeated the three sentences to me carefully, softly, and firmly, pausing in between as I imagined she did when she spoke the words as a child. Riassah then said, "He never hit me again—not once during the whole time we were growing up. When I heard you today, I realized that I had made a non-defensive statement. I hadn't tried to convince him to agree or threaten him with anything. I just told him how I felt about our hitting each other."

Whenever we add extra force to our words, presenting them as truth and trying to compel others to agree with us, we usually meet a great deal of resistance. It is sometimes hard for us to realize how much effect our words can have when we let them stand on their own, when we let them convey the inherent power of our personal message.

A thorough statement can become a story within itself that moves others to respond sincerely. The Greek Sophist Gorgias said that *logos*, the word "with the smallest and most invisible body accomplishes the most god-like works. It can banish fear and remove grief, instill pleasure, and enhance pity." I agree with him. I think we have barely tapped into the true power of our expression, because we have stayed tied to a tradition that prescribes "objective" statements over subjective ones and persuasion over openness and vulnerability.

Mental preparation

- Am I willing to speak about my own viewpoint and experience without generally applying it to everyone?
- Can I express myself without trying to convince anyone else to agree?
- Can I recognize another person's experience as providing equally important information?
- Is my statement open? vulnerable? subjective? descriptive?

Effect: Courage, Freedom—and More

We are often reluctant to express our own position in any circumstance where we think it would fall on deaf ears or where we fear initiating a conflict. As a result, we make our position fully clear only when we believe it will achieve a desired outcome, and in so doing we lose clarity that gives shape and direction to our lives. By contrast, when we make a non-defensive statement, we do not expect the results we want to boomerang back to us immediately.

Establishing Our Own Position

A non-defensive statement can give others thorough information without causing polarization and resistance. At the same time, it can powerfully establish our position, even when we anticipate having no control whatsoever over the outcome. Sojourner Truth emerged from slavery to be the first African American woman to speak in Congress. She used her powerful voice in situations where she had no realistic hope of altering the outcome. In one incident, her words were so strong that someone in the audience decided she was a man in disguise, and she was ordered to go into the bathroom and bare her breast to prove she was a woman. The power of the words she uttered has passed the test of time: "It is to your shame, not mine, that I do this." She didn't argue or try to convince; she simply established her position.

When Riassah said to her brother that it was not in her nature to fight, she had no reason to think her words would have the power they did. Had she held them back, she and her brother would probably have given each other many more bruises throughout their upbringing. Likewise, if Geneva had decided that telling Clyde her need (to have separate holidays) and her fear (that he would hold up her alimony) would make her too vulnerable, she would probably still be cooking his turkey.

José was frustrated that his partner, Idalia, allowed her bright and popular teenage daughter, Carmen, to be sloppy and rude at home. They had argued over the situation and gotten nowhere. Finally, one day, José completely and non-defensively stated how he felt about the situation.

"I feel so much frustration and pain and anger when I watch what happens between you and Carmen. I get angry when I hear her speak disrespectfully to you and see you in pain—but you just take it, except when you scream back at her sometimes. And I feel helpless to do anything about it. I see you get angry at me if I tell her to respect you. You probably think I am interfering, but what I see is that you are defending her bad treatment of you. I see how well she does in school, and yet she is unwilling to pick up her own clothes and you follow her around, doing it for her. I not only feel anger at her and sadness for you, I also feel anger at you for letting this happen, and sadness for her, that she is learning to treat family like servants."

Idalia thought, and then began to defend her position, but without her usual anger. She was quiet, subdued. "I put Carmen through so much pain with the divorce and all," she said, "I swore I'd do everything I could to make her life better now."

José said just one more thing: "When you pick up after her and let her speak rudely, I don't think you help her. I think you teach her she can treat people she loves badly and hurt them."

Still subdued, Idalia responded, "Well, she'll be graduating in a few months. I'm not going to change anything now."

José told me he realized that if he had said more at this point—trying to persuade Idalia how important it was and that it wasn't too late to change—he would have slipped into a power struggle. It is often very difficult to catch ourselves before we slip across the line into attempting to convince someone else. We can start out making statements that are subjective, but if our counterpart mounts a defense, we may ratchet up the intensity or urgency in what we say. Soon we are back at it, trying to "get" the person to listen, up to our ears again in the power struggle.

Having said what he wanted to say, José ended the discussion. He realized it felt good to him, "good in capital letters" as he described it, just to say with such clarity how he felt and what he saw. He felt less entangled in the whole conflict. He had established his own position. Even having exposed his own feelings of helplessness, he felt stronger and freer, although Idalia had not budged. When we state our own position non-defensively, our feelings and passion are often more present rather than less. José's own pain, helplessness, frustration, and anger, as well as his love, were very powerful. He didn't need to raise his voice to express himself.

José felt satisfied about what he had said, yet he was stunned at what happened later that evening. From the living room, he heard Idalia saying to Carmen in a strong but calm tone, "I don't want you to speak to me rudely anymore, and I want you to do your share around here. I don't help you to be a strong young woman when I let you get away with all this." When José had expressed himself without holding back and without trying to get Idalia to agree, she had heard him.

Disarming

When José first made his statement to Idalia, he really did not expect her to do anything differently. Something in how he spoke enabled her to listen better. She became open to receiving information that was important, not only for her but also for her daughter.

In many cases, if a person continues to be defensive after we have asked a sincere question, a non-defensive statement can prompt the person to open up to genuine conversation. After Mihn had asked an angry student a question or two, she would express her own reactions if the student continued to speak rudely. She sometimes said, "When you shout at me, it is hard for me to get the details of what has happened, and I can't think about how to solve the problem so that I can help you."

Mihn's non-threatening directness often caused the upset student to calm down and answer questions or explain the situation more clearly.

After Selma acknowledged that she wasn't carrying her share of the workload on their joint projects and had been feeling guilty about it, Gordon went on to tell her about his own reactions. He described not only his frustration with her but also his concern for her struggle as a single parent. He shared his reluctance to ask too much of her, his subsequent awareness that he was burning out, and his decision to talk to her once he realized how his marriage was being adversely affected. Selma was very moved by what he said.

When we balance the expression of our vulnerability with direct observations about others, they often find it easier to hear us. They sense such statements are not designed to control their response and recognize our integrity in exposing our own experience. Feeling more trust in us, they are less likely to lock into resistance and blindly object to whatever we say.

The information others receive from us can be very valuable to them. Marie, in whom Celeste had confided about an eating disorder, decided to take a risk and talk to Celeste about her reactions.

"I wasn't totally honest with you the last time we saw each other. I was having some difficult reactions to what you told me, and I was afraid to share them. When you said that you had never told your partner about your eating disorder, I was shocked. I see you as so competent and successful—the idea that you were allowing such a fear of rejection to dominate your life made me feel discouraged for all of us as women."

Rather than devastating or alienating Celeste, as Marie had feared, her statement brought them closer. Celeste had felt similar discouragement that she was then able to voice to Marie. Their conversation gave Celeste the courage to work toward taking the risk of being more open with her partner.

Separateness

When we remain focused on defending ourselves and controlling how the other person is reacting, we usually inhibit the power of what we say and spend most of our energy countering what we are told. Betsy, a workshop participant who worked for Head Start, had a difficult conversation with a man who was objecting to any form of national health care on the grounds that "there is too much government bureaucracy already." Her retort had been, "Well, then, what difference does a little more make?"

I asked her if her own position on national health care had anything to do with how much bureaucracy there is. She looked blank for a minute and then said, "Well, no, it doesn't." I then asked her what her own position was, and she replied, "I have worked for years in a Head Start program in a small community, and I have watched children come to school with chronic colds, bronchitis, and ear infections. They are not sick enough to end up in the hospital, but they are too sick to concentrate on their schoolwork. I watch these children grow up and, after years of not being healthy enough to do well in school, they become dropouts, get hooked on drugs, get pregnant—and it breaks my heart!"

What Betsy said was impassioned and insightful, and people were moved. Only an hour earlier, she had protested, "But Sharon, we could never be as eloquent as you are." She had not been eloquent in her response to the man who was sick of bureaucracies because she used her energy to counter him instead of speaking to what was true for her. In the struggle, she lost her own verbal integrity and clarity.

Rebecca, who had been involved in local politics for many years, decided to try the non-defensive approach one evening at a political meeting. She found herself alone in her position, talking with five other people who opposed her viewpoint regarding a city planning issue. First, she asked some questions about their respective positions; then she stated her position independently, as she would to a friend, without trying to answer their arguments point for point and without trying to convince anyone to agree with her. They concluded their conversation and parted company.

Typically, during a discussion of political differences, people part more polarized rather than less. Yet during the course of the evening, two of the five people sought her out and said essentially the same thing: "You caused me to reconsider my position with regard to this issue."

Accountability

Often, when others do things that are harmful to us, everyone involved is aware of what is happening. But because we are communicating from within the war model, we are afraid to expose the other person's behavior or attitude and so become complicit in doing ourselves harm. Geneva knew Clyde would hold up her alimony check when she didn't invite him to holiday meals, but she was afraid to say so. She initially held back, thinking Clyde would have more power over her if she spoke up.

When we do speak up and bring what we see out into the open, we expose the person's manipulative behavior and reduce its power. Much of the strength of manipulative games comes from their remaining unopenly acknowledged, even when everyone knows they are going on. Once Geneva named Clyde's behavior, he felt more accountable for it.

Colin, who worked at a mill, sought out a local attorney for some legal advice. Each time he asked her to explain certain aspects of the legal proceedings, she replied (as George had about my tires), "That's not necessary for you to know," or "That's too complex to explain." Colin felt fairly certain that the lawyer thought he would not be able to understand because he was not college-educated. He began by asking her directly, "Do you think I would not understand because I don't have a college education, or do you say that to every client?"

She stumbled around a bit verbally and denied treating him differently from anyone else. Once she had responded to his question, he was able to state his own opinion without trying to prove his point and get her to admit something.

"I know you are saying that you don't treat me differently. I am not sure I trust that. I still have the feeling that you might speak differently to a college-educated person. In either case, I think it is important for everyone to understand as much as possible about their own legal matters, and I would like for you to answer my questions."

Although the attorney never admitted treating Colin differently, she began to provide the information he asked for instead of putting him off. Colin said her tone also became more respectful. Even if they don't admit to wrongdoing or bad intent, people often respond with increasing respect and take more responsibility for their behavior when it is brought out into the open. Even though the lawyer overtly denied her accountability, it was harder for her to repeat the behavior once the issue was clearly on the table. It is as if the mirror of Colin's statement continued to shine on her.

In the same way, if Frank had denied being sexually inappropriate when he grabbed Nancy, saying, "Don't be so uptight," she could still have held him accountable by stating her position openly. "I am very clear that no one has a right to touch me without my permission, and also that your behavior qualifies as sexual harassment. I will report you if it happens again."

Nancy does not have to convince Frank to agree with her viewpoint. If she tries to convince him, she loses power. Nor does he need to acknowledge responsibility for his behavior in order for her to establish her intention of holding him accountable. By simply making her position clear, she will be more influential in stopping the behavior.[1]

If the woman at the school district office had spoken rudely to Floyd (after he asked her about her assumption that he was applying for a bus driver's position), instead of angrily walking away, he might have said, "It's hard for me to imagine that you would think a white man dressed in a suit was here to apply for a bus driver's position, so I believe you probably made that assumption because I'm Native

---

1. In a professional situation that could involve either party incurring retaliation and/or disciplinary action, I recommend thorough documentation. For example, Nancy could document the incident and have it certified by a notary. If Frank suddenly began giving her bad performance reviews or took other retaliatory action, she could verify the date and content of the event that preceded the change in performance reviews. She could also send him a certified letter, indicating she would take no further action as long as there were no more incidents and no retaliation.

American." He could end by saying he hoped she would consider why she made an assumption about which position he was applying for and how hurtful such assumptions can be to people. After hearing his words, the staff member might be more conscious of her behavior.

When we feel vulnerable, we typically want to hide it, especially from someone who is being disrespectful. However, I believe that when we are clear about the effect other people have on us, we enhance our ability to hold them accountable. They may reflect upon their behavior when they receive information in a way that does not incite power struggle—as Idalia did after José told her how he felt about her letting Carmen treat her so badly. Even if other people do not accept responsibility for their behavior, stating our own position clearly can help us to walk away with a sense of integrity and strength.

When we speak non-defensively, we often take more responsibility for our own choices as well. When Brandon told Camille he believed she was coming back to him between boyfriends because he didn't have the guts to say no to her, he heard himself describe his own feelings and behavior, just as he described hers. He felt less victimized by her. He saw how he had repeated the same cycle each time, first deluding himself that she was sincere and then feeling rage and blaming her for being manipulative when she left. Though he still felt some legitimate hurt and anger at her willingness to take advantage of him, he was less angry because he saw his own part more clearly.

Clarification

There are many times when our understanding about another person's meaning or intention is still not accurate, even after we have asked some questions. Often, in our interactions, we witness only the tip of the iceberg. We can't see the bulk of the issue that is hidden below—the body of information, emotions, beliefs, and previous behaviors. A defensive reaction will not reveal the hidden information, but a non-defensive statement can take us to it quickly. If we speak non-judgmentally, other people will often provide us with more information, even if our interpretation of their behavior is inaccurate.

Instead of attacking and accusing Jason, Trina might have expressed herself more non-defensively. "I've been frustrated because I didn't know where you were. I thought you forgot you were going to fix dinner, and I had no plan in mind for fixing it myself."

In response, Jason might have said, "I *am* planning to fix it. I believe I have made dinner every time I have said I would. If I'm late and it's my night to make dinner, I usually fix something quick, which is what I planned to do tonight. I don't understand why you don't trust me to follow through, and it really frustrates me."

These statements provide the clarity Jason and Trina need to begin to resolve the issue. Based on a similar interchange, the couple did begin to get to the root of the problem. Despite Jason's memory of always making dinner when he said he would, Trina remembered two recent occasions when he was late and she had assumed responsibility by beginning dinner before he got home. When he had protested, she had said, "It's OK, I don't mind." She stuffed her frustration until the third incident and then blew up when he walked through the door.

Jason didn't think of those incidents as breaking his commitment because he had clearly intended to make dinner and had even offered to take over the preparations once he arrived home. He said that, if the situation were reversed, he would not have felt pressure to begin cooking unless he really wanted to, so he didn't realize it upset Trina to start the meal.

Jason had resented how nervous Trina became about his fulfilling his commitments because he felt he was basically very responsible. Since he resented her mistrust, he would resist picking up the phone to let her know when he would be late. Doing so, he felt, would somehow confirm her false assumptions about his being untrustworthy. And because Jason didn't call, Trina's tension increased, as did her feeling that he was inconsiderate about keeping commitments.

By using non-defensive statements, Trina and Jason could each express memories and reactions that allowed them to gain clarity and understanding. When Jason said he didn't understand her lack of trust, Trina thought carefully and realized the source of much of her nervousness. Her father—occasionally and unpredictably—would arrive home intoxicated and irritable. On evenings when he was late, her mother would anxiously begin preparing the meal, hoping to feed him as soon as he arrived. Yet if she started the meal too early, the food would be overdone and he would be irritable about *that*. Trina was replaying her mother's anxiety about her husband's unpredictability. When Jason realized the depth of pain underlying Trina's reactions, he was able to offer comfort and support.

As Jason listened to Trina describe her hurt, he realized he had resisted the simple courtesy of calling to let her know he'd be late. As he thought about why, he too made a vital connection. No matter how hard he tried to please his parents, they had been highly critical of him. In seeking their approval, he had become very responsible. But he would show his resentment of their criticism in small ways, such as not calling when he was late. Jason realized that when Trina expressed mistrust he had subconsciously begun to repeat his defensive response to his parents. He too felt sad when he realized that he was beginning to see Trina, like his parents, as never thinking he was "good enough."

By using non-defensive statements, we can turn even a mundane argument into a genuinely enlightening and healing conversation. Instead of letting this issue become progressively worse and spread to other areas of their relationship, Trina and Jason were able to resolve it and achieve deeper intimacy. It made a significant difference in the kind of foundation established by this newly married couple.

Quantum Leaps

The preceding examples have demonstrated how a non-defensive statement enables both the speaker and the receiver to make quantum leaps in personal growth. The remainder of this chapter will focus on how such statements increase our sense of freedom and personal strength.

The act of making a direct, vulnerable statement often causes people to remark, "I felt so *free* after I said it." It's as if a person has been bogged down or anchored in one spot and is now able to leave that place and move freely to a new one.

Keeping so much of what we think and feel inside is analogous to carrying around a heavy bundle of things we want to hide. The bundle keeps us from moving easily, but if anyone comes close and wants to see what is inside, we fight the person off. We may know very clearly and precisely what its contents are. Or, having kept things hidden for so very long, we may no longer know ourselves what is in it.

Once we put the contents of our bundle out on the table, we can examine and identify them. We no longer have to spend energy hiding them, carrying them, or resisting anyone who wants to see them. If part of it belongs to someone else, we can give it back—whether the person wants it or not. We don't have to control whether it is accepted or thrown away. We can keep what we find valuable, return what belongs to others, discard the rest, and move on, free of a cumbersome burden.

Being able to move freely also allows us to experience our own strength. Instead of hunkering down in a psychological corner, hiding our experience and perceptions in a misguided attempt to protect ourselves, we have openly declared, "I don't have anything to hide." Such openness empowers us, even if the other person does not value what we have said.

In the movie *Powder,* a young man born with an advanced state of consciousness tells a teenage friend that people have no need to hide themselves or lie. "It's possible to talk to someone without any lies, without sarcasms or deceptions, without exaggerations or any of the things that people use to confuse the truth." Wide-eyed, she responds, "I don't know a single person who does that."

I think *we* can begin to do it, and to a far greater degree than any of us have in the past. When we stop misusing statements to bolster our defenses, we give our words an entirely different kind of power. I believe the essence of what Gorgias said: "The power of speech has the same effect on the condition of the soul as the application of drugs to the state of bodies." Some ways of speaking "bewitch the soul with a kind of evil persuasion," others "instill courage." I believe nondefensive statements instill courage and give us freedom.

9

Formats for Making
Non-Defensive Statements

For months Jamal and Renée had been remodeling the old house they bought some years earlier. They had discovered extensive dry rot in the floors, walls, and part of the ceilings, all of which had to be torn out and replaced. Late one Friday evening, they stood amid a huge pile of debris and watched the construction crew leave. On Monday another crew would arrive to begin rebuilding.

Jamal and Renée had decided to haul the rubbish to the dump themselves in order to save money, but there was more than they ever imagined. Old pieces of insulation had cascaded down from the rafters, piled up two feet deep on the bathroom floor, and floated through the house like sea foam on the wind. With the crew gone, Renée began shoveling the insulation into a wheelbarrow, but trying to catch and carry the foam made her feel crazy. After struggling to get the first load out to the canopied truck, she came in and leaned against what was left of a living room wall, slid down into a heap on the floor, and announced, "Jamal, we've got to have a break." The conversation, which escalated into sneering and shouting, continued as follows:

RENÉE: Let's just go to the beach for the weekend and deal with this when we come home.
JAMAL: Are you crazy? No way. We have to clean this mess up before the next crew gets started on Monday!
RENÉE: You're always so damned responsible!
JAMAL: I am not. I just don't run away when there's a job to be done!

146

After this blowup, they both stormed around and resumed working in angry silence. About a half hour later, Renée began a conversation.

RENÉE: Will you talk to me about this?

JAMAL: OK. But I don't know what good it's going to do.

RENÉE: Well, I don't either, but we can't just go on this way.

JAMAL: Oh? Why not? *[small laugh]* I don't see how we are ever going to agree.

RENÉE: Well, I'd like to start by each just saying what we think, without trying to solve anything.

They had been working on communicating non-defensively. Jamal agreed to Renée's idea and asked her to go first.

RENÉE: Well, what I think you're telling me is that we have to keep working all weekend and that my need to have a break means I am irresponsible and not really committed to our remodeling project. It sounds like you think we have no choice but to work right into next week without any break.

I'm watching you clench and unclench your jaw so fast it looks like you are chewing gum, and you have dark circles under your eyes. I think you are exhausted, totally stressed out, and don't know how to stop. I know I am. *[starts crying]*

I'm going to blow if I have to work all weekend and then face even more next week. I want to scream. I don't have any reserves left, and I don't know how I can cope if I don't get away from all this and relax for a little while.

Jamal took his turn next.

JAMAL: It sounds like you think I'm just being compulsive about wanting to keep working and that I demand too much of you as well—and that the only reason I keep working is because I can't stop myself. And I think you're saying we need immediate relief even if we don't get this garbage to the dump.

I don't understand where you got the idea that I think

you aren't committed to the project, 'cause I believe you are. But I do get the feeling you just want to escape from this mess without thinking about the consequences. I don't think you are considering how much stress we will be under if this rubbish isn't cleaned up when the crew gets here Monday.

I can't even imagine how horrible that would be. That's what I couldn't cope with. If we just leave, I could *never* relax. I'd worry the whole weekend about how in the hell we were going to get it all done when we got back.

At the outset of this conflict, Jamal and Renée had both stated their own opinion as fact. Each was trying to convince the other about the best course of action. When this failed, they hurled accusations, then withdrew in mute anger. Arguing in this way, they did not find—probably could not have found—a genuinely satisfying solution.

When they decided to make non-defensive statements, they changed their entire dynamic. They spoke with feeling, but without defensive anger—the rage that flares when we are determined to make others see how wrong they are, prove our point at any cost, and then hurl blame when we can't get through to them. By exchanging information and getting out of the power struggle over who was "right," they were able to find a crucial point of agreement—the need to relieve stress.

In their last exchange, Jamal and Renée used four specific non-defensive formats that will be presented in this chapter. The first three formats convey, as completely as possible, our *subjective* interpretation of the other person's statement.

- Format 1: conveys our understanding of the overt message
- Format 2: conveys our perception of any covert message
- Format 3: describes any additional meaning we attach to the message, such as underlying cause or motive
- Format 4: Expresses our own reactions

The first three formats comprise our translation (our perception, assumption, interpretation, understanding) of that person's messages through the lens of our own experience. They are our observations regarding the other person's meaning. As with a non-defensive question, all feedback through these interpretive statement formats must be neutral in tone. If we inject such observations with our own feelings, they are more likely to become accusatory judgments. Only the fourth format goes beyond translation to our reaction.

These formats enable us to make a position statement. We convey thorough information while minimizing the tendency to state opinion as fact, persuade others to agree, or level them with harsh judgments.

Interpreting the Overt Message

We can begin our feedback by reporting our understanding of what we "hear" a person saying. We state what we believe the person consciously wants to tell us.

Identifying Our Assumptions

This process is similar to responsive listening but has some distinct differences. The guidelines for responsive listening often instruct us to paraphrase as closely as possible what we understand the other person to be saying. When people do this, they frequently resort to synonyms for the other person's words, rather than state their own assumption of what the other person means to say.

Had Renée used "escape" as a strict paraphrase of what Jamal meant when he said she wanted to run away, she would not have accurately stated her own assumption that he meant she was "irresponsible" and "not committed" to the remodeling project.

Furthermore, when we attempt to paraphrase closely, if we can't think of a parallel word, we often repeat word for word what the other person said. Had Renée replayed Jamal's words verbatim, "It sounds like you are saying I just want to run away," she would have ushered in a frustrating, dead-end process. We can avoid these pitfalls with a clear statement of our own *assumption* of what the person means. He or she can then accurately confirm or deny our interpretation and thereby make the exchange of information more accurate.

Varying the Beginning Phrase of the Feedback

Traditionally, when people use active or responsive listening, they begin with "I hear you saying . . ." and then paraphrase what the person said. Many people are tired of this phrase, perhaps because it is often used to practice proper communication and therefore can sound like a stilted script. Also, many people have used this phrase as an automatic response to what someone else says, rather than first asking sincere questions. Finally, people have used the phrase as a way to avoid making a clear statement of their own reactions.

Our feedback sounds much more natural when we vary our beginning phrases:

> "What I think what you are telling me is . . ."
> "It sounds like you are saying . . ."
> "How I interpret what you're telling me is . . ."
> "I assume from what you are saying that you mean . . ."
> "It seems to me you are saying . . ."

Confining the Description to the Overt Statement

When we initially begin our feedback using format 1, we should focus solely on the *overt* statement rather than address some covert "double message." A contradictory covert message expressed through the person's tone or body language usually comes across more strongly than the overt statement. Therefore, even when we are trying to describe what we "hear" the other person saying, we often describe the *covert* message instead. For example,

> NORA: *(in a tone that pleads for help)* I can weed the garden myself.
> ED: I hear you asking for help.

Here, Ed is describing the message he hears in Nora's tone of voice instead of the one she consciously seeks to convey—that she *doesn't* need help. If he were to focus only on her overt message, he could say, "I think you are telling me that you feel confident about getting the garden weeded today without my help."

When Ed states his assumption about what Nora *consciously* wants to say to him, she has the best opportunity to evaluate (1) whether he has understood what she intended to communicate, and (2) whether what she said is actually true.

Interpreting the Covert Message

The second format only comes into play when we perceive a contradictory message in certain word combinations, tone, or body language. A covert message can slip though unconsciously or semiconsciously. It may even be a conscious message that the person doesn't want to take responsibility for. Nora knows Ed has a major report due on Monday, so she consciously wants to convey that she can do the weeding herself. But her tone imparts a second message she is trying to suppress—that she really *would* like some help. The irony is that even though Nora is trying to support Ed, her mixed message can cause conflict.

When we are on the receiving end of a double message, we often find it hard to respond without getting defensive and hooked into a power struggle. If Ed doesn't believe Nora really wants to do all the weeding, he may say, "OK, I just wasn't sure you really wanted to do it alone," then worry all day about whether he should be helping her. Or he may react sarcastically: "Yeah, right, you look real happy about the idea." Or he may start convincing. "I know you don't *really* want to do it without my help. I can get this report done later."

Separating the Interpretation of Overt and Covert Messages

When we react to covert messages, we often ignore the overt message and just respond to the covert one ("I know you want help with the weeding"). We also frequently link our interpretation of the conscious message with that of the second and contradictory message: "You say you feel fine about doing the weeding, *but* I can tell you really want help."

By linking the two messages with the word "but," Ed has used his own observation to discount Nora's overt statement. He draws attention to the contradiction in a way that sounds accusatory—a point-proving habit ingrained in many of us. When describing our interpretation of a person's covert message, we are better off to state it independently, using phrases such as the following:

> I see . . .
> When I look at you . . .
> It seems to me . . .
> What I perceive . . .
> What I am observing is . . .
> I notice that . . .

Thus, instead of using the word "but," Ed might respond with two separate sentences.

> NORA: (making assertion) I can weed the garden myself.
> ED: (describing overt message) It sounds like you are saying you feel confident about doing it without help.
> ED: (describing covert message) What I see is that you are frowning and that your voice sounds high and intense.

By describing the two contradictory messages separately, Ed provides clarity without accusation and harsh judgment. He describes the covert message simply in terms of what he observes. He does not draw any conclusions about what his observation means. He has removed himself from the bind of either accepting a statement that does not seem true or getting into an argument.

Making Detailed Observations

Vague observations are less effective than precise ones. Suppose your teenage daughter is slouched in a chair with a scowl on her face, yet says nothing is wrong. You might respond to this denial by saying, "Well, you look upset to me." The word "upset" is general and does not provide her with specific information. Instead you can say, simply and directly, "I see you slouched down and frowning." This observation is neutral, specific, and non-judgmental.

Contradictions between overt and covert messages typically fall into three general categories: contradictions between words and voice tone or body language; contradictions within a statement; and contradictions among VERB elements.

Contradictions between Words and Tone or Body Language

This is one of the most common discrepancies. If you ask a man for help on a project and he agrees while sighing and rolling his eyes, you might say, "I hear that you are saying you feel willing to help me. [pause] What I see is that you are sighing and rolling your eyes." You are using the two formats together to describe a perceived contradiction between the person's words and tone.

Contradictions within a Statement

We can also make observations about contradictions in a person's actual words.

If your partner says, "We're both tired tonight—let's just go out to dinner. At some point, though, we're really going to have to spend less money," you might say: "It sounds like you are saying you would like to eat out. I noticed that you quickly went on to say that we need to keep a tighter budget."

Sequentially stating the contradictory aspects makes the contrast more apparent and helps you deal with the issue in a more straightforward manner.

Contradictions among VERB Elements

Often, we notice inconsistencies in a person's values, emotions, reasoning, and behaviors (VERB elements) but don't name them unless we are "accusing" the other person.

For example, you might say to your partner, "It sounds like you are saying you want to handle the conflict with your mother without my help [reasoning]. At the same time you often talk to me about your hurt and anger [behavior and emotion]."

Here, the discrepancy is between reasoning about how to handle the problem and behavior—constantly discussing the emotions involved. Your partner overtly says no help is needed while covertly subjecting you to the stress.

Rather than arguing with Beth, Corey might say to her, "It seems that you believe [value statement] I am unfair for asking you to do the dishes tonight. What I have noticed is that you say I am unfair each time I ask you to help with housework [behavior]."

A clear and neutral statement of our observations gives the other person a chance to reflect and also to respond and clarify. It also keeps us out of a no-win argument.

Describing the covert message makes it possible to deal with painful situations with integrity. Perhaps your sister, who has been hooked on drugs, comes to you and pleads, "If you give me a loan, I will pay it back." Instead of arguing with her, you can describe the contradiction between her reasoning and her past behavior. "I understand you to be saying [reasoning] you will pay me back. What I have seen is that you have borrowed money four times, failed to pay it back each time [behavior], and have never mentioned the money again."

When we describe, first, the overt message and, second, any contradictory messages that come through tone, body language, words, or actions, we have simply named each of the messages as we understand them. We have not discussed their contradictory nature or what we think the contradiction means. We can do that next, using the third format for statements.

Interpreting Cause or Motive

When we hear any message from another person, we usually have our own subjective interpretation of what that message means. This interpretation goes beyond the scope both of translating what we believe the person is consciously telling us and of drawing attention to the covert messages. We express the conclusions we have drawn about the cause or motivation we believe is underlying what the person is saying and the meaning of any contradictions we perceive.

Our interpretation may pertain to the person's conscious motive. Ed may say to Nora, "I believe that you are not being fully truthful when you say you can weed the garden yourself. I think you would like help but you're not asking because you know I need to finish my report."

The Importance of Verbalizing Our Interpretation of Motive

Stating our interpretation of another person's motives aloud can be difficult. Even when we do so meticulously and sincerely, we are taking the risk of exposing our misunderstanding, being perceived as judgmental, or sliding into actually *being* judgmental. But when we withhold such information, we are not being fully open and honest. Here are some of the problems that can occur when we fail to verbalize our perceptions.

1. If we don't verbalize directly, we may do so covertly. You might say to your sister who wants to borrow money, "I feel like I can't trust you to pay me back." Here you have said "I feel," as if describing your own emotions, then slipped into your interpretation of *her* motivation—that she wants a handout and doesn't intend to pay you back. This becomes a covert accusation.

2. When blending our own feelings with our observation about another person's motivation, we may become confused about what our feelings really are. If you were to say to your sister, "When you ask me for money, I feel manipulated," you have identified "manipulated" strictly as your feeling. You not only do not indicate that you see manipulation as your sister's intention, you accept it as your own emotion, which may not be accurate. This can lead you to take on feelings that aren't yours and ignore others that are. In so doing, you undermine the accuracy of the communication and lose some degree of self-awareness.

When we take on another person's intention as our own experience, the person will often insist that it is solely our experience and even blame us for feeling the way we do. Your sister might say, in response to your statement about feeling manipulated, "Well, if you want to feel manipulated when your own sister asks for a little help, that's *your* problem."

3. If we don't verbalize the interpretation, we may deny it even when the other person points it out. When others sense our conclusions or interpretations, we often deny them instead of saying clearly, "Yes, that was my perception."

Your sister may say, "You don't trust me. You just think I want this money for drugs!" And you reply, "I do trust you. I'm just *worried* about you." Such a response sends its own contradictory message. You claim trust and then imply there is cause to have misgivings.

Presenting the Interpretation of Motive Respectfully

Using the following guidelines can help you ensure that your position is conveyed non-judgmentally.

1. Speak only in terms of the specific issue at hand rather than making a generalized statement. After your initial statement to your sister about how many times she has borrowed money and not repaid it, you might conclude, "I believe you are saying you will pay me back without having a genuine commitment to doing it," or "I don't believe you will take responsibility for paying me back." Here, your interpretation involves an underlying issue of either commitment or responsibility.

You might also make a longer statement, based on her involvement with drugs. For example, she may have promised that she is clean and just needs help to "get a new start." Yet she is unwilling to take a drug test or get support services and appears to be in desperate need of a fix. In this case, it is appropriate to say directly, "I believe you have told me you are off drugs in order to manipulate me into giving you more money. I think it is likely you would walk out the door and go spend what I give you on more drugs."

In this case, you name manipulation as an underlying motive. Any of these straightforward statements—expressed as a respectful, neutral *description* of your perceptions—are more useful than the covert judgments we so often make. They are far less judgmental and inflammatory than an angry accusation, such as "You never pay me back!" or "You're just trying to get more money for drugs!"

Should your sister accuse you of not trusting her when you state your interpretation of her motives, you can confirm it rather than deny it. "I do believe there is reason not to trust what you will do with any money I give you. I know the power drugs can have over any person, and I believe you are still hooked."

Here you specify the exact area of mistrust and identify your perception of the cause of her behavior instead of simply labeling your sister as "untrustworthy." This kind of statement can remain respectful as long as it is neutral in tone and not designed to persuade the person to get help.

2. After you have offered your non-defensive observations about another person's motivations, avoid repeating yourself. If you hold your statement as a "truth bat" with which to pummel someone into submitting to your view, you move back into the war zone. This kind of statement is intended to serve as a mirror, not a club.

3. Should the other person not want to hear your observation, stop respectfully. Persisting when someone does not want to hear what you have to say, or continuing to repeat the same observations, can become harassment.

The Benefits of Using the Three Interpretative Formats

When we offer feedback regarding how we interpret the other person's message, we accomplish two key purposes: We examine our assumptions and provide insights.

Examining Our Assumptions

Once we state any interpretation aloud, it is available for examination and reevaluation. The other person may verify our assumption or respond with information that causes us to lay aside inaccurate judgments. (People often realize they have made an erroneous assumption the moment they verbalize it.) An erroneous judgment that is held within, unscrutinized, can become a basis for greater misunderstanding or entrenched prejudice.

Providing Insights

Our perspective on the other person's reactions may contain insights that help in increasing the person's self-awareness. Many of us hold back observations which could be useful to another person's growth. Although people have for centuries offered wise counsel to others, today many hold unsolicited observations to be "judgmental." The result is that we sometimes throw out the good principle of giving feedback along with the bad practice of doing so inappropriately. Thus, we tend either to stuff our judgments inside (often unsuccessfully), express them covertly, or periodically blurt them out in moments of stress and anger.

"Judgment" can mean anything from moral superiority and censure to wise discernment—the thoughtful observation that can give guidance. If we were to rid ourselves of *all* judgment, we would not only eliminate dogmatic abuses of personal power but also discernment and wisdom.

We interpret another person's words and actions every time we interact. Whether these judgments are completely erroneous, reflect real differences in philosophy and experience, or offer wise counsel, they contain important information. Although Jamal and Renée partly misunderstood each other's motives about continuing or discontinuing the construction cleanup, each made some astute observations about the other.

By using these interpretive statement formats to give neutral (non-accusatory) feedback, we can often influence others to identify and change dysfunctional patterns voluntarily. José demonstrated the simple power of this genuine feedback when he said to Idalia, about Carmen, that "you teach her she can treat people she loves badly and hurt them."

Although she resisted at the moment, Idalia later that day began to change her expectations of Carmen. She was able to hear José because he described his observations without trying to convince her to agree, and she ultimately felt supported instead of attacked. His counsel helped her make important changes almost immediately. When we offer subjective observations and interpretations in a neutral tone, if what we say rings true, the other person is much more likely to hear the bell.

Expressing Our Reactions with Integrity and Passion

The three formats covered so far involve our observations about the other person's reactions. Only when using the fourth statement format do we talk about our own reactions apart from our interpretation of another's messages. Now we can describe our own personal beliefs (values), feelings (emotions), thoughts (reasoning), and actions (behavior) related to the issue at hand.

For example, once you have stated your observations regarding your sister's behavior and motives, you may find your feelings are no longer contaminated by subtle—or not so subtle—accusations. You can then express yourself with more openness, vulnerability, and, compassion.

"I don't believe I should give you money unless you enter a drug rehab program, and yet I get terrified when I think about turning you down. I have visions of you having no place to live and dying on a street corner. Sometimes after I give you money, I get very angry, at myself and at you. Mostly, I feel so sad I can hardly stand it. I love you so much, yet I know I can't force you to want to quit, and I'm not sure what to do to genuinely help you."

This statement weaves back and forth from belief to feeling to behavior to feeling to reasoning. If it is purely sincere—and you don't slip into trying to persuade her to go into a rehab program—your words will carry the passion of your feelings and can give you more clarity. They may also give you the courage to say no to this new request for money, if that is what you believe would be best.

Staying Focused on Ourselves

Our statement can address all four VERB elements or just one or two. The example from chapter 7 involves a combination of feelings, beliefs, and behaviors. Remember that Riassah told her brother, "I don't like it when you hit me. It is not in my nature. I don't like for you to hit me, and I don't like to hit you."

When we focus on our own reactions, the emphasis shifts away from the other person. Had Riassah said to her brother, "I wish you would quit hitting me. You are so mean, I can't stand it. You should just go kick the stone wall over there if you want to kick something so much," she would have blunted the power of her non-defensive statement. When we are emotionally focused on the other person, we usually become defensive and attack, even if we are just trying to protect ourselves or help someone else.

Renée originally said she needed to get away, and when Jamal replied, in effect, No way, she became defensive. She moved immediately into attacking him for always being "so damned responsible." Only when each of them focused on their own feelings, separate from their observations of the other person, did they gain more complete understanding.

The Initial Goal Is Clarity, Not Solution

When Renée focused on expressing her own feelings, it became clearer to both herself and Jamal that she could not face another week without a break. When Jamal expressed his feelings, it became equally clear that he could not stand the stress of leaving the mess until Monday. What would relieve the pressure for each of them seemed to be diametrically opposed: leave and take a break versus stay and clean up. Yet they also realized that Jamal needed a break as much as Renée, and that postponing the cleanup would create more pressure for her as well. Once they each accepted this reality, neither one wanted to coerce an agreement.

Expressing feelings, thoughts, and needs does not necessarily create a magic solution; it simply creates clarity—which can then provide the basis for a creative solution. A number of options opened up. In the end, Jamal and Renée enlisted the help of a young neighbor, who wanted to earn some extra money, and Jamal's brother, who brought another truck. Having finished the cleanup by noon on Saturday, they were able to go to the coast and drive back early Monday morning.

Jamal's compulsion to keep going and Renée's desire to escape from pressure had been central to many arguments over the years. After this incident, he became more able to examine his habit of working compulsively as a way to relieve pressure; Renée in turn began to work more effectively with her desire to escape from pressure-ridden situations. As they expressed their own feelings and needs more clearly, without reverting to defensive accusations, they found it easier to come up with satisfying solutions.

Using the Statement Formats Together

In some cases we may use one format by itself. For example, if someone says, "I'm ready to go for a walk now," we may respond, "Great, so am I" (Format 4). Here, there is no need for any of the three interpretative forms of statement. In other cases, we may interpret the person's conscious statement and then simply respond to it without naming a covert message or our perception of the person's motive (Formats 1 and 4). Likewise, we can state our understanding of the overt message, name a covert message we perceive, and tell the person our reactions (Formats 1, 2, and 4). In this case, we do not state our interpretation of the meaning of or the motive for the contradiction. In yet other cases, we might name what we hear the person consciously saying, what we believe the motive to be, and our own reaction, without naming any covert message (Formats 1, 3, and 4). Thus we can use one format alone or two, three, or all four.

An Abbreviated Form of Statement

Often, we can put two, three, or even all four of the formats into an abbreviated form of a position statement. In one or two sentences, we can describe the overt message, the covert message, how we perceive the meaning of the contradiction (or person's motive), and our reaction to what the person is saying. [1] "When you say you can learn this computer program without help, and at the same time [2] I see you frowning and speaking through gritted teeth, then [3] it's hard for me to believe that you feel confident, and [4] I feel confused about whether to leave you alone or offer to help you."

In another example, you might say to your partner, [1] "When you ask if I want to go out to dinner and [2] you follow it with a statement about how we have to tighten up our budget, *then* [3] I believe you have mixed feelings about spending the money, *and* [4] I get so tense I don't even want to go out."

The short version usually works well, because it is succinct and fits easily into the natural speaking pattern of many people.

Abbreviated Position Statement

- *When* you say (my interpretation of your overt message)
- *And* I see (my interpretation of your covert message)
- *Then* I think (my interpretation of your motive and/or some underlying cause of your reactions)
- *And* I react (with certain feelings, thoughts, beliefs, and behaviors)

The Longer Version

We can add thoroughness and power to our statement—with little additional investment in time and energy—by adding just a few more sentences. The following example uses the longer version of a position statement.

Lynette said to Walter, [1] "It seems to me that you believe being an attorney requires being paid for any legal services you provide. [3] I believe that, as a result, you devalue the work I do for Legal Aid and even see it hurting my reputation as a good attorney. [4] My own belief is that any legal services I offer are of value, whether I charge for them or not. When I offer free services to nonprofit organizations in need of them, I feel good about giving something important back to the community that supports me."[1]

In a similar fashion, Maggie might say to her social work supervisor, Claudia, who thinks Maggie should be "objective" and unemotional, [1] "I hear you saying that I am being too emotional. [3] It seems to me that you see having emotional reactions about our client's situations as unprofessional. [4] My own belief is that, if I show compassion, the client will at least know that I care, even if I can't help get the funding back. And when I care about a client, I am more likely to be motivated to find an alternative funding source. I personally be-

---

1. In this and the following example, the speaker did not use Format 2 because the other person did not provide contradictory information.

lieve that I can do my job with the greatest integrity when I honor my emotions."

While their responses are longer than the single-sentence version of a position statement, both Lynette and Maggie respectfully clarify significant differences in philosophy in about thirty seconds.

In a host of situations, we are at a loss regarding how to respond to the messages others give us. This non-defensive process for giving feedback—about what we hear and see, how we perceive the underlying causes and motivations for the person's reactions, and the effect this has on us—can provide us with an effective way to respond in a wide variety of situations.

When we sort out the kinds of information we give to another person—as if we were sending four different letters in four separate envelopes—the information doesn't get mixed up. Our messages are clearer, and others are more likely to receive them.

The Feedback Loop

Fritjof Capra, author of *The Tao of Physics,* gained understanding about human relationships from studying ecology. He describes "feedback loops" as a key element in the earth's ecosystem, which has had billions of years to evolve effective methods for sustaining itself. Every action has implications and affects every part of the ecosystem. Changes are transmitted through feedback networks that help it to stabilize and maintain a healthy balance. Capra applies the same principles to our human relationships and communities. Through feedback loops that inform us about the effect we have on one another, we can self-regulate and learn from our mistakes.[2]

The formats discussed in this chapter are mechanisms for increased informational exchange, analogous to the feedback loops Capra describes.

Non-defensive statements often reflect our conscious awareness of the implications and effects of someone else's behavior, both negative

---

2. Fritjof Capra, in a speech for the Mill Valley School District at Walker Creek Ranch in Marin County, 1994, and in his book entitled *Web of Life.*

Statement Format Summary

1. **Overt messages:** Reporting what you "hear" the other person consciously saying
2. **Covert messages:** Making observations about anything [tone, body language] you "see" in the person's message that contradicts what you heard him or her say
3. **Interpreting cause or motive:** Offering what you believe to be the "cause" or motivation that underlies the person's statement or makes it contradictory
4. **Your own reactions:** Describing "your experience" (thoughts, feelings, beliefs, and behavior) to the other person and/or situation

and positive. If the feedback loop is functioning effectively, we will give and receive information regarding how others affect our lives and we affect theirs. According to Dr. Sandra Lewis, "If this feedback loop breaks down, then the health of our relationships will break down."[3] Power struggle inhibits the feedback loop in our communication system and blocks the open flow of information. By using non-defensive statements to keep our feedback system open, we can better sustain healthy relationships and communities.

---

3. Sandra Lewis is a psychologist and an organizational consultant with Growing Community Association in San Francisco.

10

The Prediction

A New Prescription for Security

Security is the missing element in our habitual way of making predictions, just as curiosity is absent from our questions and vulnerability is absent from our statements. Either by manipulating with a covert bribe or by coercing with an overt threat, we have conventionally used predictions to get others to comply with our will. While Corey had a legitimate need for her daughter to do more of the housework, her intention when she threatened—"I won't buy your prom dress if you don't shape up and help around here!"—was to make Beth feel insecure and frighten her into helping.

Parents have typically said to me, "I told Johnny he couldn't watch TV unless he got dressed, but it didn't work." When I ask what they mean by "it didn't work," the response is invariably, "Well, he didn't get dressed"—in other words, he didn't make the choice they wanted him to make.

We act in a similar fashion with other adults. Hans was upset that Franklin's laxness about time always made them late for important events. One night, Hans made the following prediction: "If you are not ready to leave for the theater promptly at seven, I will drive my own car." When Franklin remained true to form and was late, Hans drove to the theater by himself, frustrated that his prediction "didn't work." He had succeeded in carrying it through, but he believed he had failed because Franklin hadn't made the choice Hans preferred. Hans remained locked in the power struggle even though his prediction had fulfilled its purpose—he *had* made it to the theater on time.

Many of us think a prediction is not effective unless the other person does what we want. But when we try to control what choice another person makes, our prediction backfires. We usher in more resistance and power struggle, and we pay the price of eroded trust and diminished productivity.

Nature: Protective and Firm

The character of a non-defensive prediction is not coaxing, manipulative, coercive, or threatening. It is secure, predictable, and stable.

Protective

I believe the essential character of a non-defensive prediction is protective. When a wilderness guide describes the respective nature of two paths issuing from the fork in the trail—one becoming steep and rocky and the other meandering along a river—the intention is not to dominate. The guide's purpose is to offer accurate information so we can make an informed choice regarding the probable consequences of following one path or another. We are told, as clearly as possible, what we will encounter before we decide upon our path. In direct contrast to our traditionally threatening ways of using predictions, this offers us a glimpse of the future so we can feel secure in knowing that we are mentally and physically prepared to manage what we encounter.

Foretelling

Our eyesight guides us through our physical environment and allows us to anticipate the consequences of our movements. If we miscalculate the distance of a stair when we step down, we may fall or violently jar ourselves. When we cannot accurately predict the consequences of our movement, we may be unprepared to respond quickly enough to prevent injury.

In our human relationships, we also need to be able to anticipate the consequences of our actions if we are to feel mentally and emotionally prepared to handle a given situation. Unexpected results can be jarring to the psyche. Companies that take the time to prepare employees for potential changes reap the benefits of improved morale and production. In contrast, when employees unexpectedly experience the consequences of decisions already implemented or of changes that have already occurred, the damage to their equilibrium is severe.

Predicting changes in our personal relationships is equally important. Any time we make a prediction, we help the other person know, as much as possible, the consequences of the various available choices. When Hans made a prediction, he gave Franklin the ability to visualize, to preview, what the consequences would be if he were not ready on time. Franklin had the opportunity to evaluate his choices in advance.

When we make a prediction we *hypothesize* about something that hasn't happened yet. Neither party can be absolutely certain that the predicted consequences will happen, because they are postulates about the future based on current data. Hans might have gone to his car and found the battery dead, in which case he would not have been able to drive his car as he had predicted. While it provides us with advance information, a prediction is still a statement of probability.

Neutral

If we are truly neutral, we are not invested in influencing how the other person chooses to respond. We predict only how *we* intend to respond to the various choices another person might make. By not trying to control *which* choice, we neutralize the power struggle dynamic.

When we make a prediction, as with questions and statements involving interpretive feedback, we must convey neutrality in our tone of voice and body language. This takes practice and vigilance, since a prediction can easily slide into a threat if it is infused with our feelings. Neutral tones and body language help to communicate that we are not seeking to dictate choices, that our prediction is not about power struggle.

Consider the difference in the following motives:

Defensive/Controlling: Hans predicts that he will take his own car if Franklin isn't ready on time because he wants to coerce Franklin into changing his habit of being late.

Non-Defensive/Neutral: Hans predicts that he will take his own car if Franklin isn't ready on time because he is unwilling to continue to

arrive late for events. (In keeping with this, he is prepared to drive to
the play alone and prepared that Franklin might not show up.)

In order for Hans to be non-defensive, he must be prepared to leave
punctually in his own car and let Franklin decide what he wants to
do. Franklin's thinking could go along any of the following lines:

> It's worth it to be ready on time. It will prevent a conflict and we
> won't have to take two cars.
> If Hans leaves for the play without me, I'll have to drive myself.
> If he leaves without me, I'll just stay home.

Definitive

A non-defensive prediction defines very specifically how we will respond to choices another person might make. You might say to a family
member, "If you don't bring your dirty clothes to the laundry room,
then I will not do your wash."

Geneva could tell Clyde, "If you hold up my alimony check the
next time I don't invite you for a holiday meal, then I will ask to sit
down with you and the children in order to decide how to deal with
holidays in a way that feels fair to everyone."

Our prediction thus provides precise information about how we
will react to a particular choice the other person might make.

Absolute

If the walls and floor were to shift unpredictably as we walked across
our living room, we would be totally disoriented. We need a structure
to remain solid and stationary if we are to walk safely through it. I believe we need the same kind of safety in our interactions with each
other. If our prediction is to provide a structure that lets another person anticipate, as accurately as possible, the consequences of a specific behavior, the prediction must be non-negotiable.

Hans must be willing to drive his own car every time Franklin is
late. Once we predict a consequence, if we change it at all, we move
the wall, so to speak; it doesn't matter if we move it a few inches or a
mile, its position has changed. We have made a false threat and lost
credibility. When we don't follow through on the consequences we

predict, we fail to provide the kind of stable, secure structure each of us needs to feel safe in our relationships.

Double-Sided

Any prediction we make has at least two alternatives. If we don't state the second alternative directly, it is present by implication. When your partner says, "If you continue to interrupt me, I will not finish telling this story," you can easily infer the flip side of that prediction: if you stop interrupting, your partner will finish the story. While the unstated part of a prediction is usually present by implication, the prediction is clearer when both sides are specifically verbalized.

Each prediction spotlights two parallel scenarios—what will happen if a certain set of circumstances *does* occur (if the person makes a particular choice) and, conversely, what will happen will happen if that set of circumstances *doesn't* occur (the person makes a different choice).

You might say to your teenager, "If you mow the lawn today, it's OK with me for you to use the car tonight. If not, then I won't give you permission to have it." If you state only the first half of the prediction, you may sound coaxing. And I've known more than one teenager who is apt to argue later, "Well, you told me I could have the car if I *did* mow the lawn, but you didn't say I *couldn't* have it if I *didn't*."

If you state only the second half ("If you don't mow the lawn, I won't give you permission to use the car tonight"), you are likely to sound punitive. When parents verbalize both sides of a prediction, they often tell me their children respond with much less anger and argument.

Avoiding the Power Struggle

We can offer a neutral and clearly defined prediction that will meet our needs and keep us out of power struggle, regardless of how the other person chooses to respond. If a student calling the financial aid office at the university continued to shout at Mihn after she had asked a non-defensive question or made a non-defensive statement, she could make a prediction: "If you continue to shout at me, then I will hang up. If you stop shouting, then I will do my best to help you."

Mihn realized she didn't have to try to control whether the student stopped shouting or not; her prediction was effective in either case.

In the same way, any non-defensive prediction we offer to either children or adults can be effective. You may say to your child, "If you don't pick up your toys and put them away, then I'm not willing to give you permission to watch TV; if you do pick them up, then I'll give you permission to watch."

Toys scattered around—permission denied; toys picked up—permission granted. Barring the influence of unforeseen events, and as long as you aren't invested in trying to control which choice your child makes, there is no way for these predictions not to work.

Function: Creating Security through Predictability

When we provide clear information about how we will respond to various choices a person can make, we create a sense of security both for that person and for ourselves.

Creating Security for Others

When others cannot foresee the effect that their behaviors, attitudes, or even feelings have on us, they are often blindsided by our response. If Hans had suddenly departed for the theater and driven off without warning, Franklin would quite likely have been much more upset. He would have found Hans's behavior unpredictable and he might even have been frightened. Was Hans going to the theater? Was he leaving the relationship? When Hans gave Franklin a clear forecast, he was much better prepared, even for consequences that might seem unpleasant.

Suppose you simply asked your teenage daughter to mow the lawn and she did not do so. As she prepares to leave for a movie with her friend, you say, "You can't have the car tonight. You didn't mow the lawn today as you were asked." The odds are high that your daughter would feel she was receiving unfair punishment. She might say, "If

I'd known that, I would have mowed it! It's not fair! You didn't tell me!" While you might think she should know she won't get privileges if she doesn't do what you ask, she will still be jarred by a consequence she had not considered. This is more likely to cause power struggle than encourage her to follow through on her responsibilities. Most people will feel more secure and make more informed choices to the degree that they know the consequences of their behavior in advance.

Creating Security for Ourselves

In addition to allowing others to anticipate the consequences of their actions, making clear predictions prepares us to handle a variety of situations with less conflict and stress. As the person making the forecast, we have security, even though we do not attempt to control what the other person does. Once Hans defined how he would consistently respond to Franklin's lateness, he felt more secure about meeting his own need to be on time. Ultimately, if we make a non-defensive prediction, it can provide increased security both to us and to the other person.

Mental preparation

- Am I willing to make a clear prediction about how I will react to various choices a person might make?
- Will I accept whatever choice the other person makes?
- Is my prediction protective? foretelling? neutral? definitive? absolute? double-sided?

Effect: Respect, Reciprocity—and More

If your partner has a habit that you find frustrating, such as backseat driving or asking questions in an accusatory tone, the behavior may seem of little consequence to the overall picture. Yet many of us have discovered that these seemingly small issues give shape and texture to the whole relationship, whether with a professional colleague, family member, or friend.

Unfortunately, most of us just "live with it" and go on for years without ever setting effective limits. But if we use predictions to disengage ourselves from even *one* irritating or painful habit on the part of someone else, we are likely to enhance the quality and durability of the entire relationship.

Protecting Ourselves Effectively

A non-defensive prediction performs the function of protecting us as well as possible in our interactions. It is a constructive alternative to putting up with mistreatment or fighting ineffectively to get others to stop behaving in hurtful ways.

Doug and Virginia came to see me because Doug was feeling increasingly attracted to Mary Anne, a mutual friend. He realized that his marriage could be in jeopardy and was wise enough to talk to Virginia about it and to seek help. In their initial session, Doug seemed unclear about what attracted him to Mary Anne. He knew that he loved Virginia, but he had been feeling increasingly distant from her. When I asked him to list the qualities that drew him to Mary Anne, he mentioned, among other things, that she was "a good listener."

A key issue turned out to be that Virginia habitually interrupted Doug. While she was genuinely warm and spontaneous, she could also be self-absorbed. And, having grown up in a family where everyone interjected their words into someone else's, she regarded such interruptions as lively conversation. Virginia thought Doug was rigid, making too big a deal out of, as he put it, "wanting to finish a sentence by myself."

Doug felt Virginia's interruptions meant that she did not respect him or appreciate what he had to say. She did not know how to stay focused on him; she was too busy blurting out whatever entered her mind. He became increasingly guarded, holding back his feelings and thoughts so they wouldn't be shattered by her assertions. Mary Anne, on the other hand, was attentive to what he said. He felt increasingly drawn to her and alienated from Virginia.

Doug learned how to make a specific prediction in order to protect himself from Virginia's interruptions, such as, "If you interrupt me when I am talking, I will not continue with this conversation right now." Virginia gradually began to change, to interrupt less often and listen more intently. As she confronted her habit of interrupting, she also had to confront the issue of learning to focus on Doug when her mind was on other things. She began to take the time to know her own husband in new ways.

Doug began to discover more about himself as well. He found that there were times when he still tended to withhold his thoughts and feelings, even when Virginia was very supportive of him. He sometimes had to struggle to take up as much psychic space as he had always thought he wanted. When he did share his feelings, he found that he initially often felt very vulnerable. He could no longer blame Virginia when he avoided expressing himself. As he learned to be heard, he also learned to speak.

The void Doug had experienced in his relationship with Virginia, the void Mary Anne had begun to fill, ceased to exist. A few months later, Doug reported that he was shocked to realize that, when he looked at Mary Anne one day, he couldn't figure out why he had been attracted to her. He found it hard to believe that changing one aspect of his relationship to Virginia could completely alter a physical attraction he had developed for another woman.

By making a prediction, we can take constructive action that may effect pervasive changes. We do not have to acquiesce to mistreatment or react by complaining, persuading, arguing, or becoming emotionally aloof—all hallmarks of a victim mentality. We can choose what we are willing to live with and what we are not, taking one issue at a time if need be, knowing that how we decide to protect ourselves will play a crucial role in how others treat us.

Creating Clear Boundaries

When we predict for another person how we will respond to opposing choices he or she might make, we essentially define our own boundaries. Recall Dick, the orthopedist who felt defensive when another physician—with inadequate prior knowledge—questioned his medical decisions? Irritated with the physician's habit of second-guessing, Dick finally said to him, "If you sincerely want to know about the factors I considered in making this decision, I'd be glad to tell you. If you just want to tell me you disagree, I'd rather not discuss it until you've studied the options I reviewed." Afterward, Dick felt great. He did not refuse to discuss the issue, but he set clear boundaries.

Even with firmly established boundaries, a prediction is still a two-way interaction, because whichever side of the boundary line the other person chooses will determine how we respond. If the other physician was critical of Dick's decision, Dick would refuse to discuss it until his colleague had done some research. If the colleague showed an open mind, Dick would discuss his decision.

Establishing boundaries in this way is often referred to as "limit setting," especially when used by parents with their children. What Dick did in setting a limit with a critical colleague is more unusual. Many of us resist setting limits with other adults; we think people "should know how to cooperate by the time they are grown up." I believe this assumption is unfortunate because limit setting is an effective way to create the boundaries necessary to any healthy personal or professional relationship.

Separation

When we use a non-defensive prediction to establish our boundaries, we simultaneously separate ourselves from the other person. We become less enmeshed, rather than allowing the other person's actions to dominate what we experience. We also respect that person's right to make independent choices.

Being comfortable with this level of separation may be hard because it requires that we consciously recognize and accept that we may not get precisely what we want. If you tell your partner that you will drive your own car to social events if he isn't ready on time, he may continue to be chronically late. Although driving your own car will resolve your stress about arriving late, the solution will not feel totally satisfactory if you strongly prefer to drive together.

On the other hand, we do not necessarily get exactly what we want when we are defensive either; in fact, probably less so. But we start out with the illusion that we can get it by trying to control the other person. The most any non-defensive prediction can do is create boundaries that give us the best protection possible without dictating the other person's choices.

Rather than experiencing a loss of power after making a non-defensive prediction, many people feel much *more* empowered because they can solve a problem for themselves rather than being dependent on gaining the other person's cooperation. Doug knew how to stop conversations with Virginia when she didn't listen to him. Since he no longer fumed as a result of her constant interruptions, his mood improved greatly, as did his blood pressure.

When we define our boundaries, we separate ourselves from the other person and create more freedom of choice for both of us. A healthy sense of separation can relieve us from guilt and anger. The relationship is likely to improve even if the other person does not immediately change some offensive or hurtful behavior.

Carolyn felt ongoing frustration because her mother, Rose, constantly complained that she didn't do enough for her. She emotionally spun around in cycles of guilt and anger. Finally, along with conversing in depth with Rose about their relationship, Carolyn made a prediction: "If you are dissatisfied with how much I do to help you, I will enjoy our time together less. If you are appreciative, I will enjoy it so much more. I also believe if you can appreciate my efforts, you will enjoy our time together more."

Carolyn said she felt an enormous weight lift from her shoulders after she made these predictions for her mother. She no longer felt that she constantly had to prove herself. She no longer felt responsible if Rose complained and chose not to appreciate her in that moment. Her prediction gave her the degree of separateness she needed to stay out of power struggle and guilt. Carolyn began to enjoy the positive moments with her mother, even before Rose made fundamental changes in her attitude. Setting clear boundaries can eliminate guilt and anger.

Accountability

Many of us know someone who shows us disrespect in some way. Whether we try to convince such a person to be more respectful or just say nothing, we typically do not hold ourselves accountable for the results. We see ourselves as abused victims and fail to recognize that the looseness of our personal boundaries may encourage others to mistreat us. But once we begin to verbalize accurate predictions for others, we act in a way that holds both ourselves and others more accountable.

In professional relationships, people often set aside their own professional expertise in order to follow the adage "the customer is always right." Don, the owner of the printing company, would acquiesce to his customers' wish if they didn't accept his advice, then be upset when they didn't like the results. When he subsequently complained that "you just can't satisfy people," he was not taking responsibility for his own part in the problem.

Don decided to take more responsibility by making clear predictions for his customers regarding the probable consequences of their choices. "If you use too many colors, then, based on my experience, this logo will be less crisp and you will not be satisfied with the outcome. If you use fewer colors, it will be more crisp, and I think you will be pleased." As a result, they were much less likely to blame him if the results were unsatisfactory. And an increasing number of people responded by taking his advice from the beginning.

In our personal relationships, we sometimes put up with behavior we don't like until we get so frustrated that we withdraw from the relationship. We may never hold ourselves accountable for not having done anything to alter how we are treated.

You may remember Regina, who was resentful of Carla's pressure to get together during a hectic week. Regina complained about Carla to others and thought about withdrawing from the friendship. She felt victimized and reluctant to admit that she participated in creating her problem by caving in when Carla wanted to see her at inconvenient times.

When, instead of withdrawing, Regina got up the courage to make the following prediction, she held both herself and Carla more accountable. "If you remain dead silent when I say I don't have time to get together, then I give in and make time, I end up resenting it and feel less like seeing you."

Here, Regina included three consequences in the same sentence—giving in to seeing Carla, resenting it, and feeling less like seeing her. She also predicted, conversely, "If you can accept it when I say I'm too busy for coffee this week, then I will feel more like seeing you another time." Regina also held Carla more accountable for her entrapping silence.

Carla acted huffy and hurt; she did not call Regina again. When Regina realized that Carla's withdrawal demonstrated Carla's unwillingness to respect her time constraints, she found it less difficult to let go of the friendship. Later, she realized she had habitually done much more for Carla than Carla had for her. Sometimes we hang on to relationships because we don't want to hurt the other person or lose certain limited benefits. After we have set respectful limits, the other person—unwilling to be either understanding or accountable—may make the choice to withdraw.

Sometimes people are afraid to set clear limits for this very reason—out of fear that their counterpart may be unwilling to be accountable and may therefore decide to leave the relationship. When, in order to keep a relationship going, we neglect to set protective boundaries, we lose our self-esteem and suffer increasingly as the other person's victim. I believe everything is progressive—the more we fail to set clear limits, the more abusively we will be treated. We may still lose the relationship no matter how much we put up with. If the person is a partner, "someone better" may come along—perhaps someone who still has some self-respect left. In this case, we lose either way, because we hold neither ourselves nor the other person accountable for how we are treated.

When we hold both ourselves and the other person more accountable for our respective contributions to a destructive conflict, we must be willing to focus on and struggle with issues that affect our own growth. We can't simply blame the other person for the problem.

Marcus and Sally had come a long way in dealing with both his resistance to talking about upsetting issues and her drive to make him talk. But changing their habitual pattern still took time. Sometimes, when Marcus became disturbed and withdrew automatically, Sally said, "If you want to tell me what is going on, I would like to hear it. If not, I don't want to force you to try to talk to me."

This prediction does not have what we might call teeth. To some it might appear that Sally was just giving him what he wanted. I believe, however, that she gave Marcus accountability for deciding whether he wanted to talk or not. If he chose not to talk, instead of being sidetracked by an argument, he would be left alone to reflect on and deal with his own mood.

By predicting that she would not try to pressure Marcus into talking, Sally also became more accountable for her own behavior. This was difficult for her, as it was for many of the people in these examples. She really had to work with her own emotions and thoughts in order to let go of trying to induce Marcus to open up. She knew her prediction would not be genuine if she did not focus on his right to make whichever choice he wanted. Sometimes she had to go for a walk or find another activity in order to take her focus off his mood.

In each of these cases, the person making the prediction first held himself or herself accountable for making clear predictions and following through on them. When we do this, holding the other person accountable seems to follow more naturally.

Disarming

We often turn to predictions after our efforts to ask questions and offer position statements have not brought resolution. In such a case, the other person may still be locked into power struggle and therefore be less likely to disarm immediately.

The first time Corey told her daughter she would not drive her to a slumber party if she continued to speak to her in a demanding, rude tone, Beth threw a royal fit, even though she could easily ride with a friend who lived nearby. As adults, we may also throw varying degrees of tantrum. Virginia initially sometimes got furious when Doug wouldn't finish what he was telling her after she interrupted him.

Many people report that, though their immediate response to a prediction was to shift internally toward being less defensive, they did not show the change on the outside right away. Often, in response to clear boundaries, especially where there have been none before, disarming is a gradual, stop-and-start process. When Sally would predict that she was not going to try to convince Marcus to talk, he said he could usually feel a shift in his attitude. Sometimes he opened up and sometimes he didn't. Though some people don't ever disarm, my experience tells me that most people will gradually do so if we maintain clear and consistent boundaries.

On occasion, a person will *immediately* become less defensive in response to a clear, non-punitive prediction. Gerard had basically a good relationship with his daughter Colette, who was eighteen. They were able to discuss many issues in depth. Yet Colette would strongly resist Gerard's advice, even though she frequently adopted it later on. Once, in the middle of an argument, Gerard became fed up and decided to use a non-defensive prediction. He started with a position statement, followed by a prediction: "It feels too stressful to try to talk to you about issues like this when you resist what I have to say. From now on, if you're interested in having my advice so you can consider it, you'll have to ask for it. If you don't ask, I won't offer."

Gerard remarked that he was stunned when Colette instantly burst into tears and said, "I *like* your advice, Dad. Please don't stop giving it, even if I don't think to ask for it." He replied, "I will, if you will be clear about whether you want it or not. I just don't want to fight you." When Gerard decided not to force his advice on Colette, she immediately began to regard it as something valuable that she didn't want to lose.

One reason people seem able to shed their defensive armor is because, as previously discussed, the non-defensive prediction simply outlines our responses to *their choices* rather than dictating to them what they "should" do. Thus, instead of putting all their energy into keeping their own willpower intact by resisting ours, they can more neutrally consider which option serves them best.

Second, since a non-defensive prediction doesn't have to carry a big club—we just predict honestly how we will react to another person's attitude or behavior—our predictions are more likely to expose our own vulnerability.

Just as Doug was able to predict what he would do when Virginia interrupted him, he gradually was able to predict for her how it made him *feel*. "If you interrupt me when I am saying something that is important to me, I feel invisible to you and disappear inside myself."

Here, Doug no longer hides his feelings of loneliness behind angry attempts to get Virginia to listen or periods of withdrawal. His prediction forecasts his own authentic feelings. When another person sees our own vulnerability—rather than trying to take more "power" over us, the person is often apt to "disarm" also—to become vulnerable as well.

Quantum Leaps in Personal Growth

The traditional war model for communicating offers us little recourse to stopping mistreatment other than giving in, coaxing, arguing, or threatening punitive action. Should we succeed in protecting ourselves in a defensive manner, we are often left with a relationship permeated with stress and hostility. When we make non-defensive predictions, we can make great strides in creating stronger, more respectful relationships.

When we ask questions and make statements, understanding usually precedes any change in behavior. The behavioral change often comes before the growth in understanding when we make predictions. Virginia might refrain from interrupting so she can hear the end of the story, but still think Doug is being too rigid. Later, after her ability to listen becomes more established, she is likely to understand better that she is being more respectful. Even the person making the prediction may only later understand—in experiencing being treated differently—how much disrespect had been allowed before.

With regard to predictions, I'd like to focus on the quantum changes that take place take place in four specific areas: respect, competence, self-esteem, and reciprocity.

Respect

When we make non-defensive predictions, we increase the respect others have for us. Marlene was dating a man who sometimes went out of town during the week. While they occasionally saw each other on weeknights, their set pattern involved getting together on Friday evenings. Dan would usually call her about six and they would make their plans for the evening. Sometimes they spent the rest of the weekend together, sometimes not. Despite the consistency of their Friday engagements, periodically Dan would call on Friday, talk for a while, and then unexpectedly say good-bye.

Marlene said these unexpected collapses in routine wouldn't have bothered her if she had been given any indication that Dan had other plans, or if he had even said, "I'm just too tired to get together tonight." But since he offered no warning or explanation, she felt hurt and taken for granted. She thought he was inconsiderate not even to mention the change in their usual habit. She always held Friday evenings open for him and sometimes turned down invitations from other friends.

Marlene finally discussed this problem with Dan. He told her that he didn't consider his spontaneous cancellation disrespectful, because they didn't have "a commitment" to see each other every Friday. He also said he would not mind if she wanted to make other plans. His response began to affect her confidence in the relationship. Although he canceled only once in a while, she found herself wondering every Friday, Am I going to see him tonight or not?

This kind of situation can cause a relationship to break down. Marlene and Dan might have spoiled the time they did spend together by arguing about Dan's inconsistency. Marlene's confidence might have further eroded, which could have resulted in Dan's being less respectful in other ways. Although Marlene was learning Powerful, Non-Defensive Communication, she found it difficult to think of a limit she could set. At first it didn't seem legitimate to say she wouldn't see him unless he called ahead, especially if she had no other plans that night. But then she decided she could set whatever limit she wanted as long as it made her feel more respected.

The next time she talked with Dan, she told him straightforwardly what had happened to her confidence. She told him that she didn't like the stress of wondering whether or not they would get together and felt disrespected by his unwillingness to recognize that unexplained deviations from a set pattern deserved some discussion. Then she said, "I've decided that I'd like to know by Thursday if you are planning to get together on Friday. If you don't call on Thursday, I won't plan to see you. If you want to see me during the week, then I'd also like to know a day ahead of time."

Marlene expressed this in a neutral tone and told Dan directly that such an arrangement would make her feel much better. The next time Dan called, the conversation went like this:

DAN: What nights do you have free this week?
MARLENE: Tuesday, Wednesday, and Friday. When would you like to get together?
DAN: I'll take all three if I can get them.

Marlene said she almost fell off her chair. While Dan did not seem to be conscious of having taken Marlene for granted, his desire to see her increased dramatically after she set clear limits about wanting advance notice. And Dan began to show that he valued and respected her more in various other ways.

Competence

Lawrence Steinberg of Temple University writes in *Beyond the Classroom* that children raised by "authoritative" parents who "combine warmth and strictness" perform better in school and are less likely to use drugs or alcohol than children from either "authoritarian" homes, where the parents rule with an iron hand, or children from "permissive" homes, which lack discipline. I think Steinberg's "warmth and strictness" equate to firm, consistent predictions that are implemented without anger.

Corey had been a permissive parent until she began making consistent predictions. She made it clear that if Beth did not do her homework and her chores with a respectful attitude, she would not give her permission to attend certain activities with her friends. As Corey effectively carried out the consequences she had predicted, Beth's behavior and attitude improved at home, as did her grades at school. Corey had also been worried that Beth was starting to drink too much. That, too, tapered off. The effect of a few consistent predictions at home began to have wide-reaching effects in how competently Beth managed her life.

I think the kinds of improvement Steinberg finds in teenagers (regarding academic performance and responsibility around alcohol and drugs) would translate into adult behavior if we used non-defensive predictions more often. When any of us—adults or children—have clearly defined consequences for our behavior, we are likely to improve our level of competence.

Unfortunately, when we want to help other adults become more competent, we're apt to coax and encourage them until we burn out in the face of their resistance. After her husband died, Gladys became despondent. They had traveled in their motor home for a large part of every year. They loved being in the outdoors and often joined up with friends at various campsites. Now the motor home sat unused in the driveway, and Gladys sat in the house.

Her son Derrick had tried to encourage Gladys to go camping with friends, or even take the motor home herself and meet her old camping buddies. She objected to all his suggestions. "I wouldn't want to impose on my friends," she'd sigh. Or, "I could never manage that motor home. Charlie always drove it." Dismayed at watching his mom's spirit fade, Derrick kept trying to coax her into more activity, which she resisted with increasing stubbornness. He thought of going camping with her himself, but, to his parents' disappointment, he had never enjoyed camping much. In fact, it was a family joke that someday he'd get old and wise and love it as much as they did.

After learning about non-defensive communication, Derrick became excited by an idea. He went to his mother and asked her questions about what she would do if she *could* drive the motor home and whether she thought it would be difficult—or actually impossible—to learn. She replied that it would be "actually impossible." Instead of coaxing her, he told her he had always admired her spunk and now felt sad to see her feeling defeated. Then he made a prediction: "If you think it is impossible, I believe you will never try to learn and you will sit here, miserable. If you do try to learn, I think you might be surprised at how competent you could be. If you decide you want to learn, I'll go to school with you and learn too. If not, I won't keep bugging you about it."

Gladys replied, "No, thanks anyway," and Derrick left. Though disappointed, he was clear that he would not bring the subject up again.

The next time Derrick saw Gladys, she asked him, "Do you *really* think I could learn to drive that thing?"

"Sure!" Derrick replied. "Even truck drivers have to go to school to learn to drive their rigs. I might as well learn too. I might get old someday and want to go sit in the woods."

Gladys learned how to handle all the mechanics of the motor home. The first time she drove it out to a nearby riverside campground, she took along her three bridge buddies—two experienced campers and one greenhorn. She had the time of her life and came home with a host of funny stories that Derrick delighted in recounting.

Sometimes, another person's lack of competence in a particular area has a major effect on our own lives. Long past trying to encourage the person to learn, we feel constant anger and frustration, yet we are still picking up the broken pieces caused by the incompetence. Sandra was a professional bookkeeper who also managed her husband's business accounts. An independent contractor who made a lot of purchases, Jake frequently wrote checks without recording them. He had even been known to grab a new checkbook, write out a check, and toss the book on the floor of his truck without telling her. Sometimes he wrote checks for his business on their personal account without making any notation for tax purposes. He also sometimes forgot to give deposits to Sandra.

Sandra kept straightening out the confusion Jake created. When checks bounced and she angrily confronted him, he either responded with a half-baked apology ("Sorry, hon, you know I'm not good at that stuff like you are") or shot back defiantly ("Well, I had to get the materials if I was going to finish the damn job!"). Sandra complained to her friends and to their grown children, but she was afraid to turn the accounting over to Jake because she feared for their financial stability. It seemed like a no-win situation.

Finally, Sandra realized the stress from Jake's money handling was jeopardizing their relationship. If they continued down this road, they could end up divorced, in which case she would turn his business finances over to him anyway. So she sat down and figured out how to create boundaries that protected herself from picking up Jake's slack, while still giving him support. She made several predictions for him.

"If you delay in giving me a deposit or write checks without checking the balance, then I won't take the deposit to the bank or take care of sorting out the account. And I won't talk to any supplier who calls about a bounced check.

"If the account is overdrawn, then I'll expect you to take care of it. If you need help to learn the process, then I'll sit right by you and show you, but I won't do it for you.

"If you don't take care of it, then you will have to either hire someone to do it or bounce checks and let your business suffer the results.

"If you do give me the deposits and make sure I know what checks you've written, then I will be happy to do the rest."

Jake was furious, but the deterioration in the accounting and the bounced checks soon caught up with him. When he did ask Sandra to show him how to balance the checkbook, he was irritable and rude. So she added another prediction: "If you're rude, then I won't help you. If you are civil, then I will." Jake didn't want his business to go under, so he contained himself.

In the past, Jake's financial laxness had cost Sandra time and embarrassment with creditors; it had not cost him anything. Now that he was held accountable, he found it took much less effort to be methodical than to repair the damage if he forgot. He struggled with the accounting for a while, but he quickly learned to record transactions carefully and not write checks before giving Sandra the deposit. His increased competency was not only a great relief to Sandra, it became something he was proud of himself.

Self-Esteem

Anytime we are enmeshed with someone else who treats us disrespectfully or functions incompetently, we drag ourselves down and deplete our own self-esteem. When we set clear boundaries with other people, we assert our right to protect ourselves from mistreatment. Such action can enhance our sense of self-worth regardless of how others react. Usually, they respond by showing more caring, which further adds to our self-esteem. In the process, we gain more creative energy to develop our own talents.

Reciprocity

Reciprocity involves how well we engage in cooperative give-and-take with others. Ironically, when we make non-defensive predictions, we do not need other people's cooperation in order to create more balanced reciprocity. We simply base how much we do for others on their willingness to contribute and be respectful. In response, most people begin to function more competently and are increasingly willing to do their share. Making non-defensive predictions can start a cycle that continually strengthens each person's self-esteem and enhances the flow of reciprocity. Ultimately, this stability fosters a new kind of security within ourselves and in our relationships.

11

Formats for Making Non-Defensive Predictions

When Sandra predicted that she wouldn't take care of Jake's financial blunders if he continued to write checks she didn't know about, she wanted to spare herself the embarrassment of dealing with the bank. She felt particular chagrin because she was a professional bookkeeper married to the owner of the company. Yet making a prediction for another person, particularly when we prescribe consequences that we will initiate, can feel like an overwhelming responsibility.

Her prediction opened the door to several possible consequences that could have a major impact on their marriage. Jake might hire a bookkeeper and incur an additional but unnecessary cost to his business. In that case, Sandra might lose whatever control she had over the finances (which might or might not please her). Or, if Jake did nothing different, he might seriously jeopardize his financial standing and his business's reputation. Sandra was aware that increased conflict could be the final blow that caused a divorce. At the same time, if she did nothing, she would continue to deal with increasingly intolerable stress.

The kind of prediction Sandra finally used was limit-setting. When we make a prediction to set a limit or create a boundary, we predict specifically how *we* will respond to various choices the other person might make. Limit-setting is the most common form of prediction.

The second kind of prediction is a *challenge–choice*. In this case, we predict for someone what kind of consequences we believe will result in the person's life if certain choices are made. This *challenges* the person to consider the *choices* carefully; however, we do not do anything to cause specific consequences.

186

Limit-Setting:
My Consequences

It is important that we carefully consider any limit-setting prediction we are going to make because its ramifications may be far-reaching. We must be clear that we can live with its consequences. This chapter will present three new facets in using this tool:

1. Evaluating the needs and core issues we want to address with a prediction.
2. Discerning how to create a specific prediction.
3. Effectively following through on a prediction.

Preparing to Make a Prediction

Advance preparation before making a prediction can help you to follow through successfully.

Determining the Problems in an Interaction

Many of the problems we encounter involve recurring patterns in relationships. Following three steps can help you decide what consequence to predict.

1. Determine the specific parts of the interaction that are causing a problem.
2. Based on that, decide what you need to change in order to meet your needs in that situation.
3. Consider how this incident fits into the recurring pattern to figure out how your prediction may influence the overall relationship.

When you are examining the recurring problem in a typical interaction, it is helpful to identify how you and the other person are each contributing to the conflict. If your partner continually tells you what routes to take when you are driving, you could ask yourself, What are the aspects of this that bother me?

You might decide that you don't like being:

- given directions you haven't asked for
- told which route to take when you know which one you prefer
- told not to take a certain route because it might take longer
- given orders
- spoken to in a harsh tone of voice

This list is very specific. (It even distinguishes being given orders from being spoken to in a harsh tone.)

The next step is to ask yourself, What are the various reactions I have to this situation? Your list might include the following responses:

- I sometimes give in to keep the peace
- I sometimes give in and get stony silent
- I sometimes give orders back ("Don't boss me around!")
- I sometimes argue about which route is shorter
- I sometimes take one route going and another route coming back and time them to prove there's not much difference
- I sometimes just take the route I want
- I sometimes stay angry for at least an hour

Determining What Needs You Want to Meet

From the first list, you can identify the specific issues that are bothering you. From the second list, you can evaluate the ways in which you react defensively. Using these two lists together can help you identify your needs.

In this situation, I see two basic needs: (1) A need to stop your defensive reactions so you can get out of the power struggle, and (2) A need to make clear predictions that protect your right to determine your own route and clarify how you will respond to orders given in a harsh tone of voice.

Identifying the Core Issue

The "core issue" is the underlying meaning we attach to a particular interaction. Core issues are often triggered by seemingly trivial incidents, but they touch us at the center of our being and spread out to affect the entire relationship.

Chapter 9, on Statements, discussed giving feedback (Format 3) about conclusions we draw about a person's behavior. These conclusions often describe our perception of a core issue regarding a particular situation. When a sister wanted money for drugs under the guise of wanting a fresh start, the concluding observation described her attempt to "manipulate." Manipulation was an issue underlying her request for money. Examples of other such issues follow:

abusiveness	guilt
alienation	manipulation
appreciation	oppressiveness
commitment	rage
denial	reciprocity
depression	respect
fairness	responsibility
fear	trust
freedom	truthfulness

In the backseat-driving scenario, you might decide that *control* was a core issue for both you and your partner.

Most people can identify the core issues that underlie a specific interaction, although they often need to start with one to uncover the other. You might be upset that your child barely thanked you for a birthday present, and from that realization identify *appreciation* as a core issue.

On the other hand, you might first identify that you are feeling un-appreciated and then identify the incidents that brought this core issue to your awareness ("Oh, yes, it was when I got no thanks for the new bike, only a complaint that the seat wasn't right and a demand for a different one. I hid my anger and just said we could get another seat.") It may also become clear that *overindulgence* is an issue for you just as *lack of appreciation* is an issue for your child. In this case, *reciprocity* also comes into play. You are giving generously and your child is not even offering a simple thanks.

Determining Each Person's Motive in Maintaining the Current Situation

Before constructing a prediction, it is important to pay attention to why we have allowed a difficult situation to continue. Why did Corey still give Beth everything she wanted when Beth was irresponsible about housework? Why did Doug allow Virginia to continually interrupt him? Why did Sandra take care of Jake's financial problems? You can ask yourself, Why have I allowed stressful conflicts to continue without doing anything constructive to change them?

- Am I making up to the other person because I feel guilty for having been hurtful in the past?
- Am I afraid things will fall apart if I set clear boundaries?
- Am I afraid of being judged or rejected?
- Do I in some way fear the person's power over me?
- Do I lack the skills I need to make the changes?
- Do I lack the confidence to follow through on changes I make?
- Am I doing things the same old way out of habit?
- Do I feel defeated and think nothing would change no matter what I did?

Once we have explored our own motivations, we can examine what we believe to be the other person's motives. You may ask yourself, What is my child getting out of being unappreciative and demanding more? Well, for one thing, more material possessions.

Hans may ask himself, What is Franklin's motivation for being late getting ready to go to the theater? Well, he's disorganized. He also gets absorbed in what he is doing. He might be late because he has been consoling a friend on the phone. He follows his own timelines without considering me or even the audience. In identifying a list of reasons, Hans may recognize that Franklin's motivation reflects both positive and negative characteristics that contribute to the issue of not being on time for events. Understanding what causes us and others to maintain unpleasant interactions can help us anticipate areas where our ability to implement effective predictions might break down.

By carefully examining both our own and another's reactions, we can identify the problematic areas of our interactions, our basic unmet needs, the core issues involved, and the respective motivation of both parties for continuing a non-reciprocal interaction. Now we are in position to select predictions that have a higher likelihood of solving the problem.

Selecting Consequences

The next step is to identify the behavior to which we want to respond differently and select the consequences we will apply.

> I want to change how I respond to my partner's unsolicited directions when I drive.
>
> I want to change how I respond to unsolicited advice from my co-worker on how to perform office procedures.

We may create one consequence or several. Our consequences do not have to be focused on behavior or material reward. We may predict the reactions we will have to someone else's choice in terms of what we will do, feel, think, or believe—the VERB elements.

In the backseat-driving scenario, you might first predict a behavior: "If you tell me what road to take when I haven't asked for advice, then I will simply not answer you and continue on the route I planned." Here, you predict two behaviors, your subsequent silence and your choice to stick to the route you selected. You could also make predictions about how you will feel, what you will believe, and what you will think. "If you continue to give me orders when I am driving, then (1) I will feel angry; (2) I will believe that you are intent on dominating how I drive; (3) I will think you are so focused on doing things your own way that even my choosing the route makes you feel a loss of control."

Although most of us would rarely use all four predictions together, predicting various kinds of behavioral *and* non-behavioral reactions can be very effective. It creates a complete picture of how you will react to your partner's orders and provides clear information regarding the consequences. Just as a position statement puts information into the "feedback loop," so do predictions.

When Doug predicts he will feel invisible if Virginia doesn't listen to him more carefully, he is predicting an involuntary emotion. If he conveys through his tone and body language that his goal is to make her feel guilty and change her behavior, he is using his prediction to punish her. Because such guilt trips are offered and received as criticism, they rarely cause the "guilty" party to change behavior. On the other hand, if Doug is truthfully revealing his reaction so that Virginia can better understand the consequences of her behavior, his prediction is neither punishing nor controlling.

Evaluating the Selected Consequence

Once we have thought about a consequence we want to articulate, we can evaluate it according to the following four standards for an effective prediction.

1. Select as small a consequence as possible to meet your need. Having made an initial selection of the consequences, you can ask yourself, Is this the smallest consequence available that addresses the problem I want to solve?

Small consequences can create positive change more effectively than large ones. If your supervisor told you at 4 P.M. that you have to finish typing a document before 5 P.M. or else it would show up in your performance review, you would probably feel pressured and be likely to make errors. If you were told to type the document by 5 P.M. or else stay until you finished, you would probably feel less pressure, make fewer errors, and still be motivated to finish as quickly as possible.

When Marcus wouldn't talk to Sally about what was bothering him, she sometimes threatened to end the relationship. "If you can't talk to me when you are upset, we might as well not even stay married!" Uncounted threats of rejection have been tossed out by people trying to persuade someone to talk, have sex, buy a certain house, agree to a vacation, or stop watching football.

When Sally asked herself what she needed *most* when Marcus was brooding, she realized it was to not be affected herself when his glowering energy filled the room. To this end, along with predicting that she would not try to convince him to talk, she sometimes also predicted, "If you don't want to talk, then I will go in the other room and do something else. If you change your mind, or get in a better mood later, I'd like to spend time with you."

If we are in power struggle, we often predict consequences that exceed what we need to protect ourselves. "If you don't stop bossing me when I drive, I'm never going anywhere with you again!" By selecting the smallest consequence necessary—simply driving the route we want and not arguing about it—we are much more likely to follow through on our prediction than if we threaten to take separate cars forever after.

2. Create a consequence that is self-contained. It is important not to add consequences later that we do not specify originally. You can ask yourself, Is the consequence I'm predicting the only one I am going to implement, or will I have other reactions that I haven't clearly predicted?

For example, Renée might have said to Jamal while cleaning up the remodeling debris, "If you are not willing to talk about how to get a break sometime this weekend, then I will plan to take one for myself and let you know what my plan is. If you are willing to talk about it, then I would love to plan some kind of relaxation with you."

If Jamal refuses to discuss the issue, the only consequence Renée can implement non-defensively is to make her own plan and inform him of it. If she argues, sulks, or slams things around as she is cleaning up, she multiplies the consequences and implements ones she did not predict.

Jamal, also, could predict, "If you are not willing to create a specific plan for getting the mess cleaned up before Monday morning, then I'm not going to talk about taking a break this weekend. If you're willing to create a plan for the cleanup, then I'd feel great about figuring out how to get in some relaxation time." If Renée doesn't make a cleanup plan, Jamal will not react with irritation; he simply won't discuss getting some time off.

Likewise, if you predict how you will respond to your child's lack of appreciation, your stated consequence should be the *only* consequence. "If you do not show appreciation for the bicycle I bought for you and stop demanding a new seat for it, then I will ask for it back until such time as you can appreciate it. If you *do* show appreciation and don't make demands about upgrading it immediately, then I would love for you to keep it."

Once in a while someone is appalled that I would advocate taking back a gift, even an unappreciated one. I think taking back an unappreciated gift is very different from giving a gift with strings attached, where we expect some favor in return from the other person. A person who does not appreciate a gift has not really "received" it. Unless what we do is appreciated, the person is unlikely to feel nurtured by it. Thus, when we allow gifts to be received without appreciation, we actually contribute to the person's feeling a *lack* of nurturing. This is one reason why making predictions that focus on respect and reciprocity is so important. If we do not set such limits, we not only fail to protect ourselves from abuse, we also fail to nurture others.

While we might hesitate to take back an unappreciated gift, most of us would not hesitate to implement unpredicted consequences or implement them with a negative attitude. This, I think, truly *is* damaging. Suppose that, after taking your demanding child's bike away, you continue to be angry and cancel a fishing or shopping trip together. No longer "self-contained," with absolute boundaries, your consequence has now spread into other areas and its ramifications have multiplied.

If you know you (1) will be angry and (2) will not want to go fishing with your child, you need to predict those two consequences in addition to taking back the bike. When we add extra consequences without warning, we become punitive and controlling. If you only predict taking the bike until the child can appreciate it, you would remain in a good mood and enjoy the fishing trip. If you do have an unexpected reaction to what someone does, I think it is important to discuss it and make careful adjustments. As much as possible, however, whatever we predict should constitute the sum total of our subsequent reactions to the person's choice.

3. When possible, give the other person control over the duration of any consequence. The question to ask yourself here might be, Does my prediction give as much control to the other person as possible while still protecting me?

As Corey began to make predictions that emphasized reciprocity, she consistently refused to give Beth permission to go out with her friends *until* her jobs and homework were done. Compare the difference in the following two predictions: "If you don't get the dishes done by seven, then you can't go to the party" and "If you don't finish the dishes by seven, then you may not leave for the party until you finish them."

In the first case, Corey would have predicted an irrevocable—and thus more punishing—consequence. In the second case, she made a prediction that gave Beth power to control whether or not the consequence was implemented and also how long it was in force. Beth might now test the limits. She might not finish the dishes by seven, to see if Corey "meant business," but then finish them by seven-fifteen so she could still head off to the party. Not only is determining the duration of an unpleasant consequence empowering, it also decreases the likelihood of an ongoing power struggle.

I want to note clearly here that there *are* some cases where we are wise to impose a condition that is neither small nor reversible, such as when we end a relationship that has become progressively abusive. But in most cases we can structure our predictions—for either children or adults—so that the person receiving them determines the duration of the consequence. As soon as Virginia stops interrupting and makes a commitment to listen, Doug can resume what he was saying to her. As soon as Jake is willing to correct his banking error, Sandra is willing to resume her bookkeeping responsibilities.

4. Consider the range of effects any consequence will have.

At the beginning of this chapter, I outlined many of the possible consequences Sandra might experience, depending on how Jake responded to her decision to not take care of his banking problems. While such a list can be intimidating, I think it is important to think through the possible consequences of any prediction before we make it. If Sandra can't live with the consequences of her prediction, she needs to find a different one that works better for her.

Sandra might say, "If you are willing to do certain things, such as giving me the checkbook each evening along with a record of the day's deposits so I can register the checks and advise you about the status of your account, then I will take care of the finances. If not, then I would prefer you hire someone else to take care of the deposits and any bounced checks so it doesn't interfere with our marriage. If you do hire someone else to deal with deposits and bounced checks, then I would still be happy to take care of the rest of the business finances, such as the payroll and taxes."

Anytime we decide we can't live with the possible ramifications of a prediction we are thinking about making, we can pick a different prediction and consequence.

When we consider ramifications for a consequence, we can ask ourselves questions like the following:

Am I willing to follow through on this consequence?
Is there anything that might prevent me from following through?
Am I only protecting myself and maintaining reciprocity, or am I trying to control the other person?
Can I live with the possible choices the other person might make in response to this prediction?

We are typically fearful about making predictions that can result in some sort of loss. Yet we sometimes fail to realize that, whether we consciously determine boundaries or create them by default, we are always experiencing their consequences. Many of these "default" boundaries result in far more damaging consequences than those we consciously establish in order to create more reciprocity.

Sandra was already on the edge of wanting a divorce because of the effects of Jake's financial problems on her home life. Had she chosen not to risk making a prediction, her relationship with Jake may well have deteriorated beyond repair.

Characteristics of an Effective Prediction

- The consequences are as small as possible
- The other person has as much opportunity as possible to control the duration of any negative consequences
- The consequences are self-contained
- The prediction has no foreseeable ramifications we cannot tolerate

---

Selecting a possible prediction and then evaluating it according to these standards can help prevent you from making predictions that fall apart midstream or cause outcomes you can't live with. After conceiving of some predictions and reviewing these guidelines, you can make your selection final.

As we gain more skill, this process will become increasingly automatic. In many situations, you will be able to create predictions in the moment. You might automatically say to your child, "If you speak in a demanding tone, I won't answer you. If you speak respectfully, I will." The same prediction works well for adults.

Consciously Committing to the Consequences We Predict

A few years ago, a retired schoolteacher said to me, "Setting limits is like crossing the Rubicon. When Caesar went to war, he could still return to the safety of his own city until he crossed the Rubicon River. Once he did, he was past the point of no return, and he was essentially committed to the battle." I believe we must pass our own point of no return by committing fully to a prediction in order to implement it effectively.

Making the Commitment before Verbalizing the Prediction

It is important to make a commitment *to ourselves* before we can communicate it clearly to another person. If we are not fully committed to a prediction, others often sense it and do not take us seriously.

Connie had informed a man she was dating that she did not like always being the one to initiate contact. Quinton was willing to get together when she phoned, but he seldom took the initiative to call. Finally, she predicted, "If you don't call part of the time, then I will not make more than two calls before expecting you to make the next one."

Connie made two calls and, in keeping with her prediction, decided not to call Quinton again until he called her. The days turned into weeks, and she found herself anxiously waiting for him to call. Several times, she came close to calling him herself and then decided not to. One day, as she was sitting and watching the phone, she realized, If I follow through on what I predicted, and he never calls me, I will never see him again. She decided her self-esteem was more important than seeing him, although not seeing him would be painful. Only at that moment did she make a full commitment to her prediction. Several minutes later, Quinton called, as if he had sensed the shift in the firmness of her commitment.

Abandoning Your Commitment
Is Breaking a Promise

A prediction is a promise. If we abandon a prediction after we have presented it to other person, we essentially break a promise. If you promise to take your son swimming after he cleans his room and something prevents you, you will probably hear a long and loud protest. "But you *promised!*" Even when we fail to follow through on predicted consequences that the other person would rather *avoid,* we damage the trust in the relationship. If Sandra gives in and deals with the bank when Jake bounces checks, she too is reneging on a promise.

Abandoning Your Commitment
Creates a Counter-Consequence

If you fail to follow through on a prediction, you may think you have failed to set a limit. In actuality, you have simply established a different boundary from the one you verbalized. If you tell your sister you won't give her any money unless she goes into a drug treatment center, and then give in and give her just a little, you predict one thing and do the opposite.

This counter-consequence will act more powerfully than your hollow prediction. Even if you only do it once, the person will expect, though perhaps unconsciously, the same consequence next time. Actions speak louder than words. If we renege on predictions, we will still react in ways that create specific consequences, but other people will respond through unconscious conditioning instead of through conscious choice-making.

We cannot *not* create boundaries and consequences for others and ourselves. Boundaries and consequences exist, even if tacit and unstated. If a bully kicks us in the shins and we do nothing, we create a boundary that allows abuse. Probably not many of us would want to predict, "If you kick me in the shins, then I will allow it," or, "If you tell me how to drive, then I will tell you I am not going to answer you and then I will argue with you anyway." We might evaluate our boundaries more thoroughly if we did make conscious statements about the ones we usually implement by default. By making a conscious commitment to our prediction, we can be clearer about the effects of our actions and how, with others, we create our joint reality.

Implementing the Predicted Consequence

Our commitment to ourselves is tested when we follow through on a prediction we have made. We must also be careful about not falling back into any kind of power struggle: giving in, defending our actions, or blaming the other person.

Responding in a Timely Manner

The timing of our response to a prediction is important. The cause-and-effect relationship is experienced most powerfully if the cause (the person's choice) and the effect (our response) are closely linked in time.

You may predict to someone in your family who is arguing with you, "If you only want to prove your own point, then I am not going to discuss this issue with you right now. If you can talk to me about it openly, and listen to what I have to say also, then I'd like to continue." The family member might respond, "Yes, but I *know* you are *wrong* about this!"

That very moment—after that first sentence—is the time to terminate the discussion. If you or say anything more, you will not implement the consequence as predicted.

Responding without Discussion

It is sometimes hard to know how to put a consequence into effect without getting caught in a power struggle. A crucial part of the process is to carry out the predicted consequence with *no discussion* other than what is necessary to enact it. Sometimes this is difficult. If you predict that you will not continue to argue and a family member retorts, "Yes, but I *know* you are *wrong* about this," you have limited choices about how to respond if you are to adhere to your prediction. Following are three different approaches you might take.

1. Simply stop talking about the topic and not answer the person. You could respond to the argumentative statement with silence. You might walk away, pick up a book and read, or even change the subject and talk about something else. (You have not said you wouldn't talk at all, only that you wouldn't continue to talk about the controversial topic.)

2. Maintain silence regarding the topic under discussion, but make a transition statement. For example, "I am going to quit talking about this subject now." You don't even want to add, "because you are still arguing." The person knows that, and it is easy for the additional comment to sound blaming. Further, it can incite a new angle on the argument, such as "I am not arguing, I am just telling you my opinion." (If there is actually a need to define what you mean by arguing, you can do that with questions and statements, before you make the prediction or sometime later, after you have followed through on the prediction at hand.) Once you say, "I am going to quit talking now," both people have a moment of transition time.

3. Make a second prediction. State it either following the transition statement (which I prefer) or by itself. "If you decide later that you want to talk to me about this without arguing, then let me know and I will continue the discussion."

I have found that any discussion, clarification, or argument at the time a consequence is to be implemented will severely disable it. Even a single word or sentence can undo the power of a consequence. If you say, "I don't think I am wrong, so I am not going to continue talking to you about this," you have already contradicted your prediction because, however briefly, you have become defensive and argued back. Not only does this violate the boundary you set and break your own commitment to the prediction, it also means you have attempted to get in the last word before you stopped talking, which the other person will rightfully take as an effort to win the power struggle. *Any* continued response on your part—even a sarcastic "Sure"—will encourage the other person to attempt further to get you to alter the consequences you have predicted.

It can be difficult—especially at first—to follow through immediately and without discussion when it is time to implement a consequence. The first time Doug predicted he would stop talking if Virginia continued to interrupt—even though they had discussed the whole process in a session with me—she practically begged him to finish what he was saying, and he did give in. But the next time he kept his promise. Once we have made the same prediction several times, it usually gets easier not to give in or get caught up in a discussion that pulls us into power struggle. Even if we don't perfectly implement every consequence we predict, I cannot overestimate the importance of being precise about how we do it. It is the same precision we expect when we fix an automobile or type an important letter.

Avoiding Bargaining after the Consequence Is Implemented

Once a person has decided how to respond to our prediction—either behaviorally or by telling us—the point of no return has been reached and we implement the consequence. If the person changes the decision, or promises to change the behavior at that point, it is too late to eliminate the consequence without breaking both our promise and our commitment to ourselves. From time to time, my daughter Ami did her part to uphold the reputation of the "terrible twos," which to my way of thinking was part of her learning to discriminate between when it made sense to exert her will at full volume and when it did not. I would tell her that she would have to go to her room if she kept throwing a tantrum. Sometimes she would continue until I said, "I would like for you to go to your room now," at which point she would stop crying instantly and say, "I'll quit, Mommy, I don't have to go to my room."

The problem was that she didn't stop her tantrum until *after* I asked her to go to her room. Had I not followed through on *sending* her to her room at that point, she would have succeeded in dismantling the consequence, which would have increased the likelihood that she would throw another tantrum soon.

Instead of discussing whether or not she had to go to her room, I simply added another consequence: "If you don't go to your room now, then I will take you."[1]

She would walk to her room, often screaming all the way. Just through the doorway she would make a U-turn, stop screaming, come back out, and say, "I won't fuss anymore, Mommy." Having followed through on the consequence, even though it may have only lasted a few seconds, I dramatically reduced the odds that she would soon repeat the tantrum.

---

1. If a child has chronic control problems, and there is any risk of a physical altercation, I would not physically carry the child. In such cases, I recommend seeking professional advice before creating appropriate consequences.

I make it clear in advance that, once I start a consequence, it is too late for the other person to change course and make a different choice before experiencing the consequence. If you make a prediction without such a clarification and encounter this issue, you can just say something like, "I already said I want you to go to your room, so I want you to do that first before you tell me you are ready to stop screaming." Frequently a child will revert to a high-volume protest at this point, demonstrating that the statement about not needing to go was an effort to take control over the consequence rather than to return to respectful interaction.

The same principle applies to adult relationships. Perhaps your partner persists in giving directions after you have predicted you will drive in the other car the next time this happens. Your partner says, "Oops, I forgot. Sorry, I won't do it again. You don't need to drive the other car tomorrow." It is too late to stop the consequence because the changed behavior came *after* the consequence was activated. Just as with a child, if we maintain the consequence we predicted, our partner is likely to exhibit a sudden bad mood. "Well, if you're going to be so picky, I give up. I said I wouldn't do it again. I think you just enjoy controlling me."

Maintaining Firmness in the Face of an Intimidating Response

Sometimes it's hard to follow through on a predicted consequence if the other person initially intensifies in resisting to any of the choices available under the terms of our prediction. This commonly happens because we so often apply predictions to situations in which we have previously accepted rude or non-reciprocal behavior. The other person may not initially welcome the change and may, in fact, hate it. For example, Beth would not initially *want* to do the dishes, nor would she *want* to miss any of the party. Jake would not *want* to have to remember financial details, nor would he *want* Sandra to stop keeping the books. Intense resistance or anger can be intimidating—so much so that we may back down and return to coaxing, arguing, and making idle threats instead of continuing to follow through on clear predictions.

It was initially very hard for Corey not to argue with Beth or give in when Beth protested, "It's not fair that I have to do the dishes before I go to Jane's party." In a situation like this, if you find it difficult simply to respond to the argument with silence, you may make a transition statement that respects the person's freedom to choose. "I have made myself clear. What you choose to do is completely up to you."

Sometimes a person threatens to make the opposite choice from the one she thinks we want her to make. Beth might say, "Fine, I'll just leave the dishes to rot and stay home and listen to my music. I didn't really want to go anyway."

It can be very easy to get hooked into a power struggle at this point, perhaps slipping into an "encouraging" statement, such as, "It will just take a few minutes. If you do them now, you can go and you won't even be late." Rather than getting caught in this way, reiterating a simple statement about the person's freedom to choose can help us stay out of the power struggle: "It's your choice."

We then need to disengage from further conversation and leave the room if necessary. If we have to say something, simply acknowledging the person's freedom to choose (once or twice at the most and in a neutral tone) can help us make sure we implement the consequence. As you become more comfortable and the other person adjusts to the change, I recommend that you say as little as possible.

We can follow through just as meticulously when dealing with other adults about household responsibilities, although the consequences may be different. If your partner leaves personal items strewn around the living room and says you are obsessed with neatness, you may feel stuck between living with it or picking it up yourself. However, there are many consequences you might predict. Some of them take a bit of effort on your part, but not so much as the stress around constant argument or doing it all yourself. You might say, "If you do not keep your personal belongings out of the living room, then I will put them in a box in the garage when I pick up rather than putting them away for you."

Adults who live with messy housemates have found a variation of the "box" prediction to be effective. If the housemate does not respond to intermediate steps, a person may predict, "If you do not wash your dishes after using them, I will designate certain pots, pans, dishes, and silverware to be yours and not give you permission to use ours/

mine, and"—second prediction—"if you don't wash those, I will just put them in a dishpan in the garage so we don't have to deal with the mess. You can wash them whenever you need them."

The person may be a great housemate in other ways, but issues such as messy kitchens often ruin living arrangements. Instead of fussing and fuming, you can do something rather simple about it. Once again, since adults are not used to having consciously predicted consequences for their inconsiderate behavior, the initial reaction may not be pleasant. I encourage adults who are beginning to set more constructive limits with each other to remember what usually happens when we begin to set limits with an unruly child: first, a tantrum; then a happier, more pleasant person.

Implementing the Consequence Thoroughly

When Corey predicts that Beth will not have permission to go to the party until the dishes are done, she must not give permission until Corey has thoroughly and completely finished her task. Beth must not leave anything, such as the pans, for later or fail to wipe the counters properly. If we apply the same exacting evaluation to task-related consequences for co-workers or other adults, I think we would live in a more productive world of competent people.

Implementing the Consequence Consistently

Following through consistently means *each and every time* a consequence is called for. As vital as consistency is, for most of us it is very difficult. Suppose, for example, you have told your partner you will not continue a conversation if he argues with you. If he then brings up a point in his argument the next day, you may automatically respond, instead of refusing to engage in the argument. In order to be consistent, you might reiterate the prediction, "If you want to argue, I am still unwilling to discuss this issue."

Although you could also simply not answer, people often react more angrily to dead silence than to another prediction. I usually recommend restating the prediction the first two times someone attempts to restart an argument. After that, I would just implement the consequence with no conversation.

Guidelines for Implementing a Predicted Consequence

- Respond in a timely manner
- Respond without discussion
- Avoid bargaining after implementing the consequence
- Maintain firmness if the person's initial response is intimidating
- Follow through thoroughly and consistently

Incremental Consequences

If we make a prediction and the other person becomes increasingly rude, angry, or abusive or becomes more aggressive in asserting a demand for non-reciprocal services, we may need to add additional consequences in response to the person's reactions.

For example, if I see my toddler headed toward the living room wall with a crayon, I would say, "If you try to color on anything besides the paper, then I will ask you to give me the crayon; if you color only on the paper, then you can keep it."

If the child is still preparing to color on the wall and refuses to give up the crayon, I can add another prediction. "If you don't give me the crayon, then I will take it."

If I have to take the crayon[2] and the child begins to throw a tantrum, I can add a third prediction. "If you pitch a fit, then I will ask you to go to your room. If not, you're welcome to stay in the living room."

If the child continues to cry and refuses to leave, I can say, "If you don't walk to your room yourself, then I will carry you. If you do go by yourself, then I won't carry you."

Such small, incremental consequences at each stage of the person's reactions offer the greatest opportunity to respond cooperatively.

Sometimes incremental predictions evolve on a trial-and-error basis. We may make one prediction and find it doesn't solve the problem as

---

2. If I am preparing to take the crayon, I walk slowly to avoid a chase scene—unless the wall is in imminent danger, and then the chase would be a preferable distraction. When I take the crayon, I move slowly and carefully, almost in slow motion, to avoid having the process accelerate into a physical struggle. Again, if there is a serious control problem I recommend seeking professional advice before making any prediction that could cause physical conflict between parent and child.

well as we had thought it would. Or the person may react in a way we hadn't anticipated, and we need to respond to this unexpected reaction. Or we might simply have gained more insight after our first prediction has been in effect.

Sometimes a new problem arises that we couldn't foresee in our first prediction. In this case, we can add a new consequence that deals with the current situation. When Franklin drove his own car to the theater and arrived late, he would whisper questions to Hans about what he had missed. This infuriated Hans, but instead of just getting angry, he added a second prediction to his first one. "If you come in late and distract me with questions, I won't answer them."

Once we add a second prediction to the first, we do not have to repeat either one. We actively and consistently apply them both.

Offering a Series of Incremental Predictions in Advance

In many cases, we may wish to present a series of incremental predictions ahead of time. A supervisor may be dealing with someone who is always handing in work projects late and holding up other team members. All too often, warning follows upon warning while everyone gets frustrated and little is actually done to solve the problem. In some cases, the problem gets recorded in the person's performance evaluation and eventually causes the person to be fired. In other cases, the dilemma continues indefinitely. If supportive efforts to discuss the issue and identify problem areas do not correct the situation, the supervisor might offer a series of predictions.

"If you turn in another late report, then on the next project I will ask you to outline your progress to me one week before the project is due so we can address any problems that might stop you from completing it on time.

"If you are still late, then I will ask you to develop 'project phases,' which break the project into parts, each with its own deadline.

"If you persist in handing work in late, then I will ask you to keep a time-motion chart of how you spend your time so we can examine your problem in more depth.

"If your work starts to come in on time, I will be glad we solved the problem and make note in your evaluation that you have demonstrated the ability to make difficult changes."

The advantage of giving all these predictions at once is that it presents a clear picture of of choices and consequences. If the employee just needs more supervision to learn necessary skills, the time is well spent in eliminating the problem instead of allowing it to continue to affect a wider circle of people. If, however, the employee is ultimately unwilling or unable to change, it will be much clearer that this person is not suited for the job, even after being given ample opportunity to learn it.

Managers often initially balk at such suggestions, thinking of the time and energy such supervision requires, but they usually discover that the process ultimately saves time and money by improving both morale and production. Of course, this type of process would not apply in situations where delay is unavoidable or where some built-in flexibility is appropriate for everyone.

We may also present a series of predictions in advance, and still add one or more later, as needed. Akiro's wife became jealous and angry whenever his children from a previous marriage came to visit. Kiko's behavior depressed Akiro, but during one visit he had an insight. He was depressed partly because he kept trying to answer Kiko's jealous comments ("They need too much attention" and "We can't ever watch the movies we like when they are here"). In his effort to be fair, Akiro had tried to answer each objection and ended up consuming much of the weekend in stressful discussion, which further diminished his time with the children. The children were also affected by the conflict, which they could sometimes see and almost always sense.

Akiro realized that even though some of Kiko's complaints were legitimate, most were due to her jealousy. He decided he would no longer discuss them during the children's visit. Eventually, he decided upon some incremental predictions.

"If you have complaints, then I don't want to be distracted by them while the kids are here on the weekend. If you try to talk about how we manage our time with them, I will refuse to do so until after the children leave. If there are any changes we want to agree upon, then I'm willing to discuss them before their next visit."

By making a series of incremental predictions, Akiro protected himself from being distracted by Kiko's jealousy. He hadn't changed Kiko, but he had identified and taken steps to deal with the issue surrounding the children's visits most important to him—being able to relax and enjoy the time he had with them.

When, at first, Kiko still tried to complain during the visits, Akiro felt more confident about not discussing the issues because he knew he had a commitment to do so later. When she persisted, he was able to add another incremental consequence. "If you continue to make unpleasant, jealous remarks, even when I don't answer you, then I will take the kids out for a walk or to a movie."

These predictions ultimately gave him and the children protection from continual conflict during their visits. At first, Kiko became more angry. However, the incremental predictions gave her the opportunity to shift her attitude at various points during any weekend. Gradually, she began to join in and enjoy family time together.

Challenge–Choice: Life's Consequences

While limit-setting predictions are most common, challenge–choice predictions can also have a powerful effect. When we make a challenge–choice prediction, we simply forecast consequences we believe the person will incur independently if he or she makes certain choices. A challenge–choice prediction does not involve *our* response or any consequence we will personally implement. If someone is acting in a way that could be harmful, I believe it is appropriate to give a subjective accounting of what we perceive and call upon the person to question the action and take stock of the consequences.

When used as a tool for punishment or domination, a challenge–choice prediction can be an ominous warning, such as when the insurance agent told an employee, "If you leave here, you will fail—you'll be back." In non-defensive communication, the goal is focused on protection and personal growth.

Doug might say to Virginia, "I believe that if you frequently interrupt others, they are likely to feel less respected, be less willing to talk to you, and less willing to listen to what you have to say. If you do listen without interrupting, I think others will feel both more respected, want to talk with you more, and be more attentive to what you have to say."

Virginia has been challenged to take account and can choose how to respond. Doug makes no reference to any reaction he personally will have to her interruptions; he is not defining his own boundaries and consequences. In this case, Doug is predicting how he believes people in general will be inclined to draw their boundary lines in response to Virginia's interruptions. He is challenging Virginia to consider the ramifications of repeatedly interjecting her own thoughts when others are speaking. She now has the option of examining her behavior. She also has the choice of changing the behavior, if, after her self-evaluation, she believes a change is warranted.

Guidelines for Making a Challenge–Choice Prediction

Keep in mind two vital points about the challenge–choice format:

1. Avoid repeating a challenge–choice prediction. The effect of doing so is badgering, or hammering the point home.
2. Offer the prediction in the form of a subjective statement rather than objective fact. Say "I believe," "I think," before the "if . . . then" of the prediction. If you present your statement as a conclusive, this-is-the-way-it-is pronouncement, you are more likely to encounter resistance.

When parents lecture children, they often use the same challenge–choice predictions over and over: "If you don't bring your grades up, you won't get into a good college." Adults do the same: "If you don't stand up to your father, he'll have you under his thumb for the rest of your life." When we use challenge–choice predictions repetitively, we browbeat the other person. I recommend stating this prediction clearly but not repeating it frequently.

Ways to Use Challenge–Choice Predictions

As with a limit-setting format, we can use the challenge–choice format to make predictions about feelings, beliefs, reasoning, and behavior. I often also use challenge–choice predictions in conjunction with limit-setting predictions. When I do so, I usually offer the challenge–choice prediction last. For example, you might first tell your partner that you will not respond to unsolicited directions when you are driving and then predict, "I believe that if you could stop worrying so much about which route we take, you would be less frustrated."

Corey used a challenge–choice prediction that provided Beth with food for thought. It helped her to understand that her choices ultimately would affect herself far more than they would affect her mother.

"I think you will find that if you put off doing basic tasks such as washing dishes, then you will create a habit of procrastination that will make daily routines seem overwhelming. You might also hurt your ability to be a productive person.

"If you practice doing routine tasks now, then I believe it will help you build good organizational habits so daily routines will seem easy. That can strengthen your ability to be a productive person."

I think teens often forget that they will live with their parents for only a few more years, but will probably live with themselves for sixty years. I like to be clear with teenagers about the impact of their choices on their own lives.

You might also make a challenge–choice prediction for the child who is not showing appreciation for a present. "I believe that if you don't appreciate your bike, it will mean less to you and you will actually enjoy it less. If you appreciate it, I think you will also have more fun with it."

Sandra could use a challenge–choice prediction with Jake so he might think about the effect of his choices on himself rather than perhaps only seeing her as trying to control his behavior. "If you don't learn how to prevent some of these banking problems, I think you will feel more stress even if I do fix the immediate mess. If you learn a few things that enable you to avoid the banking problems, then I believe you will feel much less pressure yourself."

Likewise, Akiro might make a prediction for Kiko that would help her to consider how her choices affect her own ability to feel loved. "I believe that if you continue to see the children as taking me away from you, then your own jealousy will make you feel less loved. If you accept the children as part of our family together, I believe you could have even more love than just what you get from me." Each of these challenge–choice predictions provides information about the impact of people's choices on themselves as well as on others.

The Tools of Non-Defensive Communication

THE QUESTION

Nature: Curious, open, innocent, neutral, inviting
Function: To gather information

THE STATEMENT

Nature: Open, vulnerable, direct, subjective, descriptive
Function: To provide information

THE PREDICTION

Nature: Protective, foretelling, neutral, definitive, firm, dual
in nature
Function: To provide security through predictability

Clear Predictions Balance Responsibility with Freedom

Years ago, Frederick (Fritz) Perls, most well known for conceiving Gestalt therapy, made a comment that was seized by the counterculture and later appeared on greeting cards. The original version read

I do my thing, and you do your thing.
I am not in this world to live up to your expectations
and you are not in this world to live up to mine.
You are you and I am I,
and if by chance we find each other, it's beautiful.
If not, it can't be helped. [3]

While I understood the intention of Perls's assertion is to move away from controlling or co-dependent relationships, I do not agree with how this philosophy was (and is) sometimes interpreted by those

---

3. Frederick S. Perls, *Gestalt Therapy Verbatim* (Highland, N.Y.: Real People Press, 1969; reprinted 1982).

The Effects of Non-Defensive Communication

Separateness: Each person is able to maintain the clarity of his or her own position instead of getting caught in power struggle

Disarming: Each person is likely to respond with openness and sincerity

Clarification: Each person has an opportunity to affirm, deny, or qualify a position

Accountability: Each person is accountable for what he or she says and does

Quantum Leaps: Each person has the opportunity to take quantum leaps in personal growth

---

who do not want to take responsibility for the effect they have on others. Out of this reasoning comes the all-too-simplistic retort, "If you choose to feel hurt by what I did, that is your problem."

On the other side of the spectrum is what the fox taught to the little prince: that we have responsibility for others "forever."[4] I used to like this idea far better, though I also believe we can feel too much responsibility for other people's choices and become enmeshed in their lives in unhealthy ways.

My experience has been that non-defensive predictions can combine the best of each of these philosophies without retaining their limitations. We can understand that, whether we make conscious predictions or not, insofar as we all create boundaries that affect each other, we have responsibility for each other. We can also understand that, by making predictions that do not try to control another person's choices, each of us can maximize our freedom.

---

4. Antoine de Saint Exupéry, *The Little Prince* (New York: Harcourt, Brace & World, 1943).

The Eight Formats for Powerful Non-Defensive Communication

QUESTIONS

Ask questions about the *content* of the topic under discussion

Ask questions about the *process* of the interaction, including attitude or feelings that are affecting the discussion

STATEMENTS

Describe for the other person in your own words what you hear his or her conscious or *overt* message to be

Share with the other person any contradictory *covert* message you see from your perspective—including any discrepancies you perceive between his or her words, non-verbal language, and behavior

Describe what you perceive as the cause or motivation for the other person's reactions

Describe and express your own reactions—thoughts, feelings, beliefs, and behaviors

PREDICTIONS

Using "*if-then*," tell the person how you will respond to various choices he or she might make in a given situation (limit-setting)

Using "*if-then*," tell the person what consequences you believe he or she will experience in life as a consequence of certain choices—(challenge–choice)

12

The Non-Defensive Mind and Heart Set

In order to integrate the process of asking sincere questions, exposing our thoughts and feelings, and making firm predictions, we need to make internal shifts in our attitudes and expectations. Non-defensiveness is not a technique that involves a script. Any single topic presents us with countless ways to express ourselves non-defensively.

Preparing to Be Non-Defensive

Because the cornerstone of non-defensive communication is sincerity, a vital part of strengthening our non-defensive skills involves consistent focus on being more sincere and open. We can learn much more rapidly if we prepare ourselves with a non-defensive mind set and heart set.

Pacing Ourselves

As a child, I had some trouble with the story of the Tortoise and the Hare. I really had to concentrate to understand why the tortoise won the race instead of the rabbit. I remember thinking, "Well, if the rabbit can run so much faster, how could the tortoise win? If the rabbit ran around and did other things and didn't stay on the track, maybe he just didn't care if he won. He could have won if he wanted to. Besides, maybe he was having more fun than the tortoise was, just plodding along. At the time, I liked the rabbit better and felt protective because of the bad press he was getting. As I grew older, I learned to appreciate one of the fable's lessons: Haste makes waste. Now I appreciate both the tortoise *and* the hare.

The Costs of a Frenetic Pace

The increase in the pace of people's lives in the last few decades would leave both the hare and the tortoise in the dust. A corporate manager recently told me he wasn't sure his job was worth its six-digit salary because he had not had a full day off with his family in three years, including Christmas.

It's been jokingly said that every yuppie family has to have three calendars to keep their various schedules straight—a family with only one or two calendars loses status. Yet there is nothing truly funny about couples who barely see each other before they fall into bed at night and seldom see their children except during transition times in the car. In single-parent families or two-parent families, the parent(s) may be working two jobs; they see little of their families and get little rest. Millions of us are functioning in a workaholic frenzy.

Many people are in such a hurry that they overlook important details and thereby usher in confusion or even a major crisis. Then they get angry at others for not being competent enough to have solved the problem. They fail to realize that their own inattention to vital details is a major source of the dilemma. We fall into a vicious cycle, too busy putting out the fire of one crisis to pay enough attention to prevent the next one.

Our frenetic lifestyle also contributes to the number of crises we face because it amplifies our defensiveness. When someone is left at day care, each parent thinking the other was to pick the child up, it is easy to argue about who is to blame. When people are not notified of an important meeting about one phase of an ongoing project, their resentment carries into the next phase.

Because of this sustained pace, the idea of taking the time to shift to being non-defensive may seem unrealistic. How long it takes to communicate non-defensively is a crucial issue, to which I have a dual reaction: The hare and the tortoise both win the race on this one.

Slowing Down

We do have to slow down in preparing to speak non-defensively. Unlearning our defensive reactions is a deliberate process.

- *First* we stop and catch ourselves when we react in old habitual ways
- *Then* we think about how to do it differently
- *Then* we actually do it

This is frequently difficult, especially during interactions that may be loaded with conflicting feelings and thoughts. For this reason, and the ones discussed below, we may need to walk with the tortoise for a while.

Learning a new skill can create confusion. Learning a skill that is very similar—yet different—from another one we already know can cause confusion and add difficulty to the learning process. If, after learning to type, we undertake learning to ski, typing would not in any way interfere with our skiing. On the other hand, if we are skilled at tennis and decide to take up racquetball, it will be harder because there are subtle but critical differences in gripping the racket and in the timing and motion of the swing.

When we shift our way of reacting from defensive to non-defensive, we still use questions, statements, and predictions, but our intention and tone are different and our phrasing is sometimes different too. Because these differences can be subtle, they may be hard to notice as we attempt to change our way of speaking. If we expect to have some difficulty making the transition and know we need to pay careful attention, we can make the process more relaxed.

It helps to try a gradual approach. Once people learn this non-defensive process, they invariably say, "I now see how constantly defensive we all are. If I dealt with every defensive reaction I saw in myself and others, it would take me twenty-four hours a day and I'd still never get through it all!" The sheer quantity of material we are dealing with can make the change seem time-consuming. Because it's overwhelming to most people to think about making a major shift to interacting non-defensively, I think it is essential to embrace the effectiveness of a gradual approach.

Presence of mind is essential. A critical part of slowing down is to focus carefully on our own words and those of the other person. When another person is speaking, we cannot let our minds wander or rush on to our next point. Non-defensive communication requires genuine dialogue. It requires presence of mind.

Saving Time and Energy—Getting Quick Results

Although we initially may have to slow down and expend some energy on creating the proper mind and heart set, this slower pace can ultimately save us time and energy and afford quick results. As I mentioned at the end of Part I, I think we waste massive amounts of energy in power struggle—a process that binds us to others through adversity. Think, if you will, about how much time you can spend absorbed by what one person has said that upset you. Learning, even a bit at a time, to be more non-defensive can free up our energy for more creative use.

Even novices can use these skills with a high degree of effectiveness. It is reasonable to expect that we may get some quick results from speaking non-defensively. We can start by figuring out how to use a single question, statement, or prediction in one interaction. Anyone can practice using these tools in various situations without having all the skills integrated. In many cases, effective ideas for handling a situation non-defensively are passed from one relative novice to another.

Even after a one-hour training session at a conference, people often go home and give advice to someone else, who then successfully uses these skills. One example is that of the woman who suggested a question for her daughter to pose to a student who was using offensive language and calling her names. The next day, the eleven-year-old girl got on the bus and with that one question—"Do you believe I want you to talk to me that way?"—eliminated the trauma of enduring daily verbal harassment. Her mother told me the story at the following year's conference. The boy never bothered her daughter again, although she witnessed him harassing other students in the way he once did her.

Time is relative. When I describe a non-defensive response, people sometimes comment on how long it would take to say it. Yet the actual time can be counted in seconds rather than minutes. It may seem to take a long time because people are venturing into unfamiliar territory. When we drive someplace new, it often seems to take forever to get there. Once we travel the same route again, even on the return home, the trip seems shorter.

Monitoring Our Own Intentions

Once we slow down and prepare to approach a situation non-defensively, it is still important to consciously monitor our own intentions. We are all quite capable of deluding ourselves into thinking we have crystal-pure motives, while allowing tainted ones to slip into our interactions. I see two attitudes that often cause people difficulty when they practice being non-defensive.

1. Now I have the ultimate weapon. One woman said to me gleefully, "Aha, the next time he says *that* to me, I'll be prepared!" Unfortunately, her tone and attitude suggested that she was still more invested in winning a power struggle than in preparing to keep her integrity.

2. Others will certainly disarm in response to my non-defensive approach. The danger here is that, if one has that expectation, others will probably sense it and resist, and from there the power struggle can accelerate. With the expectation thwarted, the first person feels frustrated that the new tool didn't succeed.

If we let an increased sense of personal empowerment and the excitement about communicating more effectively become distorted in this way, it is too easy to slip back into the war-model framework (and perhaps we have not yet fully left it). Here, the bottom line is still "them against me."

Because we often experience an almost magnetic pull back into the power struggle pit, it is possible to use non-defensive methods, be more effective than we have been previously, and still walk away feeling the pleasure of having won a battle. Once when I went into my small neighborhood grocery, I couldn't remember something I was going to buy. An employee gave me permission to use the phone to call home for a reminder. While I was on the phone, another employee ducked under the phone line and went behind the deli counter. After I hung up, she said, in an accusatory tone, "Next time you want to use the phone, why don't you ask first!"

I was completely taken aback, particularly because the employees there were usually friendly. I was mute for a minute, while I thwarted my initial defensive urge to retort, "I already *did* ask!" My mind raced, and I asked her a question about what I thought motivated her remark.

SHARON: Are you assuming that I didn't ask for permission?"
EMPLOYEE: (*with a frown and a tone of slightly subdued irritation*)
            Well, yeah.
SHARON: I did ask and was given permission.

She mumbled a response, yet I knew I didn't feel satisfied with the interaction, so I said, "I would have felt much better if you had asked me about this instead of assuming I hadn't gotten permission."

Even though she did not change her attitude, I walked out the door, congratulating myself: Yes. I did it. I remembered to ask a question, and there she stood with the egg on her face. *Oops!* As I heard my own thoughts, I realized I was relishing having won a power struggle. Despite feeling good about my effort to be clear instead of defensive, it was only in retrospect that I realized part of my intention had been to retaliate against her rude treatment and prove her wrong.

Slowing our process down and questioning our motivation *before* we speak can help us to shift into non-defensive mode. It is also useful to develop the habit of questioning ourselves *afterward*, a practice that creates awareness and helps promote future change. Such self-examination can be used with all three non-defensive tools: questions, statements, and predictions.

Asking Yourself about Your Questions

Is my question sincere?

Is it entrapping?

Do I really want to know the answer, or am I trying to prove my own point?

Do I think I already know the answer? If so, why am I asking the question?

Did I load it with my own feelings?

How did my tone sound? Was it neutral or coaxing or attacking?

Did my body language (frowning? shrugging?) convey my feelings?

Are there other questions that would elicit more information?

Asking Yourself about Your Statements

Have I tried to convince the person to agree with me?

Have I stated my opinion as fact?

Am I hiding some of what I thought or felt?

What else am I thinking and feeling?

What am I thinking that I would not want the person to know?

Am I stating the parts of my position that don't show vulnerability and hiding the parts that do?

Am I expressing the part of my statement that shows my insecurity and hiding the part that clearly reveals my opinion?

Have I said what I *hear* the other person saying?

Have I named what I *see* in the other person's body language or attitude that contradicts what I hear?

Have I shared my own insights and observations about the other person's reactions?

Have I stated my own thoughts and feelings?

Did I express my observations neutrally and confine my feelings to statements about my own experience?

Asking Yourself about Your Predictions

Am I using this prediction to threaten the other person into doing what I want?

Am I trying to punish the other person for considering a choice I don't like?

Am I wanting just to protect myself, or am I trying to control the other person?

Is my goal simply to be treated with respect and maintain reciprocity, or is there something else I want?

Is my tone neutral or filled with my own feelings (hurt, judgment, anger)?

Am I feeling respectful of the other person's right to make an independent choice?

What is my body language like?

Monitoring our internal process to keep our own *intentions* non-defensive is crucial. If, before speaking, we realize we are not completely non-defensive, we can acknowledge feeling defensive to the other person. We can also simply continue to use the non-defensive format, knowing our intentions are not crystal-clear. When I asked Rhonda what she meant when she compared what I was teaching to charm school, I clearly didn't feel totally non-defensive, but I forced myself to use a non-defensive format for a question. A more sincere and open conversation resulted. I don't subscribe fully to the saying "Fake it until you make it," but many people have reported to me that, just by using a non-defensive *format,* they could feel an internal shift settling into place, a shift that resulted in a sense of calm and freedom from power struggle.

Each step is important and leads to the next. I didn't do a top-notch job in the grocery store, but I did manage to ask a question (instead of just defending myself) and state how I would prefer to be treated. With practice, the internal shift toward non-defensiveness begins to become more automatic.

Releasing the Outcome

Using non-defensive speech contributes to our own growth, regardless of how the other person responds. Anticipating how the other person will or will not react can severely limit us. (This is different from anticipating *various* reactions a person might have and considering how we would respond to *each* of them.) If we anticipate that the other person will not respond positively ("What's the use? Trying to *talk* won't do any good"), we may give up before we start and withdraw from using our own verbal power. On the other hand, if we anticipate that the other person *will* respond non-defensively, he or she may sense our expectation and (as indicated earlier) be more likely to resist.

We can't ever know how someone will react when we speak non-defensively. We may often be surprised. I once was awakened in a hotel room at 6 A.M. by a pounding racket I later learned was caused by someone repairing a washing machine. That noise was followed by employees shouting back and forth about who was cleaning which room. I complained to the manager that the level of early morning commotion was beyond the limits of my flexibility.

The manager fairly snarled, "What do you want me to do, give you your money back?" I don't know how others would react, but his attitude would have left me feeling angry even if he did give me a refund. I asked him, "Why are you angry at me when I am the person who was inconvenienced?" He looked down and away from me, rapidly clenched his jaw, and said gruffly, "*I'm not angry!*"

I then said, "I see that you are not even able to look at me."

In a second, his previous demeanor vanished. He looked me squarely in the eye and said warmly, "You know, I should get walkie-talkies for the maids. They have to talk back and forth while they clean the rooms, and that way they could do it quietly." He had taken the quantum leap. When I described how I saw his behavior, something must have clicked in his head and allowed him to acknowledge his defensiveness. Not only did he begin brainstorming about how to solve the problem, he also offered to cut the charge for the room in half. We shook hands and parted smiling. Seconds earlier, I would not have bet a penny on his capacity to respond to anything non-defensively, much less try to solve the problem of how to meet the needs of his staff as well as his guests.

Being Willing to Be Both Vulnerable and Direct

The next step in attitude development is to cultivate a willingness to be both vulnerable and direct. We expose our *own* motivations, feelings, and thoughts as well as giving others feedback about how we perceive *their* reactions. People sometimes find this more difficult than monitoring their intentions and assumptions. When Susan told

Elaina she looked great in her dress and then followed it by saying, "Isn't it nice that they are making better clothes for large women now?" Elaina walked away devastated. The idea that she would speak to Susan directly about the comment—whether on the spot, later in the week, or after three years—entails a directness that, to many, carries with it extreme vulnerability. According to the traditional war model, Elaina's directness could cause her to be accused of making a big deal out of nothing or expose her to further "attack." For a person who feels self-conscious about her weight, reopening the subject is painfully humiliating.

Avoiding the topic with Susan will not heal the wound that Elaina carries inside herself. In fact, she will revisit that pain each and every time she sees Susan. When we hide our vulnerability, we *accept* the hurt we believe someone intended. We take it in and walk around as though stuck with invisible knives.

Having another person's motive exposed, even a cruel one, does not have to increase the hurt I feel. Nor does letting her know the kind of impact she had on me mean that I have to lose more self-esteem. In fact, my clarity can give me strength. This lesson is a hard one for many of us, when we feel devalued by someone who ridicules our personality, weight, race, sexual preference, age, disability, religion, or intelligence.

Even though approaching these issues can be terrifying (and therefore requires preparation), I believe it is through our vulnerability that we experience our greatest power. If we can shift our thinking toward being open and direct and vulnerable, we will have the greatest possible exchange of accurate information, achieve the greatest clarity, and increase the likelihood that the other person will respond in kind.

Dealing Effectively with Hurtful Feedback

Developing a willingness to be vulnerable and direct goes hand in hand with developing a different attitude about how we deal with another's hurtful words. Since one goal in being non-defensive is to gather as much information as possible (as opposed to giving in, withdrawing, or counterattacking), asking questions of someone who says something that feels hurtful can be very valuable.

I want to make it clear that I do not support continuing to receive feedback when others are simply using us as whipping posts. However, sometimes, if (and only if) I feel strong enough, I may ask for more information even when a person isn't completely respectful, because I want the information. It may provide an accurate understanding that will help me deal with the situation more effectively.

In a world where being non-defensive was considered normal, Elaina might have a different attitude about dealing directly with Susan's comment. She might have asked, "When you followed your compliment about how nice I looked with a comment about how wonderful it is that they now make better clothes for large women, how did you think it would affect me?" Or she might have asked, "Were you trying to hurt me by saying that, or did you have some other reason for the comment?"

Elaina could also have made a statement. "When you followed your compliment with a comment that put me in the category of a 'large woman,' it seemed to me that you were setting me up with a compliment and then knocking me down with an insult. I felt like I'd been stabbed." Once Elaina brings her feelings out into the open, she can free herself from the power of Susan's judgment.

Elaina might have been surprised by Susan's answer. "Oh, no, I wasn't trying to hurt you. I'm so sorry, my comment was thoughtless. I lost a hundred pounds not long before I came to work here—which you had no way of knowing. I always used to hate how they plastered polka dots and wild designs on dresses for large women, making us look even bigger. When I saw your beautiful dress and how great you looked in it, I just blathered out my next thought."

Even if Susan's comment had been the thoughtless utterance of a thin woman, she would still have a chance to learn to be more compassionate in the future. Or, had Susan been a person who was using intimidation (consciously or unconsciously) as a way to establish her own power in the office, she would have exposed a mean-spirited part of herself.

By preparing ourselves to deal openly with another's responses, we can hold others accountable, free ourselves from the grasp of judgment, and possibly find some valuable gems of information.

Acknowledging Our Own Accountability

Another tough challenge for many of us is to openly acknowledge our own accountability. Holding ourselves accountable, regardless of whether or not the other person acknowledges any responsibility, requires us to keep focused on our own non-defensive philosophy and values.

Phil told me about a situation where some fellow members of an organization were doing things he regarded as unethical. He felt disturbed about the course they were creating for the organization. While talking with one of the men during a meeting, he asked questions in a tone he realized was accusatory. He thereupon apologized for his tone, only to have the other man respond condescendingly and without acknowledging any responsibility for *his* own actions.

Phil found it very hard to apologize for asking an accusatory question; it seemed minor compared to the some of the other person's violations. He found it even more difficult to sit there and not try to get the other guy to admit anything. After inwardly railing against himself, almost believing he was weakening his position, he realized he didn't have to maintain a martyred silence. He could continue with his own statement and predictions. What he said was this: "Your response feels condescending to me, as if I made a major error and you made none. My apology is for my own defensiveness, and it doesn't change my viewpoint. In fact, it was hard to apologize for asking an accusatory question when that feels small to me in comparison to some of the things you and others have done, which I believe are unethical. If you are not willing to change your course of action, I will ask that the board investigate this issue."

Holding ourselves accountable, especially when someone else denies being a part of the problem, can be a stretch. Yet when we do so, we often gain rather than lose. By being accountable for his own defensive behavior and then continuing his efforts to deal with the issue non-defensively, Phil added to his strength rather than diminishing it. After witnessing this conversation, two other people who had been fence-sitting requested that the course of action be changed.

Respecting the Other Person's Right to Refuse

As we build our non-defensive frame of reference, we should also be mentally and emotionally prepared to accept another person's resistance to giving us information or hearing our feedback. When we ask non-defensive questions, we are asking for the other person's willing participation, not attempting coercion. Likewise, if we make an observation about how we perceive someone's body language or motivation and the person says, "I don't need *your* feedback, thanks anyway!" then it becomes invasive to continue. A closed mind does not hear.

I believe that in order to remain non-defensive in such cases, we must not pursue any attempt to have the person give or receive information. I have found this is very hard, but vital, for people to learn. Forcing a person to give or receive information can be a psychological assault. Trying to draw out information a person wants to keep carries the energy of theft. Trying to force-feed a person with unwanted information carries the energy of rape. Non-tangible violations have power, just as tangible ones do.

If someone does not want to give or receive information, the alternative to trying to force a continued conversation is simply to make a prediction. With the prediction, the other person chooses whether or not to hear us. We simply forecast our own intentions. We put on record how we will respond to each of the other person's possible choices. This is as useful in volatile situations (refusing to discuss alcoholism) as with lesser annoyances (disclosing the cause of a bad mood).

Maintaining a Non-Defensive Posture

It is still possible to start out non-defensively but at some point slide back into defensiveness, especially when the other person remains invested in the power struggle. A key factor in maintaining a non-defensive posture when someone is still trying to draw you into conflict is to be very clear that you are doing this for yourself, so you can become a more open, direct, and competent person. Though you might also be motivated to provide a model for your children, or to be more compassionate toward others, the primary goal of a non-defensive attitude is to develop your own character and strength.

I think keeping this goal fresh in our minds is essential. If we lose sight of it, our ability to monitor our intentions vanishes along with other aspects of a non-defensive attitude, especially when we are challenged by others.

Although talking non-defensively is often disarming, others sometimes do respond by trying harder to pull us into the power struggle.

HARRY: What do you mean when you say . . . ?
ARNIE: You know what I mean!
HARRY: (*now hooked into raising his voice*) If I knew, I wouldn't have asked the question!

A person may directly attack the way we are communicating by accusing us of trying some new technique, engaging in psychobabble, or attempting psychoanalysis. When others increase their efforts to knock us off our non-defensive stance, we can be pushed to the edge and may fall, thinking on the way down, Well, I tried and it didn't work. But if we focus intently on maintaining our own process, we do not have to give up just because someone wants us to. We can prepare ourselves to continue—with neutral questions, statements, or predictions such as these:

Would you like to know why I asked you?
Are you willing to answer my question, or would you rather not?
I won't be able to tell you what I think until I understand what you mean.
If you don't want to answer me, then I'd rather not continue this part of our conversation right now.

The process we use determines the outcome. If we give in to people's demands and then gossip about them, we "become" a passive-aggressive person. If we defend ourselves by blaming others, we "become" an aggressive person who is intimidating, even though we may feel intimidated ourselves. A client of mine once rolled her eyes, sighed, grimaced, and shook her shoulders with a kind of disgust as she declared, "I don't even want to *bother* telling him how I feel." I asked her, "Do you want to become a person who rolls her eyes, sighs, and doesn't even care whether she communicates clearly?" She looked at me, startled out of her dramatic posturing. Often we forget that how we communicate does much more to shape our own lives than it does anyone else's.

I want to emphasize again that if we stay focused on our own non-defensive process there is no way for us to fail, regardless of how the other person responds. We can strengthen our own confidence and self-esteem by maintaining our own clarity and not getting drawn into the power struggle. We can walk away with a sense of integrity and dignity, no matter what challenge we have faced.

The Non-Defensive Predisposition

- Slow down
- Monitor your own intentions
- Avoid predetermining whether or not the other person will remain defensive
- Be willing to become more direct and vulnerable
- Cultivate openness to hearing the perceptions of others
- Hold yourself accountable regardless of what the other person does
- Accept that someone may not want to give or receive information
- Maintain a non-defensive posture in the face of continued defensiveness

Selecting Practice Methods

If someone says something that pushes our buttons, the reaction can set in instantaneously, in every cell of our body. People often ask me, "How can I practice this? How can I be non-defensive when someone has just said something that makes me furious?" I remind them that once they begin to speak non-defensively, they are likely to be encouraged by their effectiveness, which diminishes any difficulty they are having. It usually becomes easier with each application.

I also suggest that people think about the various ways they can practice—I present several techniques in the following pages—and then choose ahead of time those that are most suitable to their own learning styles. If you simply assume that you will be able to employ a non-defensive tool spontaneously in the moment of interacting, you may have a hard time escaping the pull of old habits.

Observing through a Non-Defensive Lens

To practice, I often suggest people simply start by carefully watching patterns of defensiveness in themselves and in others. Seeing patterns clearly can defuse the power they have over us. Perhaps we are angry at a woman friend who continually breaks commitments. After observation, during which it becomes clear that she is surrendering and sabotaging, we may see her vulnerability as well as her covert hostility. We may feel genuinely curious about why she first surrenders and then hurts us by breaking commitments. The separateness or detachment that comes with acting as an observer can give us enough room to shift gears and respond differently.

Mentally Replaying a Non-Defensive Interaction

After an interaction has left us frustrated, we often replay it in our minds so that we come out on top ("I *should* have said . . . !"). We attempt mentally to rescript the battle we feel we have just lost. If, instead of staying locked in the power struggle, we begin to replay the scene using non-defensive questions, statements, and predictions, we will be better prepared the next time a similar situation occurs. Behavioral studies have shown that people who mentally visualize doing yoga or playing basketball can acquire a significant portion of the skill level attained by those who practice physically. We can surely benefit by mentally practicing how to say things non-defensively before doing so in an actual situation. Also, even within the context of our own minds, a non-defensive resolution can build our self-esteem more than a defensive "win."

Modeling a Non-Defensive
Voice Tone and Body Language

One of the hardest aspects of practicing non-defensive voice tone and body language is shifting away from habitual defensive patterns. In workshops, when I have people practice in groups, I almost always—even after others have found a person's tone and body language to be acceptably non-defensive—find signs of defensiveness. After I help the person to eliminate all of these signs, what the person says sounds *so* different that the others will make audible sounds and comments such as "Oh, yes, that's it!"; "Now you've got it!"; "I feel much more like answering you"; "My walls came right down when you said it like that."

Mirrors are valuable aids in learning about body language. I remember once when I was angry with my then three-year-old daughter. I said in an accusatory way that I didn't like the look on her face. She looked surprised and said, non-defensively, "But Mommy, you're looking at *me* like that too." How she had deduced that her look and mine were the same, I don't know, but I stopped cold, intentionally froze my expression, and proceeded straight to the bathroom mirror. There I was—with tight lips, clenched jaw, squinted eyes, and intense frown. After that, I learned much about myself by looking in the mirror when I was feeling different emotions and wanted to communicate non-defensively.

We often do not see ourselves as others do. For example, many people frown intensely when they ask a question and have no idea how accusatory they look. They may think they look intently interested. Practicing in front of a mirror, looking at ourselves as if we were the other person, helps us learn how to make our questions *look* as well as *be* sincere and inviting. We may also see more of our own charisma and warmth when we look in a mirror.

You can use tape recorders to monitor your voice tone, but keep in mind that the tape recorder always mutes intensity to some degree, whether the tone is warm or harsh.[1] Gary, a lumber mill manager, was frustrated because, as soon as he was promoted to manager, his co-workers started to treat him differently. He found himself getting very defensive. So he began to keep a tape recorder in the car and used his forty-five-minute commute to practice what he wanted to say non-defensively. The routine helped him immeasurably.

We can also practice our tone of voice with someone who is sup-

---

1. The audiotape "Powerful Non-Defensive Communication" covers the material in this book in abbreviated form and demonstrates the difference between defensive and non-defensive tones.

porting our non-defensive learning process. We may tell the person what we want to say to someone and then ask if it sounds defensive and, if so, how. We can also ask a person we are talking to at the moment, "Did I sound defensive when I said that?" Although some people may want to reassure us rather than state the truth, others will often provide us with accurate information.

Planning How to Use Non-Defensive Tools

Many of us deal with a repeated situation, both at work and at home. You may therefore find it useful to sit down and plan some questions, statements, or predictions to use the next time a certain type of interaction occurs. You could even list the questions, statements, and predictions you would use to address a certain situation. Planning ahead in this way is not the same as trying to control the situation or use a technique "on" another person. When we are planning how to be sincerely open and direct, we are preparing to act with respect and not be caught up in our own destructive habits.

You may also decide to practice by simply picking a certain number of non-defensive questions, statements, and predictions to practice in a given time frame ("I think I'll ask a minimum of one non-defensive question every day this week"). Or you might also plan to use a single non-defensive question, statement, or prediction during any given interaction. You can also practice with a store clerk, a service station attendant, a telephone solicitor, or someone else with whom you do not have an ongoing relationship.

Stopping a Conversation and Identifying It as Defensive

You can also plan to practice by stopping certain conversations—but only in relationships where you feel comfortable doing so—as soon as you notice you are reacting defensively. Even if you aren't sure what to do differently, you can stop and say, "I think I am reacting defensively to what you are saying." This can help you shift to a non-defensive mode.

Another valuable practice exercise is to decide to reapproach non-defensively a previously difficult or unresolved conversation. I have sometimes had people come back into a workshop late after a break and tell me, "We were just resolving something that happened a year ago." For some reason, we tend to think that once we have said something, it is over and done with, unchangeable and irreparable. I see every conversation as a piece of clay that we can work and rework—as long as both people are willing.

Choosing the Right Situation

Some people have successfully applied non-defensive communication immediately after learning about it—and in difficult situations. For others, trying something totally new in a high-stakes situation may be hazardous. Each of us can gauge the level of risk we feel. If your job does not feel secure, it might not be advisable to practice a new way of speaking, first off, with the person who has the power to fire you.

When I was training some security police who often dealt with gang members, I advised them against experimenting with a new way of talking in situations where they feared physical harm. Although they later used non-defensive methods successfully to reduce the escalation of potentially violent situations, they first tested the waters during less intense interactions.

We can integrate non-defensive ways of speaking best if we allow them to develop gradually and not try to force ourselves to use them in situations that feel too difficult. Some people find it easier to practice first in a personal relationship, others in a professional relationship—wherever they feel the safest and the most empowered.

Evaluating the Timing

As we develop greater skill in communicating non-defensively, we still need to consider when we choose to use the process. You may not want to raise an issue about something your partner says that upsets you when you are visiting family and your partner is already feeling tense. Or you may agree to hold off on a discussion about the bank account if you are both too tired. You may decide not to give your college-age son feedback about time management when you are working to change roles. You may want to decide carefully on the timing of talking to a co-worker about a disagreement regarding a project you both need to work on.

You can evaluate factors such as the other person's mood, your own confidence, the condition of the relationship, and the current activity or environment to determine optimal timing for practicing PNDC. The risk here is that you might find reasons to procrastinate about dealing with a certain issue forever, although there *may* be some issues you choose not to deal with at all. There are other times when you might jump into the frying pan and deal with a hot issue at what seems to be the worst possible time, and it could turn out extremely well. Timing is a complex issue. While the sincerity of being non-defensive can help you deal with many situations on the spot, thinking ahead and being sensitive is still vital. A commitment to PNDC can and should go hand in hand with discernment about timing so that your potential for positive results can be maximized.

Selecting Ways to Practice

- Observe through a non-defensive lens
- Replay interactions non-defensively
- Model a non-defensive tone and body language
- Plan how to use non-defensive tools
- Stop a conversation and identify it as defensive
- Choose the right situation
- Pay attention to timing

Accepting Imperfection

Any notions of perfection have to be tossed out the window when we use non-defensive communication. I still sometimes find it difficult to think fast enough to use this process as effectively as I would like (although it gets easier with practice); I can almost always think of ways I could have said it better. Our imperfection does not necessarily mean our interactions are ineffective. The conversation I had with the hotel manager about noise could be a textbook example of several things *not* to do. Let me review two sentences I said to him: "Why are you angry at me when I'm the person who was inconvenienced?" and "I see that you are not even able to look at me."

Here, I assumed that he was angry instead of asking him how he felt. When I stated that he wasn't *even* able to look at me, I added an unnecessary quality of judgment to my observation. But because my tone was neutral, he still dropped his defensiveness.

I believe it is good for us to remember that perfection is finished, static, and therefore outside the realm of the living. Our imperfect efforts to become non-defensive are simply a part of our being human.

Communication as a Transfer of Energy

Ultimately, questions, statements, and predictions are tools for using energy. Energy is our source of power. When we make the internal shift to a non-defensive mind and heart set, we change how we use our energy and therefore how we use our power.

The essential change we make, I believe, is to move away from seeking to control the choices of others. Even our attempts to get someone's attention or respect are controlling efforts that usually result in some kind of psychological warfare. Instead, we can develop the internal motivation to speak and listen in a manner that focuses on strengthening ourselves.

The personal empowerment that results from this kind of energy shift has been recounted in examples throughout the book. In many instances, the shift can be so potent that it can seem to be broadcast telepathically, over time and physical distance. Barbara was a workshop participant who had not spoken to her sister Sherry for several years. During the workshop, Barbara focused on getting out of power struggle and opening her heart again toward Sherry. On the way home she decided to call her sister. When she walked in the front door, the phone was ringing. Sherry was calling *her* after a seven-year silence.

Shifting the focus of our internal energy can also give us more conscious control over how or whether we receive the energy sent from others. According to a martial arts teacher, our bodies are "transformers" of energy.[2] We have the capacity to take in one kind of energy and transmute it. When we neutralize our tone of voice and our body language, we literally take the charge out of the situation and defuse the energy. In the process, we get our ego out the way so that a true encounter and communication can take place.

Once we recognize our ability to work with our own energetic make-up, we realize we can refuse to take in any negative energy directed toward us. This is an important qualifier to the principle that we need to be open in our mind and heart set.

Marilyn told me the story of how her husband, a professor well known in their community for his charm and intelligence, used to blame and criticize her to the point that she felt torn up inside. Charles could level her with his anger, which he usually seemed able to turn on and off at will. After consciously working hard to build her own self-esteem, Marilyn realized one day when Charles began criticizing her that his anger was not having the usual effect; she wasn't taking it in at all. It was as if they were having two separate experiences, his and hers. Marilyn felt as though she had just put a protective shield over her heart, like the covers used to keep children from poking into electrical outlets and getting shocked. Able simply to watch Charles's anger from a distance, she said, "I feel so good that your anger doesn't tear me up into little pieces anymore."

Simultaneously, Charles stood staring wide-eyed at his hands. He snarled, grabbed a newspaper, tore it in half, and threw it on the floor. Marilyn said it was as if he had been left holding a ball of angry energy, anger specifically intended to tear, as it had done to her before.

As we strengthen our non-defensive disposition, we can better manage how we use our own energy resources. It is this capacity to work with energy and to transform it that gives us the ability to develop and maintain a non-defensive stance regardless of how the other person reacts.

People often ask whether our defensiveness is genetic or cultural in origin. The cross-cultural pervasiveness of defensiveness suggests

---

2. Vicki Dello Joio, a Chi Kung teacher, artist, and founder of The Way of Joy, Oakland, California.

that a shift of evolutionary proportions[3] would be required to change human beings on a broad scale. This indicates that our defensiveness might be genetic, a residual quality left over from baring our teeth, growling, and putting up our claws whenever we felt threatened. But the speed with which a person can drop all defensiveness suggests an instantaneous energy shift that is psychological and spiritual in nature, rather than genetic. Whatever the sources of our defensiveness, we can concentrate on our own power to shift our energy, interaction by interaction.

---

3. Jane Mara, M.S.W., a therapist in Waldport, Oregon, was the first person to refer to non-defensive communication as an "evolutionary step."

13

The Practice of Becoming Non-Defensive

Internal shifts and external practice are like the chicken and the egg; it's hard to tell which comes first. Each one promotes the other. Shifting internally and practicing the various formats for asking questions, making statements, and predicting consequences are equally essential as we move toward becoming non-defensive.

I have discussed each form of communication separately—question, statement, and prediction—in order to clarify its non-defensive nature, function, and effect. This next-to-last chapter will include a variety of examples to demonstrate how these tools work together in three areas of interaction. Some examples will demonstrate using them briefly and some will model how to use all the formats together. My hope is that you will practice this process in a way that fits your own needs and life experiences.

Short Versions of the Non-Defensive Process

Putting too much emphasis on proper "technique," or trying to do each step every time we practice, can create more pressure, cause unnecessary awkwardness, and impede the learning process. For this reason, I want to start by focusing on how to use short versions of the non-defensive process in commonly occurring interactions.

Varying the Order: Using the Statement First

In many situations, the order of questions first, statements second, and predictions third seems like a natural progression. It is organic, in the sense that we gather as much information as possible before we react, then share our reactions, and, if necessary, make predictions to indicate how we will respond to choices the other person might make.

The most common variation is to start with a statement. We may want to clarify why we are having a certain conversation. Elaina might go back to Susan and say, "Something happened several years ago during a conversation we had that upset me, and I realize it still affects my relationship with you. Would you be willing to talk to me about it?" By making a clear statement before she asks Susan to discuss the dress incident, Elaina is letting Susan know her intentions. Susan will not feel surprised or set up when Elaina brings up an incident that happened years earlier.

Another time we may make a statement first is when we have a very strong reaction to something a person has said or done. If our feelings—anger, hurt, or fear—are strong, they could leak into a question, observational statement, or prediction and contaminate its neutrality. Here we may want to acknowledge our feelings in a statement before asking a question or making a prediction.

"I felt so angry about what you said that I am having a hard time asking you a sincere question about what you meant. But I do want to know why you said it. Would you be willing to tell me?"

Short Versions of the Entire Process

There are also many effective ways to use abbreviated versions of the entire process. We might ask one question, use the "When . . . and . . . then" version of a statement, and conclude with either a limit-setting or challenge–choice prediction.

Suppose we are responding to someone who feels defeated and finds it impossible to understand an issue, learn a new process, or complete some project. We can use a short non-defensive sequence, beginning with a question: "Do you mean you actually want to quit, or are you expressing frustration but still want to keep at it?"

If the person says, "I want to quit," we might say, "I would feel very upset if you quit because I believe that you can learn this. I think the biggest thing that would stop you is your own belief that you can't do it. If you decide to continue, I'd like to help you in any way I can."

In this case, after one question, we make a statement that expresses our reasoning, beliefs, and feelings. The statement is followed by one side of a prediction that is brief, honest, and supportive and holds the other person accountable for a decision. The relationship is likely to feel more equal and less condescending, whether the assisted person is a child or an adult.

Here, using a question, statement, and prediction together, even in brief form, helps prevent us from doing 90 percent of the work to aid someone who is resistant. It also often prompts more of a committed effort if the other person decides to continue the process. While this interchange can be expanded by going into more depth, done briefly it can still be highly effective.

If the person saying "I can't" is your son who doesn't want to do his math, you would probably not accept his decision to quit without consequence. In such a case, I would ask the same type of questions, express my faith in his ability, and offer my help only "if" he wants it. However, I would also express my unwillingness to simply agree to his giving up and not doing his assignment. I would make some additional predictions, which limit his free-time activities until he completes his homework or decides to get the help he needs.

Short Responses to Defensive Reactions

In similar fashion, we can approach many of the defensive reactions that others have. If a co-worker offers to help with a task but shrugs and grimaces, instead of either accepting the help or saying, "never mind," we can ask, "Do you feel pressured by having something extra added to your workload right now?"

If the person denies feeling pressured and says, "I'm fine, let's just get on with it," instead of being stuck with an unpleasant work partner, or trying to argue that we don't really need help, we can say, "You shrugged your shoulders and grimaced when you agreed to help, which felt unpleasant to me, so I'd rather do it myself."

Here, we may just use one question and one statement. Or we

could add one side of a prediction: "If I continue to feel as though you are irritated by my asking you for help, then I will ask someone else instead." We do not have to be caught in the bind of either accepting a moody task mate or proving that this person is irritable. We can quickly handle the situation non-defensively and protect ourselves.

Once again, how we respond depends on the circumstances. If a spouse or child gripes every time we ask for a contribution to the household's functioning, we probably don't want to handle the situation by turning down the help.

We can smooth our transition into non-defensiveness and strengthen our skills more quickly if we start by assuming that we do not have to carry out every step of this process each time we practice. Over time, we can apply the skills with increasing sophistication and reap additional benefits.

The Non-Defensive Process in the Context of Various Types of Relationships

When we use the "longer version" of a non-defensive interaction, we can ask content and process questions, use any or all of the four formats for making a statement, and use both formats for making predictions. The remainder of the chapter demonstrates how to apply this process in three general categories of relationships: peer relationships, non-peer (hierarchical) relationships, and group relationships. First, I will present a completely scripted example to demonstrate using all the parts together. Then, I will apply variations of the process to common situations in each of the three relationship categories.

Peer Relationships

For many of us, the easiest place to begin using non-defensive communication is in one-to-one relationships with peers—siblings, intimate partners, friends, or co-workers.

The following dialogue between Sally and Marcus reflects the issue—common to so many relationships—of one person who does not want to talk and the other who keeps probing. It models the sequential use of all eight basic formats for speaking non-defensively. While people rarely use every format in a single conversation, I think it is feasible to do so. It can bring clarity to a conversation, even in a matter of minutes, and provides a way for either person to respond to difficult issues without getting caught up in power struggle.[1] This example can also be applied to countless other situations where core issues such as denial, double messages, resistance, and invasiveness are present.

> SALLY: Are you upset about something? (*content question, neutral tone*).
>
> MARCUS: No, I'm *just fine!* (*denying problem but sending double message with tone and body language*).
>
> SALLY: Are you willing to talk to me about whatever you are thinking about right now? (*process question, neutral tone*).
>
> MARCUS: I told you, nothing is wrong! (*continuing denial and double messages*).
>
> SALLY: Well, I think you're telling me that you're in a good mood and nothing is bothering you (*statement, part 1, "I hear," overt message, neutral tone*).
>
> What I see when I look at you is that you are slumped in your chair, frowning intensely, and shaking your head. Your voice also sounds very harsh to me (*statement, part 2, "I see," covert message, neutral tone*).
>
> I don't believe you are feeling fine; I believe you are feeling pressured about something and are denying it, possibly because you want to figure it out by yourself (*statement, part 3, conclusions, interpretation of motivation, neutral tone*).
>
> I'm angry about getting double messages, and I have a huge urge to try to make you talk to me, but I know I can't make you. I also feel helpless because I don't know how to reach you. It's very hard for me to go about my day with

---

1. In cases where there is no conflict, using all the formats can enhance understanding and the flow of creative ideas.

you sitting here like this (*statement, part 4, full expression of thoughts, beliefs, and feelings, her own experience*).

If you don't talk to me, I believe you will continue to feel a lot of pressure inside and it may be harder to deal with whatever is bothering you (*challenge–choice prediction, part 1, neutral tone*).

If you do talk to me, I think you might get rid of some of the pressure and find it easier to figure things out (*challenge–choice prediction, part 2, neutral tone*).

If you decide you want to talk to me, then I would like to hear what's going on (*limit-setting prediction, part 1, neutral tone*).

If you don't want to talk to me, then I'm not going to try to convince you to do it (*limit-setting prediction, part 2, neutral tone*).

Marcus has eight different opportunities to decide whether to respond defensively or non-defensively. Sally may give all three parts of the position statement and both parts of both predictions consecutively if Marcus doesn't respond. It is important that Sally pause and give herself space between each part of her position statement and her predictions so she doesn't slip into an accusatory tirade. On the other hand, if Sally is silent too long between each part, she may load the silence with intense feelings or expectations. By pausing to breathe between each part of the position statement and both sides of each prediction, she also gives Marcus time to respond if he wants to, but without pressuring him.

If we are using a non-defensive sequence such as this and the other person speaks up defensively, we can just go back to what we are saying and not get hooked into argument. For example, if someone interjects, "I'm not denying *anything!*" we can just continue, saying, "I don't want to try to prove that you are, I'm simply describing how it seems to me."

In this case, Sally made the challenge–choice predictions before the limit-setting ones. She wanted Marcus to have that information to consider before she made it clear that she would not try to convince him to talk. She ended on a note that respected his freedom to choose silence. If the challenge–choice had come after the limit-setting prediction, it could well have sounded like: I'm not going to try to convince you to talk, but you are going to have a tough time if you don't. In other cases, the challenge–choice prediction might be used last.

As they work together on this issue, Marcus could also ask questions and make statements and predictions for Sally. For example, Marcus might want to talk to Sally about not pressuring him to speak when he is upset.

> MARCUS: Are you willing to not push me when I am in a bad mood and don't feel like talking? (*process question, neutral tone*).
>
> SALLY: Well, you would probably never talk if I didn't! (*resistance to accepting his unwillingness to talk and desire to control his choices*)
>
> MARCUS: Are you saying that you are going to keep trying to make me talk even if I'm not ready? (*process question, neutral tone*).
>
> SALLY: Well, no, I guess it's your choice. (*reluctant acceptance of his choice to refrain from talking*).
>
> MARCUS: I hear you saying that you won't try to force me to talk to you (*statement, part 1, "I hear," neutral tone*).
>
> Your words were that you "guess" it's my choice, and you're frowning and sighing and shrugging your shoulders (*statement, part 2, "I see," covert message, neutral tone*).
>
> I believe you sound reluctant to stop pressuring me, and I think it will be hard for you to accept it if I don't talk right away when you want me to (*statement, part 3, conclusions, interpretation of motivation, neutral tone*).
>
> I feel frustrated. I want to learn to be more open when I am upset, but not because I am giving in to your pressure (*statement, part 3, full expression of thoughts, beliefs, and feelings, his own experience*).
>
> If you do pressure me, then I will refuse to even consider talking until you stop (*limit-setting prediction, part 1, neutral tone*).
>
> If you don't pressure me, then I'll talk as soon as I feel open enough (*limit-setting prediction, part 2, neutral tone*).
>
> If you don't trust that I will talk to you after I think things through for a little while, then I believe it will be

hard for you to stop pressuring me (*challenge–choice pre-diction, part 2, neutral tone*).

If you can trust that I will talk to you after I work through my feelings a little bit, I think it would be easier for you to stop trying to control whether I talk immediately or not (*challenge–choice prediction, part 1, neutral tone*).

The conversation initiated by Sally and the one initiated by Marcus do not have to be mutually exclusive. Marcus can have a goal of becoming more open when he is upset, while Sally can have the goal of not trying to control whether he talks or not. Marcus can know that he will be more accountable for his own decisions about talking, and Sally can know she will be more accountable with regard to pressuring Marcus. Each will have consequences for their actions. This gives you one example of a conversation approached by two people when both parties are motivated to change.

How each of them responds the next time the issue comes up will determine how the interaction goes. Sally may say she won't pressure him to talk and do it anyway, or she might try to not pressure him and sulk silently herself, or she might stick to her word. Marcus might ask her not to pressure him and then never talk about what it was that upset him, or he might be able to talk more quickly.

Many times, in intimate relationships, we get dragged down by each other's problems. A thorough non-defensive process enables each person to maintain enough separateness to be accountable for his or her own behavior. If Marcus chooses not to talk, then Sally, instead of getting bogged down in a destructive conflict, must decide what to do next with her time. Marcus then has the space to think about whatever is bothering him, perhaps even his own isolation and inability to talk. Such separateness and accountability afford us a healthy independence, which I think is essential in order to support one another's growth and come together in real intimacy.

If one person is still engaging in defensiveness or power struggle, the person using these steps might take only sixty to ninety seconds to gather as much information as possible and then make statements and predictions. This small investment of time is quite different from a typical argument, which might go on indefinitely.

Carefully proceeding through these steps saves the person from entering the power struggle, while preserving openness, honesty, and integrity. The person does not have to accept the other's denial, does not need to ignore double messages, and does not have to try to prove the validity of any observations or reactions, but can deal with any issue in a straightforward way, making observations, expressing reactions, and setting boundaries clearly, even without the other person's cooperation. Likewise, the other person does not have to accept being coerced into talking or engage in long periods of sullenness as the only available means of resisting pressure.

Having both people use the non-defensive process provides the most information possible about each person's reactions, choices, and possible consequences. It keeps the feedback loop wide open. Such a conversation may last only a few minutes, or it may expand into an in-depth discussion of related issues, the kind of heart-to-heart conversation in which both people are fully engaged, the kind of mutual exchange in which new insights are gained and emotional and spiritual bonds are strengthened.

The Weight of Negative Social Sanction

In many peer relationships, one person may make a comment that carries the weight of negative social sanctions. We may be in a relationship where one person has more power in some way: psychologically, socially, professionally, or financially. Sex roles may be a factor. Marcus's refusal to talk, for example, might fall in the category of "You know how men are, they never want to talk about their feelings." Sally's insistence that he talk could put her in the category of women who nag.

In other kinds of peer relationships, such as those with co-workers, some of us may be less fearful about changing our ways of communicating. We may not care so much how the other person ultimately feels about us. On the other hand, we could have less trust and feel more risk of changing how we interact because we may fear losing our job if we create an irresolvable conflict with a co-worker. Or we may fear the person will gossip about us and damage our reputation in the workplace or community.

Although it may be difficult to be open and vulnerable when a peer makes a comment that carries negative social sanctions, I firmly believe that, when we feel able and willing to do so, we can create more strength within ourselves by using the non-defensive process.

Quita, a black woman, described the following incident during a workshop. She and a white female co-worker had entered an elevator together after the lunch hour. It was raining outside and Quita had forgotten her umbrella. The white woman looked at her and said, "You people are so lucky, you don't need umbrellas." The workshop members found it impossible to interpret, in a way that was not denigrating, a remark that suggests a whole race of people doesn't need umbrellas.

When people make jarring remarks, our most common reactions are to withdraw, make a sarcastic response, or lash back in anger. Saying nothing does not eliminate the wound, and reacting with sarcasm or anger often results in the other person's projecting blame onto us for making a mountain out of a molehill. Quita had reacted with angry silence.

Quita, along with others in the group, thought of some possible non-defensive questions, any one (or several) of which she might have asked:

> What do you mean when you suggest that I "don't need" an umbrella?
> When you refer to "you people," who do you mean?
> What is it about me that makes you think I won't get wet?
> Do you mean that I would stay dry in the rain, or that I wouldn't care if my clothes got wet (or did you mean something else altogether)?
> What do you mean by "lucky"?

We can't know the other woman's actual thought process and motivation. She may have been thinking that Quita was unwise to be out in the rain without an umbrella and made her remark as a conscious put-down. Or, without being consciously aware, she might add further injury to the insult by suggesting that she thought the nap of Quita's hair would keep her dry. Or, thinking, She's been out in the rain and her hair still looks good. Mine would be a limp, ugly mess if I did that, she might have intended her remark as a compliment, not having the presence of mind to realize the level of prejudice it exposed.

If Quita felt uncomfortable telling the woman her own reactions, without just accepting the comment in mute anger, she could let her questions give the other woman the responsibility for clarifying and exposing her meaning. If she felt comfortable saying more, Quita might state directly to the woman the kind of impact the comment had on her. The following is an example of being very straightforward without engaging in power struggle. Quita could say something like this in her own words, or anything else she felt:

"I think you're telling me that I am very lucky to be a black woman because we don't need umbrellas when it rains. While you are outwardly making a statement intended to sound like a compliment, I'm watching you making a huge generalization about black people based solely on the fact that I forgot my umbrella today.

"I don't know if you intended to hurt me or not, but I was truly upset that I forgot my umbrella. I feel angry and humiliated that you would believe my having no umbrella was related to the color of my skin."

If the woman tried to dismiss Quita's response, saying, "Oh, I didn't really mean anything by what I said," Quita could predict, if she felt comfortable doing so, part or all of the following:

"If you want to think I am overreacting, then I think that you may go away blaming me for causing a conflict. If you are willing to examine your comment, I think you might find reasons to believe that what you said was hurtful and showed prejudice by making generalizations based on inaccurate assumptions."

In the war model, to be so open with a peer who has said something hurtful, something that adds to the ongoing pain of prejudice, would be unthinkable. By war-model standards, being vulnerable would constitute handing power over to the other person. By nondefensive standards, however, if we feel able to do so, staying open in such situations enables us to maintain our awareness of what we see happening, keep our self-respect, and set our boundaries.

What our peers do and say can push our buttons about deeper personal issues, such as our fears about competency, rejection, and conflict. They can also cause personal wounds that may be magnified by prejudice.

Thus, even in the context of our peer relationships—family, co-worker, and friend—many of us do not maintain our own personal authority well. Too often we react to people who have no actual authority over us as if they do. We allow them to say and do things that make us feel disempowered. While our fears may be legitimate, we can gain much more ability to effectively process, transform, and feed back what another person puts out to us.

Non-Peer Relationships

Non-peer (hierarchical) relationships have a power differential, where one person has more authority than the other. Examples are parent-child relationships, supervisor-employee relationships, and certain professional relationships such as doctor-patient or therapist-client. The nature of the disparity may lie in the professional's having more knowledge or more legal authority.

Family Relationships

Our bond with our parents is usually our first major relationship, one in which the power differential is extreme. In some workshops for parents, I have had each person take a turn lying on the floor, while the rest of us stand around, cooing, "Oh, the baby is so cute." Sometimes we put our heads down close or pat the person on the head. Many people find the experience to be quite intense, and most come out of it knowing exactly why we have so many children's stories about giants. The person taking the part of the child looks up at the adults towering overhead like giant redwoods.

Psychologically, I think that experience exemplifies the kind of power we start out perceiving our parents to have. Even as adults, many of us have not shed that imprint. Our parents' control—over us and over how we interact with our siblings and other peers—has a huge effect on how we deal with our own authority and the authority of others. Most adults carry around a great deal of parental baggage that depletes our personal strength and ability to fully mature.

While it is possible to address issues of parental authority indirectly, most of us could do much more to develop direct non-defensive conversations with our own parents. Doing so can be a very freeing experience. In the majority of cases, I think the relationship will improve rather than deteriorate. If it does deteriorate, I think we are still faced with one of two choices: to live our lives without asserting our own individuality or to assert it and let our parents choose how they will respond.

My own experience leads me to believe that, once we decide to assert ourselves, it is often easier to assume our adult stature with our parents than we think it might be. One man said to me, "When I finally spoke up to my father, it was so easy. Suddenly, I looked at him, and he seemed so much smaller. It was shocking to think I had been afraid of him until I was almost fifty."

Differences with our parents frequently affect major events in our lives. We feel a loss of control about creating what we want, even when we plan our own commencement from graduate school, our weddings, or our children's bar mitzvahs. I would like to see adults assert their wishes more clearly and respectfully. Often we are either unassertive or we get mad and express ourselves harshly.

When Caitlin was planning her wedding, she knew her parents would object that her ceremony was not in accordance with the tenets of the church in which she had been raised. Since they were outspoken with their judgments, she feared they would express negative opinions at the wedding and dampen her joy on the occasion. She wanted to be married in a community ceremony, but her anguish over her parents' disapproval ran so deep that she thought of having a private ceremony or going to a justice of the peace. Finally, she decided to ask her parents, "Do you think you can feel happy at my wedding if I don't do it according to the traditions of your religion?"

As they inwardly struggled with their answers, Caitlin also talked about her own feelings and needs. In part of her statement—prior to making her prediction—she expressed her feelings about the choice they might make.

> Caitlin: I love you and would be incredibly sad to be married without you. At the same time, I do not want to have you there if you act judgmental or say critical things to people about the ceremony Steve and I have created. It is in keeping with our own beliefs, and I don't want to feel pressure or conflict because you disapprove. I don't want anything to damage the joy of our wedding day (*statement*).
>
> If you do not believe you can come to the ceremony

without having a negative attitude or saying critical things, then I would rather you not come (*first prediction, one side*).

If you don't come, we could plan some kind of reception with you and your church friends after we get back from our honeymoon. We could share our happiness in a way that would feel better to all of us (*second prediction, one side*).

If you can come and not express negative feelings about the wedding, I would be so happy and proud to have you there it would make my joy complete (*prediction, other side*).

Caitlin's non-defensive process was a success, but not just because her parents decided to go to the wedding. It was successful because Caitlin was willing to demonstrate her authority with regard to creating her own wedding, while offering her parents clear choices in a loving way.

I believe this process also helps to create healthy relationships between parents and young children. When we ask non-defensive questions, we honor their individuality—their unique feelings, beliefs, and thoughts. And when we make statements, we say what we hear, see, and experience in a non-lecturing way and so treat our children with more equality. When we set effective limits, we provide our children with security and encourage respect, competency, and reciprocity. A comment children often make to those of us who interact with them according to these principles is "You treat me like a real person." I believe such communication will encourage our children to be respectful without fearing authority figures or needing to engage in so much rebellion.

Many adults who were not treated respectfully by their parents have a fear of authority. They often translate it to others outside their family of origin. Harriet told me about her experience with her mother-in-law, Gwen, who would sometimes come to visit on the weekend. When Gwen arrived on Friday afternoon before her son came home from work, she would begin to move their living room furniture around, making comments like, "This would look good over here, wouldn't it?"

Terrified of the ramifications of trying to deal with her husband's mother regarding this issue, Harriet came to dread Gwen's visits. It never occurred to her to approach the situation by asking a simple question: "Do you dislike the way our furniture is arranged?"

Gwen did have skill in interior decorating, but the two women had not found a positive way to talk with and learn from each other. Harriet shut out all advice from Gwen; Gwen would rearrange the furnishings as if the house were hers. Eventually, they did talk, and Harriet was able to ask a number of questions, including this one: "What kind of effect do you think it has on me when you move the furniture without asking me?" (*process question, neutral tone*). She also told Gwen how it made her feel.

> HARRIET: I hear you sometimes asking about whether something would look good in a certain place (*statement, part 1, neutral tone*).
>
> At the same time, it seems like, rather than really asking for my opinion, you have already decided and moved the furniture before you ask (*statement, part 2, neutral tone*).
>
> When you just move things without asking me, I feel frustrated. I don't feel that I have control over my own furniture, and I start to get nervous about having you come over—which I don't like because I want to have a good relationship with you. I do like some of your ideas, but I end up resisting all of them when I don't feel I have any choice. I want to make my own choices, and I also want to consult Tom about setting up the living room so it fits both our needs (*statement, part 3, personal experience, full expression*).
>
> If you don't move things without talking to me, then I will feel that you respect this as our home and will feel more open to hearing your ideas (*limit-setting prediction, part 1, neutral tone*).

Harriet chose *not* to add another side to her prediction, but she could have said, "If you continue to move things without talking to me, I will ask you not to do it" (*limit-setting prediction, part 2, neutral tone*).

We might get so outraged thinking about such invasive behavior that we find ourselves wishing Harriet would really nail Gwen. But entrenching the power struggle would be disempowering to both women. They can gain confidence and each other's acceptance more easily if at least one of them initiates a non-defensive process. After Harriet spoke to her mother-in-law the first time, Gwen was a bit huffy, to say the least, but they gradually worked on it. Within a year they came to a place where they could laugh about their earlier conflicts. Gwen would say, "Well, I guess I was a little dominating." Harriet would respond, "And I guess I was pretty passive. I just stood there and let you move all the furniture around." Over time, as people build family ties, they can often look back and laugh over earlier problems. However, given the added difficulty of blending more than one family system, achieving such change using traditional defensive modes could take many years. And I believe there is greater risk that the changes might be for the worse.

Being non-defensive certainly does not mean we can always easily resolve issues to our satisfaction. Sometimes we can't. At each juncture here, I want to acknowledge that any situation I have described *could* become more complicated. For example, Gwen might not be open to giving up any control, and Harriet's husband might deny that there was any problem: "It's no big deal. Let her do what she wants, and we'll move the furniture back when she's gone." I think we have to evaluate any situation—"Am I ready to take this on?"—and, if so, pick a manageable piece of the puzzle to start with. For me, it's also important to remember that whatever I do *not* take on can give a shape to my life that I do not want.

Supervisory Relationships

We often carry this fear of authority into many relationships outside our families. I see supervisors at work who feel frustrated that employees refuse to speak up about important issues, upset that the employees seem to feel threatened by them in ways they don't need to be. The millworker I mentioned previously was stunned at how differently his former buddies treated him from the moment he was promoted to supervisor.

Many of us react to those who have, or seem to have, more authority than we do by using defensive modes that range from surrender and sabotage to withdrawal and defiance. For example, when Phoebe warned Wayne that a production method he was implementing had been tried in the past and had caused serious problems, she became defensive and resorted to an entrapping silence. She even failed to notify him when the problems she had predicted began to crop up.

In retrospect she realized that her behavior was not substantially different from how she had reacted to her father, who had not listened to her advice either. She remembered an incident when she told him the lawn mower was almost out of gas and he ignored her, thinking he had recently filled the tank. She thought, Fine, it will serve you right when you get out on the back forty and run out of gas. Which he did.

As an adult, she acted out the same scenario with Wayne. I never cease to be amazed at how often we run into the same situations in life until we learn to deal with them in a way that resolves the issue inside of us. When Phoebe got called on the carpet by a higher-up for not advising Wayne when the problems began to occur, she used her childhood defense: "I tried to tell him and he wouldn't listen." We can never feel completely free or fully competent until we learn how to non-defensively assert our own authority.

Even if a supervisor does refuse to listen to us, we often have appropriate options. When Wayne refused to listen, Phoebe could have respectfully asked him any one of several questions:

> Do you believe me when I tell you about the problems we had before when we used this process?
> Do you believe it will be different this time for some reason?
> Do you think I am objecting simply because I have been here a long time and don't want to try something new?

If Wayne did not become more open to discussing the topic, Phoebe could express her own opinion, and make some predictions:

> PHOEBE: I think you are saying this process will work (*statement, part 1, "I hear," neutral tone*), and what I see is that you are ignoring information I'm giving you about what happened before (*statement, part 2, "I see," neutral tone*).
>
> I feel confident it is the same process we used before and that we'll have the same problems. But I know that you're the boss, so I'll do what you want and I will continue to do my work well (*statement, part 4, personal experience, full expression*).
>
> If we run into problems, then I'll report them to you so

you can decide what to do *(limit-setting prediction, part 1, neutral tone)*. If not, I'll just keep on truckin' and doing my job" *(limit-setting prediction, part 2, neutral tone)*.

As demonstrated here, Phoebe could have asked several thought-provoking questions, confidently stated her position, and clearly predicted how she would respond, all in a respectful way. If the anticipated problems were serious enough, or if she feared being held accountable for them, she could give a written copy of her viewpoint to Wayne and keep a copy for herself. Had she done so, the odds are higher that he might have listened. Even if he did not, she would continue to strengthen her own skills. Instead of hearing the excuse that "he wouldn't listen," the next supervisor up the line might notice the wisdom, clarity, and professionalism she displayed in a difficult situation.

Group Relationships

The complexities of individual personalities, past histories, authority issues, group dynamics, and various cultural climates all come into play in the group setting. A group thus provides a fertile field for practice, be it a staff meeting at work, a public forum, a party with friends, or family members at the dinner table.

Whenever a person is added to a given group, the number of possible relationships within the group increases in progressively larger increments. A couple has one relationship. If the couple has one child, the number of relationships increases to four. By the time the couple has a second child, the number of different relationship possibilities jumps to eleven—six dyads, four triads, and the foursome itself. The different combinations appear below. We often forget to pay attention to each of these relationships, yet doing so can strengthen the entire family unit.

Father—Mother	Father—Mother—Daughter
Father—Son	Father—Mother—Son
Father—Daughter	Father—Daughter—Son
Mother—Son	Mother—Daughter—Son
Mother—Daughter	The Whole Family
Son—Daughter	

In a group of ten, there are forty-five possible dyads and over two hundred possible relationship combinations. Even though many of these sets of relationships may never be actualized, each one would have different dynamics and would contribute different weaknesses and strengths to the functioning of the group.

On the one hand, the complexity this represents in terms of effective communication can seem overwhelming. Even with a small group of people in a room, there is potential for the dynamics of a hundred or more relationships to be going on at different levels. On the other hand, there are exciting possibilities for maximizing the potential creativity inherent in the variety of relationships within a group. In professional settings, working with different mixes of personnel within a team or department can open the door to the greater creative potential of the group as a whole.

Shifting Alignments

In our traditional methods for communicating, confidentiality—keeping many things secret—is central to how we protect ourselves. Two or three people may have privately discussed an issue and come to agreement. In family dynamics, the issue may be about a reaction to something one family member has done. At work, it may involve several people discussing an issue that will be discussed at a team or staff meeting.

After the private discussion, the most vocal person may speak up at the family dinner or during the staff meeting, thinking it is with the support of the other(s). The person speaking will then feel betrayed when others, who have privately expressed agreement, either remain silent or actually disagree with what is being said to the group. Many times, such shifting alignments are based not on intentional divisiveness but on fear of speaking up in front of various family members or staff people, on shifts in perception based on additional information, or on peer pressure.

The speaker may feel in a bind and thus not expose what the others said privately, but nevertheless feel betrayed. If the speaker does bring up the discrepancy, it is likely to be in an accusatory way: "That's not what you said the other day!" Either response, maintaining confidentiality or going on the attack, will have lingering ramifications, not only for the relationship among any subgroup but also because the dynamics of that interaction will influence the group as a whole.

Even when it is not an intentional betrayal, problems of duplicity—where people's alignments shift depending on what grouping they are presently in—happen constantly. Although confidentiality has a significant place in our lives, I believe it has been overused. It has allowed people to be less accountable for what they do and say in various settings than they should be, thereby greatly affecting healthy group interaction. During the Iran-Contra investigation, Edmund Muskie said, "Every time you become overly obsessed with secrecy, you neglect process." I believe this idea is also borne out in recovery groups, which emphasize the degree to which secrecy can foster illness in family systems.

The following example depicts how one could use more open nondefensive communication at a staff meeting when someone shifts position.

SPEAKER: Has your position shifted since we talked the other day? (*content question, neutral tone*). If so, what caused the shift? (*process question, neutral tone*).

I understood you to say that you supported the course of action I am proposing (*statement, part 1, "I hear," neutral tone*), and now I see that you're expressing doubts (*statement, part 2, "I see," neutral tone*). I would like to have the security of knowing more clearly where you stand on this issue (*statement, part 3, full expression, your own experience*).

If you have mixed feelings about it, I'd like to know that and hear both sides so I have more information, rather than not know where you stand (*limit-setting prediction, part 1, neutral tone*). If you have decided for sure what your viewpoint is, I'd like to make sure I have a clear picture of it (*limit-setting prediction, part 2, neutral tone*).

I think if we hold back on expressing our thoughts and observations regarding this course of action, we might be missing important information we need for our decision-making process (*challenge–choice prediction, part 1, neutral tone*). If we all express the full gamut of our viewpoints, we can make the most effective decisions as we proceed (*challenge–choice prediction, part 2, neutral tone*).

Here, quickly using all eight steps, we can acknowledge the dynamic that is occurring, effectively protect ourselves, hold the other person more accountable, be respectful of the fact that people's positions do shift, and provide non-judgmental guidance for the group. While we could use a more compact version, in doing so we may lose important pieces of clarity. I think the same principles apply in all groups.

The risk of bringing things out into the open is that others may hold back their opinion in a private dialogue for fear it will later be publicly exposed. We often barter confidentiality for becoming privy to others' thoughts and feelings. I frankly doubt that it is necessarily a good trade because it often causes people to carry around many unresolved issues, including feelings of conflicted loyalty and betrayal.

"A chain is only as strong as its weakest link." I think this saying is more applicable when we use traditional communication methods than when we use non-defensive ones. We have had a strong tendency to allow the most negative person, whom I would consider to be the weakest link in terms of openness, confidence, compassion, and problem-solving skills, to dominate the energy and even the activities of the family or group. When we use a non-defensive process, negative people do not have so much power.

Divisiveness

Some people are more actively divisive. Such a person may be openly negative or use forms of subtle manipulation to break down trust in a group. In extended families or at work, this may be a person who gossips back and forth, appearing to be most closely bonded to whichever person is being addressed at the moment. However, this is someone who accelerates conflicts by exaggerating what each person said to the others.

Katie described a difficult situation that had confronted her during staff meetings at work. Her organization dealt with a great deal of confidential information. At the conclusion of several recent staff meetings, Simon, a team member, had stared directly at Katie and said, "Let's *all* keep this information confidential."

Katie felt trapped. She didn't want to defend herself and make it look like she had a reason to do so, but she knew her silence left her defenseless against her co-worker's non-verbal insinuations that she was somehow leaking confidential information. She feared the effect Simon's obvious but covert message would have on others. She decided she would talk to her supervisor, but realized that distrust had been planted in the minds of other group members and, unless she made "a public issue" (as she referred to it) out of Simon's seeming accusation, others in the group might feel ongoing distrust of her.

So many issues overlap when we deal with several other people at once that it is often extremely difficult to speak up. Moreover, even when others treat us disrespectfully in a family gathering or professional meeting, we are still very reluctant to deal with it in a group setting because we feel we would be creating conflict. I believe, when one person chooses to use the group as a forum for defensive maneuvers, it is appropriate to deal with it in the group. An interaction between two people in any group virtually always affects others as well. Simon's behavior had already put anyone who was not oblivious to his non-verbal message in the position of deciding whether or not to trust Katie.

It is possible to deal with such issues directly with less chance of accelerating the conflict. The next time Simon directed his implicating gaze at Katie, she asked him a question. "Are you aware that while you were talking about the confidentiality issue, you looked only at me, and that you have repeated that pattern for several meetings in a row?"

Simon flushed and said, "I don't know what you're talking about, unless it's your own guilty conscience." This mounted the attack more directly, and Katie responded.

"I hear you suggesting that I am in error and that I may be reacting in a paranoid way because I have done something to break confidence. What I have observed is that each time you begin your statement about confidentiality, you make eye contact solely with me and do not break it until you finish the sentence.

"It has felt so pointed to me that I would find it hard to believe that you're not aware of it, and I am concerned about the subtle implication it has, which I think you just made more overt—that I need to pay more attention to being confidential. Since I know that I am extremely cautious about never violating confidentiality, I am curious as to why you are so focused on me when you say this.

"If you have some concern, then I hope you will come to me directly, as I would to you. If not, and you focus exclusively on me again, then I will bring it up rather than ignore it."

When we are non-defensive, speaking openly about what we see happening in a group can often go very smoothly, as it did for Katie. Whether Simon's behavior came out of misunderstanding or an effort to be divisive, Katie resolved the situation and earned the respect of others in the group. Although Katie was able to use a thorough non-defensive process in this case, she did have other alternatives, such as using an abbreviated version of the process, or perhaps using just a question. Or, if Katie found it too difficult to address the issue in the group, she could speak to Simon privately or with her supervisor present. The main difficulty with a private meeting is that if Simon is making false implications, he could also distort what she has privately said and continue to discredit her. If Katie has her supervisor's support, either one might address the incident the next time it occurs.

Interrupting the Flow of Group Interaction

This same process can also be applied in the classroom. One student sitting in the back of the room—sighing, yawning loudly, or reading a newspaper—can disrupt the cohesiveness of the class and also injure the instructor's confidence. The instructor can speak to students directly about such reactions.

"Are you bored? When you yawn and sigh loudly, what kind of effect do you think it has on the whole group?

"I find that your behavior distracts me, and I am very conscious of your energy dampening my own enthusiasm. I often feel compelled to try to draw you in or figure out what is going on for you. I don't want to have your seeming lack of interest affect the whole class, so I wanted to bring it up and deal with it directly.

"If you continue to act bored, I will not focus on it so much. If you decide to participate, I will welcome that."

When anyone disrupts the group process, and we do nothing even though we are bothered by it (we may be withdrawing to escape), everyone feels the impact to one degree or another. One person's antagonism can affect the gestalt of the whole atmosphere.

Likewise, if a student is asking sarcastic questions to prove a point, I would ask a direct question, perhaps followed by a prediction.

"Do you want my answer, or are you asking the question sarcastically to prove me wrong? If you are genuinely curious, I'd be happy to answer. If not, I'd rather you just explained to me directly why you disagree, so I can respond as accurately as possible to the issue you are concerned about."

Dealing with one or more individual students openly often can easily solve the disruption problem.[2] They become more conscious of their own behavior. I have seen students switch quickly from sarcasm to openness and genuinely participate in learning, once the interruptive behavior is addressed directly. Depending on how disruptive and how old a student is, I might state that I will not focus on this behavior if the student remains negative, or I might ask the student to leave until he or she can be present without interfering with the class interactions. An entire class can shift to being more engaged after a teacher deals openly, gently, and firmly with one disruptive member.

The Naysayer in Any Group

We can also deal effectively—at home and at work—with the naysayer who shuts down a problem-solving process or a brainstorming session by suggesting that various ideas "won't work." We may be planning an outdoor wedding for our daughter, and one family member says, "We'll get rained out for sure." We may be deciding where to locate a hot tub in the backyard and hear a comment such as, "Everyone will be tracking into the house wet!" I have a friend who calls such people the "doom, gloom, and pestilence crowd." For some reason, we give such pessimists a great deal of power to impede the creative process. Either we drop the idea or we spend effort to con-

---

2. Disruptive boredom, hostility, and sarcasm can be dealt with in a similar way at home or in professional meetings.

vince the naysayer that it will work. Such people can kill the joy of planning any event or project.

We can deal directly with such negativity by asking questions.

"Do you believe there is any way we can plan for this and make it work, or do you think it simply won't work?"

"Are you aware that you often immediately respond to ideas with a strong negative reaction?"

"What specifically about this idea do you think is a problem? Do you see any good points?"

Depending on how the person responds, we can then express our own thoughts and make predictions. The following example has several predictions, along with the statement.

"I hear you having mostly negative opinions about any idea we suggest, and then I tend to shut down and get depressed and feel like giving up. I want to be able to hear about potential problems and still keep a positive spirit about coming up with good ideas, so I want to change how I react when you say something that negates an idea.

"If you want to tell me what specific problems you see, then I'll listen so we can address the problems and make the plan work or come up with a better idea. If you just want me to give up the whole idea, I'm not willing to do that automatically unless most of us agree that some other idea is better.

"If you stay negative, I won't try to convince you to agree. I'll just focus on talking with others who want to find positive solutions. If you contribute positive ideas as well as negative ones, I'd be glad and will feel more open to what you have to say.

"Frankly, I suspect that if you focus only on why ideas *won't* work, you'll feel more depressed and defeated. I think you'd feel better if you focused more on what *can* work."

Having such a conversation with a person whose negative energy puts a wet blanket on projects can also free up everyone else and relieve them from being sucked into a depressed energy field. A person's non-defensive dialogue with one other individual can change the entire group dynamics. It enables us to keep our own authority rather than become disempowered by the group's "weakest link."

A World of Opportunities

Gandhi once suggested that anything we do is simultaneously unimportant and vitally important. I believe that each interaction is a microcosm of a whole relationship. If we react to a current incident in ways that are based on old unproductive habits, that response may not matter so much because another opportunity to change will come along soon. On the other hand, if we do make a significant change in our patterns of response, our action will matter a great deal because it could change the whole relationship. The part can change the whole.

We have countless interactions from which to choose opportunities to practice becoming non-defensive. We can practice with or without other people's cooperation. We may practice sporadically, putting in more effort at some times than at others. We may use the process and think we are being non-defensive when we are still trying to get the other person to cooperate. We may accomplish the goal of opening our heart, even if our words aren't completely non-defensive at every moment.

For me, becoming a non-defensive person is a lifelong practice. Our whole family practices—Monza and I, our daughter Ami, her husband Jesse—as well as others in our larger circle of family and friends. Our interactions are increasingly rich, but it doesn't mean we have no conflict. It means we have more capacity to *resolve* conflict. Instead of feeling alienated, we usually come through it feeling stronger and closer.

The Breakfast Club provides a powerful example of what can happen when each of us openly reveals more of our experience. In that film, a diverse group of students—"a brain, an athlete, a basket case, a princess, and a criminal"—was put in a room, essentially without supervision, for one day as part of a disciplinary "Saturday school." Left to their own devices, the students began the day by expressing animosity, judgments, and accusations. But as they gradually shared their experiences and pain, they came to understand and care for one another and the day became a transforming experience for each of them. They learned firsthand what Henry Wadsworth Longfellow meant when he said, "If we could read the secret history of our enemies, we would find in each [person's] life sorrows and suffering enough to disarm all hostility."

In one of her college papers, my daughter wrote that "the burden of understanding is compassion, and since most of us fear the burden, we narrow our vision, not realizing that we are entrapping ourselves. The only way to free ourselves is to accept the burden." When we are in power struggle, we see openness as dangerous and avoid it, thereby missing the understanding, compassion, and freedom that can come with it. As we practice being non-defensive, we can accept this challenge to be open. We can become more fully integrated and secure, have deeper bonds of intimacy with others, and fulfill our own creative potential.

CONCLUSION

Peace and Power

Albert Einstein said, "It has become appallingly clear that our technology has surpassed our humanity." By "humanity," I believe Einstein was referring to our capacity to treat one another with compassion, to work together to solve the problems we face as a species, and to envision ways to align our destinies as *Homo sapiens* with the survival of the intricate web of all creation. Although I agree with him, I also believe we *can* change our course before we allow technology to completely overwhelm us. I think we are currently witnessing a deepening shift in human consciousness, demonstrated by the growing number of people who are affirming the relationships among quantum physics, deep ecology, feminist theory, spirituality, psychology, and social justice. Many of us realize that only if we act upon an ethic of interdependence will we ensure the survival of civilization for future generations. My hope is that Powerful, Non-Defensive Communication can be a tool for the continuing evolution of human consciousness.

In order for us to close the gap between our vast technology and our full humanity, I believe we must recognize that the methods we use for person-to-person verbal communication are tied umbilically to the expression of our human nature. How we communicate not only shapes our individual lives, it also drives our human destiny. How we talk and listen creates enormous energy, and that energy has inestimable power. One of our primary tasks, I would suggest, is to hold ourselves accountable for the power we wield with every question, every statement, every prediction we make.

Power is customarily defined as "an ability either to produce or to undergo an effect." In his article on "Two Kinds of Power," Bernard Loomer suggests that the kind of power we use determines our level of "individual and social fulfillment."[1] He suggests that "our lives and our thoughts" have traditionally been dominated by what he calls "unilateral power . . . a non-mutual power," designed to control and manipulate others. That definition, I believe, fits the understanding of power we express when we are entrenched in what I have labeled the war model of communication.

Since the focus of unilateral power is on controlling others, it follows that being influenced by someone else, or even receiving anything from others, "means weakness and a lack of power," in Loomer's terms. This causes us to ward off any influence others might have over us and breaks down the give-and-take required for reciprocal relationships. It also means that we are likely to experience someone else's gain in power as "a loss of our own power and therefore our status and sense of worth." Moreover, we often respond to someone else's efforts to control us with a unilateral attempt to be the one who controls.

Many people refer to unilateral power as the "power *over*" species of power. It *does* have "the ability to produce an effect," but that effect is rarely lasting and often unsatisfying in the long run. It simply creates ongoing struggle. Moreover, it only focuses on one half of the whole definition of power because it doesn't place a positive value on "undergo[ing] an effect."

When I think about how many people I know who feel weak, even when they receive loving help from others, or doubt their own self-worth in the face of someone else's accomplishments, I am keenly aware of how many of us share assumptions about power that we accept as givens—that power is about *over* and *under,* win and *lose.* When those assumptions are not questioned, the reality we build on them is also simply accepted as the norm. Thus, millions of people join together in the "virtual reality" created by the *unilateral* or "power over" understanding of power. And, as I have demonstrated in the first part of this book, the belief that we must have power *over* others in order to meet our needs and even to survive has had a catastrophic effect on all of us.

While I think it is impossible to have purely unilateral power, if it were, it would go all in one direction. Using an analogy of electricity,

---

1. Bernard M. Loomer, "Two Kinds of Power" (*Criterion* 15 [Winter 1976]: 10–29).

this movement is somewhat like the direct current (DC) electricity that Thomas Edison discovered.

When two people, each using unilateral power, try to interact, they are pitting their direct currents of energy against each other. While one or the other may have greater spurts of power, the ultimate effect of bringing two direct currents face-to-face is to create a series of sparks or mini-explosions. The greater the energy flow, the bigger the explosions. These are precisely analogous to the battles in the war model of communication.

Involvement in this kind of energy exchange is dangerous and frightening, no matter how often one "wins." A conversation between a priest and a "tyrant" in an episode of *The Twilight Zone* I saw long ago shows the result of committing our energy to seeking power over others. The tyrant says, "I have enemies. I will continue executions until I have no enemies. I can't live this way. I'm so afraid all the time. If a man has power, he has enemies. If you have power, you have no friends, only followers and enemies. The victory is not so sweet. It is not the taste of wine, it is the taste of ashes."

I think the tyrant aptly describes the nihilistic result of using our energy as unilateral power. Its effect on our individual lives may not result in physical death, but to varying degrees it certainly can and does destroy relationships. We defend ourselves by warding off the influence of others and assert ourselves by trying to gain control over other people's reactions. We become adversaries. Like the tyrant, we feel simultaneously victimized and justified in attacking others— we become "superior-victim attackers."

Any time we use defensive communication, we are attempting to use power over others—to control them—no matter how subtle our efforts or how much we think we have someone else's good in mind. Every interaction with another person becomes a microcosm of a use of power that ultimately skews the essential reciprocity of the whole relationship. When masses of people use power unilaterally and communicate defensively, they become the microcosmic parts of a larger community of energy, if you will, in conflict. Then each of these larger communities becomes a microcosm of the whole of human energy at war. We need to shift the power of human energy to another "current," as it were, in order to evolve to our next stage of consciousness. I believe talking non-defensively is an essential part of that process.

The second kind of power described by Loomer is "relational power," which others of us refer to as "power from within." Relational power, as it applies to communication, is the force that propels us to interact without trying to manipulate others into doing what we want. This kind of power incorporates both halves of the whole definition of power; relational power is focused on the ability both to produce *and* undergo an effect, to give *and* receive, because it is based on reciprocity. Or, to put it another way, I see relational power in keeping with Fritjof Capra's description of a healthy ecosystem or human community where the feedback loops are open.

Continuing this analogy of power, energy, and electricity, relational power, or power from within, is more like the alternating current (AC) discovered by Nikola Tesla. This form of electricity creates a steady flow because it doesn't all go from one direction to the other unilaterally. Instead, it moves back and forth, energy coursing in both directions, as in the circle-eight—∞—the symbol sometimes used to denote reciprocity. We can also relate the circle-eight to Capra's feedback loop, because each half of the loop "feeds back" into the other.

When we charge our human energy with relational power as we talk with each other, each interaction goes full "circle-eight," creating reciprocity and interdependence. Anytime one person or the other shuts the gate on the feedback or reciprocity loop, the give and take vanishes. If I apologize to you for something and you refuse my apology, you have shut the gate. If you accept my apology and give forgiveness back to me, but I don't accept that forgiveness, then I shut the gate. If I apologize, you accept my apology and forgive me, and I *do* accept your forgiveness, then the cycle is complete. Our energy flows in an alternating current.

Most of us have, at one time or another, felt the frustration of having the exchange of energy blocked. When the channels of reciprocity stay open, the flow of energy seems almost infinite. In fact, I don't believe it's coincidental that the circle-eight is not only a symbol for reciprocity but also for infinity; there is no end to the channel of energy when power from within is freely shared. On a wider community scale, we can create interlocking webs of reciprocity, relational power, and alternating currents of our energy when we communicate non-defensively in our full power from within. The hallmark of such exchange can be peace: peaceful power, even through challenges and conflict.

As each of us shifts to using our energy non-defensively, we create just such open channels. And we can still protect ourselves. Even in our open vulnerability, we are protected because we are able to make predictions that limit how much we give to anyone who is non-reciprocal.

I believe that at the very heart of non-defensiveness is the call to reject the concept of power over others as a viable understanding of sustainable power, and to use our *power from within* to manage our own energy in reciprocal ways.

I see no way to force others to change their concept of power or make one group of people stop hating another. However, I don't think we have to go out and try to persuade others to change their basic beliefs about how to use power, or even how to talk to each other, in order to succeed in using this process. Each of us who wishes to make a change in the use of our energy can simply begin to speak and listen non-defensively. Every time we do, we change how *we* use our own power. Interacting non-defensively, not bound in a struggle to gain control over someone else, we may find the other person more willing to disarm than we could have imagined. The whole process can be contagious, as each disarmed person offers the opportunity to another.

With our current view of human nature, I don't know what percentage of us would have to communicate non-defensively to create the critical mass necessary to have relational power become the norm. But I think it works as simply as adding rye flour to our bread dough. At some point, one granule of rye flour turns the dough into the makings for rye bread instead of white bread. One more grain creates a different reality.

In the same way, I think that someday one more person speaking non-defensively will shift our collective energy so that it becomes "normal" to use our power in reciprocal ways. Until that day, I think we can begin to envision the possibilities for our own human evolution to accelerate so that we honor the diversity among us, create strong and compassionate relationships, families, and communities, and become wiser about how we relate to the resources our earth shares with us. The key, I think, is to keep hope for the world, and for our capacity to change, and then focus less on the impact we are having on others and more on the integrity of our own process. If we do this, we can each truly say, "Let there be peace, and let it begin with me." Peace and clarity within each one of us contains all the power we need.

Index of Examples

General Examples

Dating

Drugs

Family

Friends

Harassment

Health

Learning

Parent/Child

Child

Teen

Adult

Index of Topics

Praise for *Taking the War Out of Our Words*

"From the time I first read this book in manuscript form, I knew that Sharon was onto something extraordinary. *Taking the War Out of Our Words* delivers every bit of its title's promise, giving us simple, powerful tools for breaking the cycle of defensive speech. This is truly a paradigm-shifting book. We're used to thinking that learning to communicate more effectively has to be a struggle. With this model profound changes can happen so quickly. It has not only helped me in my professional life and in my marriage, but in parenting a toddler as well!"
—*Caroline Pincus, manuscript consultant and former senior editor at HarperCollins*

Using Powerful Non-Defensive Communication, I feel like a camera body that has just been given a new set of lenses. A set of lenses with no distortion. No matter what I'm viewing, the images that come out of me are true.
—*Jesse di Franco*

A message that should be spread across the nation. So simple, I don't know why no one has discovered it before.
—*Rob Merlo, engineer*

The seeds of peace have been planted. I believe that if all children could learn non-defensive communication at an early age, we would have a different world.
—*Linda Bennett, Thurston Middle School, Springfield Oregon*

I have been able to test this method with the most difficult person in my life. To my absolute amazement I was able to diffuse the anger and aggression in an instant. I am actually able to speak without compromising my integrity or becoming entrapped in power struggle. I am able to stay true to myself without a need for masking my feelings in order to remained protected. I believe this book may be preventing many years of unnecessary, damaging stress to my life. I will return to it repeatedly as a resource.
—*Tifanie Hayden*

For centuries, Aristotle's model for communication has been taught in Western culture as the art of winning arguments. Powerful Non-Defensive Communication replaces this traditional model with one that gives each person the ability to communicate effectively without engaging in power struggle.
—Dr. Martin Jacobi, Chair, English Department, Clemson University

I believe Sharon has developed a program that is nothing short of revolutionary. Sharon's model is built on a peace paradigm of communication that stresses respect, clarity and honesty. Energy is spent on developing openness and clarity rather than defending, attacking, and persuading. The surprise is that this peace model is much more powerful and effective than the war model.
—Dr. Kostas Bagakis, San Francisco State University

How many times have I said "Well, I know what she's going to say, so why bother asking?" This kind of anticipation is exactly what keeps us in conflict with others. Sharon's book teaches the art of asking questions without any assumptions or expectations. And, miraculously, what we hear is rarely what we anticipated. And here is where the learning and the real communication begins.
—Janine Sternlieb, Host, A Novel Idea, KRCB Radio

If the people in Washington read Sharon's book and worked with her a while, our country would be a much better place to live.
—Marjorie Weingrow, Director, SAGE Scholars Program, UC Berkeley

I think almost any community group or grassroots organization could benefit from Sharon's methods.
—Derick Miller, President, Berkeley PTA

I consider Sharon Ellison's Powerful Non-Defensive Communication to be the ultimate language of conflict management.
—Mady Shumofsky, Conflict Management Consultant

After looking for a way to communicate with clarity and an open heart, I had the good fortune to find Sharon Ellison's Taking the War Out of Our Words. I hope this book reaches a critical mass, so we can all improve our lives personally and globally.
—Vivienne Verdon-Roe, Academy Award winner
Women for America, for the World

Sharon Strand Ellison, Director of The Institute for Powerful Non-Defensive Communication, is an award-winning speaker and internationally recognized consultant. Sharon was a nominee for the "Leadership in a Changing World" Award, sponsored by the Ford Foundation and the Advocacy Institute.

Sharon's *Powerful Non-Defensive Communication™ (PNDC)* process provides a basis for a radical shift in how we use language. It moves us away from methods that systematically create and accelerate conflict to one that defuses defensiveness and power struggle.

More than thirty years ago, Sharon developed pioneering programs for children and parents, taking her sessions out of the office and into home, school and playground environments where she taught on-the-spot parent, teacher, and peer relationship skills. Currently, Sharon teaches PNDC to individuals, couples, and families. She has a strong commitment to community and has taught these skills to children of all ages, including gang members, as well as community organizations, such as the Napa Valley Peace Table.

Sharon also provides keynotes at conferences and workshops for people in many professional fields, including business, education, government, health care, law, and social service. Some of her clients include Hewlett Packard, Nordstrom, The Smithsonian, Centre for Dispute Resolution (London, England), U.C. Berkeley, Stanford University Lucille Packard Children's Hospital, and the United States Department of Justice.

Her website (www.pndc.com) offers the opportunity to read personal stories from people who have used PNDC, exercises not included in the book, and Q & A. Her goal is to create an ongoing forum for learning non-defensive communication skills. Sharon, her partner, Monza, and her mother-in-law, Rose Mary, live in Oakland, California. Sharon and Monza have a grown daughter, Ami, a son-in-law, Jesse, and twin grandsons, Sam and Will.

You may contact Sharon Ellison at: 4100-10 Redwood Road, #316 Oakland, CA 94619; Phone: 800-714-7334 or 510-655-8086; Email: info@pndc.com; Website: www.pndc.com

CPSIA information can be obtained at www.ICGtesting.com
Printed in the USA
BVOW01s0352300514

354869BV00001B/179/P